# THE MORAL ELECTRICITY
OF PRINT

# THE MORAL ELECTRICITY *of* PRINT

*Transatlantic Education and the Lima Women's Circuit, 1876–1910*

Ronald Briggs

VANDERBILT UNIVERSITY PRESS

NASHVILLE

© 2017 by Vanderbilt University Press
Nashville, Tennessee 37235
All rights reserved
First printing 2017

This book is printed on acid-free paper.
Manufactured in the United States of America

Library of Congress Cataloging-in-Publication Data
LC control number 2016042789
LC classification number  PQ8492.L5 B75 2017
Dewey classification number  860.9/98525—dc23
LC record available at *lccn.loc.gov/2016042789*

ISBN 978-0-8265-2145-3 (hardcover)
ISBN 978-0-8265-2147-7 (ebook)

*For Clara and Lucinda*

# CONTENTS

ACKNOWLEDGMENTS ... ix

INTRODUCTION
Aesthetics of the Cosmopolitan Teacher ... 1

1 Independence and the Book in Subjunctive ... 19

2 Exemplary Autodidacts ... 47

3 Collective Feminist Biography ... 74

4 Novelistic Education, or,
The Making of the Pan-American Reader ... 107

5 Educational Aesthetics and the Social Novel ... 147

CONCLUSION
Publication as Mission and Identity ... 183

NOTES ... 191

BIBLIOGRAPHY ... 229

INDEX ... 247

# ACKNOWLEDGMENTS

This book was written with the support of two Mini-Grants and Special Assistant Professor Leave funding from Barnard College, as well as a Travel and Research Grant from the Institute of Latin American Studies at Columbia University. I am also grateful to the students in my undergraduate and graduate courses at Barnard and Columbia, where I first discussed many of the ideas included in the book.

At Vanderbilt University Press I would like to thank my editor, Eli Bortz, who provided essential guidance and support. Thanks also to Michael Ames, Joell Smith-Borne, Dariel Mayer, Betsy Phillips, Melba Hopper, and two anonymous readers. Special thanks also go out to Susan Boulanger and Steven Moore.

I would also like to thank the Wollman Library of Barnard College; Butler Library of Columbia University; the Jessie Ball duPont Library of Sewanee: The University of the South; Widener Library of Harvard University; the Library of the University of California, Berkeley (special thanks to Jutta Wiemhoff and Lisa Hong); and Yale University Library (special thanks to Jana Krentz, Robert Klingenberger, and Stephen Ross).

In Lima the Biblioteca Nacional del Perú proved to be an invaluable resource, along with the Instituto Riva Agüero (special thanks to Gilda Cogorno). Sara Beatriz Guardia, Carmen McEvoy, Francesca Denegri, Marcel Velázquez Castro, and Emmanuel Alberto Velayos provided hospitality, encouragement, and orientation.

This project has also been fueled by debates, discussions, and conference presentations, and I want to thank those who have helped shape the thinking behind it: Wadda Ríos-Font, Alfred MacAdam, Maja Horn, Orlando Bentancor, Anna Brickhouse, Ana Sabau, Alejandra Josiowicz, Felipe Martínez-Pinzón, Hernán Díaz, Lee Skinner, Amy Wright, Victor Golgel Carballo, Christopher Conway, William G. Acree Jr., and Luba Ostashevsky.

Most of all thanks to my editor-wife, Liz Van Hoose. Her wisdom and insight have informed every page, and her love and compassion have sustained me throughout the project.

# INTRODUCTION
# Aesthetics of the Cosmopolitan Teacher

> And here there is a contradiction, though only an apparent one. Poetry teaches and does not teach. In order to resolve this contradiction well, to explain and reconcile it altogether, a book would be necessary. And a wise and profound book, of which I do not feel myself capable.[1]
> —Juan Valera, "Apuntes sobre el nuevo arte de escribir novelas," published in *El Perú Ilustrado* (March 1, 1890)

## *Pedagogy and the Aesthetics of the Novel*

This study positions the hotbed of literary discussion that was Lima, Peru (1876–1910), as a point of departure for an analysis of the intersection between aesthetics and pedagogy both in nineteenth-century Spanish American letters and in the broader hemispheric realms of book publishing and educational reform. Lima's *veladas literarias*, hosted by exiled Argentine writer Juana Manuela Gorriti in 1876 and 1877, placed the city at the center of Spanish-language literary discourse. These gatherings, which were widely reviewed in the Lima press, included a veritable who's who of Spanish American writers, many of whom were women: Clorinda Matto de Turner, Mercedes Cabello de Carbonera, Soledad Acosta de Samper, Teresa González de Fanning, and others. In the decades that followed, American and European commentators would refer to this generation of female literary pioneers as Spanish America's Pleiades.

Literature and pedagogy mingled at Gorriti's salons, a fact reflected in the very layout of the house in which they took place. Emilia

Serrano, who wrote under the name "Baronesa de Wilson," chronicled for a European readership the highlights of her travels through Spanish America's social and literary scenes, and her *Vanity Fair*–meets–*New Yorker* picture of the *veladas literarias* included the observation that these evening events happened in a room adjacent to the one where Gorriti ran a school during the day: "a little room connected to the classroom, where there were only benches and slates, maps and student desks" (*Lo íntimo* 149).[2] The intimate proximity of literature and pedagogy might have been considered comically ill-suited for such formal gatherings, were it not echoed in the subject matter as well: it was no accident that readings in poetry and fiction were interspersed with talks on educational reform.

The participants in these *veladas* harbored significant philosophical and political differences, but they were united on two major issues: the need for increased educational opportunities for women and the importance of public morality as a political foundation for a functioning liberal republic. Three of the group's novelists, Matto, Cabello, and González de Fanning, harnessed these imperatives into the development of new theoretical approaches to the novel. They peppered their fictional works with arguments for the novel as a new and highly efficient form of public pedagogy, given the century's industrial development and corresponding increase in capacity for book production and distribution.[3] Cabello's published monographs on both the ramifications of naturalism for the realist novel and the importance of Russian fiction to the inchoate American republics made waves from New York to Barcelona.

The international scope of the *veladas* is, perhaps, best described in the title of Leona S. Martin's article, "Nation Building, International Travel, and the Construction of the Nineteenth-Century Pan-Hispanic Women's Network." Such networks, she writes, were characterized by "a political stance that privileged internationalism and pan-Hispanic ideals" over national literary projects ("Nation Building" 440). While increased communications certainly gave intellectual and professional networks an increased vitality and visibility for writers and professionals of both genders, Martin argues that women writers networked out of professional necessity. She cites Stacey Schlau's argument that, for Spanish American women, "creative survival may have depended on support from colleagues in a society hostile to women asserting themselves in the

## SEMBLANZA

Estaba yo recién llegada de Europa á Buenos Aires, cuando á su vez daba vuelta á su patria la excepcional escritora salteña, que había granjeado en toda América envidiable reputación literaria. No perdí momento para conocerla personalmente, pues lo que es por cartas ya estábamos en íntimo contacto. Yo había saboreado con deleite muchos de los escritos que en periódicos y en libros atestiguaban la sin par fantasía de aquella mujer por demás extraordinaria.

Al verme entrar me abrazó como á una hermana, diciendo: «¡Dios mío, qué felicidad! ¡Deseaba tanto conocerla!»

Aun ahora paréceme verla sentada á mi lado, con su erguida estatura; la presencia arrogante y hermosa; la frente ancha, muy despejada; el rostro de un óvalo perfecto, y la mirada perspicaz, enérgica y á veces profundamente melancólica. Su cabello era sedoso y finísimo. Cuando yo la conocí sus rizos parecían de plata, porque los terribles contrastes de su vida los habían blanqueado más que los años.

A la altura de un alma de acero tenía la poderosa fuerza de voluntad y el corazón dispuesto á todos los sacrificios y templado para los grandes infortunios.

Juana Manuela Gorriti era soñadora vehemente, apasionada, con imaginación fantástica, fecunda como pocas, rica en tesoros de ingenio y pródiga en narraciones, ligadas con frecuencia á sus memorias de la niñez y de la juventud.

«Güemes,» «La biografía de Belzu,» «El álbum de una peregrina» son fotografía de su historia.

Hay rasgos en su vida que harán comprender el valor moral de aquel gran carácter, que de suyo se destaca en las páginas legadas á la posteridad.

«Toda mi existencia – decía – ha sido una cadena de luchas y de episodios extraños.»

Era la época de las revueltas políticas, de los motines de cuartel y de terribles represalias, cuando ocupaba de nuevo la presidencia el general Belzu, que en años anteriores había casado con la ilustre argentina. Ídolo de los indios, para quienes todavía hoy es un héroe legendario, sosteníase apoyado más bien en aquel prestigio y á pesar de las grandes dificultades que le creaba el general Melgarejo, soldado de fortuna y uno de los hombres más audaces que figuran en la historia de Bolivia.

Hubo combate y lucha prolongada, y cuando el general Belzu podía juzgarse vencedor, fué de improviso asesinado en su propio palacio.

Las turbas propagaron por la ciudad el funesto acontecimiento, y la noticia llegó rápidamente á la casa donde habitaba Juana Manuela Gorriti, que por incompatibilidades de carácter y de costumbres vivía alejada de su marido y del palacio teatro del drama sangriento.

No vaciló un instante; el deber la llamaba y se sobreponía á desvíos y á ofensas.

Es uno de los rasgos culminantes en aquella mujer insigne.

Sin detenerse se lanzó á la calle y siguió á las masas. Se dirigían al palacio. Al entrar en él Juana Manuela buscó, encontró y colocó sobre su regazo el cuerpo inerte de su marido, y mientras se cercioraba de si aún tenía un átomo de vida, resonaban en sus oídos los gritos de *¡Viva Melgarejo!*

Todo en torno suyo debía parecer pequeño y mezquino ante la magnitud del grupo.

Juana Manuela tuvo siempre verdadera predilección por el Perú; veía en él su segunda patria, donde muy joven y hermosa le prodigaron ovaciones entusiastas y fraternal cariño.

– Lima, decíame con vehemencia; usted no sabe lo risueña y hospitalaria que es aquella tierra.

Cuando yo llegué al Perú, ya Juana Manuela había regresado de Buenos Aires, y mi primera salida fué para ir con ella y visitar la tumba de su madre, por quien guardaba profunda veneración.

Por entonces vivía de su pluma y de la enseñanza. Era infatigable para el trabajo y su espíritu inventivo no decaía nunca.

Su casa convirtióse en templo, y allí al rendir culto á la literatura descollaban sus geniales condiciones, imponiéndose á todos, comunicando su entusiasmo y sus ideas originales, en un aticismo especial.

Juana Manuela acudía á cada grupo: dejaba caer aquí una frasecilla, una acertada crítica; salía al encuentro de un recién llegado, y en dos palabras le ponía al corriente de lo que en aquella noche se trataba para que sin perder tiempo apoyase ó combatiese el pensamiento.

En aquel piso bajo que tengo tan grabado en la imaginación se reunían las entidades literarias más en boga; se desarrollaban temas nuevos, aplaudiendo y estimulando en veladas inolvidables á peruanos y á extranjeros. Para llegar al salón principal había que atravesar el que durante el día ocupaban las clases y las alumnas, donde desempeñaba su misión educacionista la autora de «La Quena.»

Yo no he visto jamás actividad tan excepcional, y es digno de notarse que Juana Manuela Gorriti ha sido la escritora sudamericana más popular; también aquella que en mayor escala obtuvo producto de sus obras, en una época en que apenas la mujer empezaba á sobresalir y á dar pruebas palmarias de su valor intelectual.

En una ocasión fuí á visitarla en Lima, cosa frecuente porque su amistad tenía tal agasajo que era imposible no abrigar el deseo de cultivarla. Me sorprendí al encontrarla mudándose apresuradamente de traje y arrojando en un cestón las prendas que se quitaba. La miré interrogándola.

– He pasado la noche y algunas horas de la mañana con una amiga querida, que ha muerto de viruelas: ¡tan buena y en la flor de la vida!

– Pero ¿no ha temido usted contagiarse?

– Cuando cumplo un deber no tengo temor á nada.

Esas palabras gráficas son un retrato completo.

Otro no menos característico:

Era en los días aciagos de la guerra entre el Perú y Chile. En el antiguo templo de San Francisco de Paula, en Lima, convertido entonces en prisión militar, estaba arrestado por cuestiones de disciplina un hijo de Juana Manuela Gorriti, joven peruano, pero recién llegado de Buenos Aires para batirse en defensa de la patria.

Con él había pasado toda la tarde la noble anciana y, como de costumbre, salió triste y preocupada, atravesando sin darse cuenta de ello la gran distancia que media desde aquella iglesia hasta el río que se cruza por un puente frontero con la línea ferrocarrilera de la Oroya – que, entre paréntesis, es la más atrevida de las construídas en América.

Extraña Juana Manuela á cuanto pasaba en torno suyo, sorda por la excesiva preocupación, no vió la lengua de fuego de la locomotora, ni tampoco oyó ni se hizo cargo de los rumores ni de las exclamaciones de angustia escapadas á los transeuntes de una y otra orilla. Todo fué obra de un segundo: Juana Manuela volvió la cabeza en el instante mismo que el eco de las montañas repetía el bramido del coloso que ya estaba tan cerca de ella que la llama podía chamuscar sus vestidos.

«La sangre fría, que más de una vez me ha servido en casos extremos, salvóme entonces de una muerte horrible.» Así me decía en una carta que recibí poco después en Colombia, frases que ha consignado también en su libro «El mundo de los recuerdos.»

De un salto se puso fuera de la vía cuando el tren pasaba á toda velocidad.

Juana Manuela sintió que la abrazaban, mientras que cien gritos de alborozo poblaban los aires, saludando la milagrosa salvación. Pocos habría entre aquella multitud que no la conocieran y la veneraren.

Hay que contar para esta popularidad que en epidemias ó en luchas habíasela visto siempre en los hospitales asistiendo á los atacados, sin temor á contagio, y curando á los heridos, sin desfallecimientos femeninos. Era un hábil ayudante, á la par que una enfermera cariñosa y consoladora.

Ruegos y súplicas la sacaron del Perú; sus amigos, sus compatriotas deseaban que pasara los días postreros de su vida en el suelo natal. Sobre su ancianidad (había nacido en 1818) pesaba ya la vida demasiado laboriosa para atender á las necesidades más perentorias.

Años atrás habíale señalado el gobierno argentino una pensión como hija del prócer valeroso de la Independencia, y por fin abandonó el país predilecto para establecerse en las riberas del Plata.

Raro privilegio, la imaginación de Juana Manuela conservó sus facultades creativas hasta los últimos días de su vida, y aunque su salud era delicadísima y su rostro mostraba las huellas del tiempo, apenas decíeron las juveniles lozanías, lo florido del lenguaje, ni la riqueza de estilo y de pensamientos.

También había en ella una segunda vida: la del recuerdo, de los recuerdos, ya risueños muchos ó azarosos otros, los que evocaba con tan pasmosa precisión y lujo de pormenores, que constituían, al decir de aquellos que la rodeaban – hasta hace poco más de dos años, – datos preciosísimos para la historia de Bolivia, Perú y la Argentina.

Juana Manuela Gorriti no murió rica, pero sí disfrutando relativo bienestar; rodeada por el respeto y el cariño de todos; acompañada por su hijo Julio; tranquila, serena, con la seguridad de que legaba un nombre ilustre y su patria y toda América honrarían su memoria.

Pocos meses antes de su muerte leí en Lima cartas suyas dirigidas á dos de sus amigas predilectas.

En una de ellas decía:

«Mi querida hija: Esto se acaba. Creo que no te escribiré más.»

Aun esa postrera frase demuestra la gráfica fortaleza y el alma de aquella mujer notable, que hoy tiene elevado puesto en el templo de la inmortalidad y es luminoso astro en la historia de la literatura hispano-americana del siglo XIX.

LA BARONESA DE WILSON

Emilia Serrano remembered Gorriti's literary salons in this piece, published in the Barcelona newspaper *La Ilustración Artística* on July 1, 1895, under her preferred pen name, Baronesa de Wilson. Courtesy of the Yale University Library.

public sphere" (Schlau 55). Martin also mentions the work of Margaret McFadden, which draws similar conclusions about the network of early feminists in Scandinavia and the Anglophone world.

McFadden argues that the use of the word "network" as a verb first comes into prominence among feminists (McFadden 11) and that the nineteenth century was marked by "a virtual explosion in the number of physical and verbal connections between women" (3). In an era in which communications took on generalized power and importance, the telegraph and the steamship became particularly meaningful for feminists and female intellectuals of all political orientations. Often isolated or denied entry into the cultural institutions endorsed by the nation-state, they formed group and person-to-person relationships that helped raise the public profiles of everyone involved.[4] As a marginalized minority within the field of literature, women writers often linked group and individual success.[5]

The recent critical recovery of Cabello, Matto, and their contemporaries in studies by Nancy LaGreca, Ana Peluffo, Francesca Denegri, Pinto Vargas, and others has been a necessary precondition for even contemplating a broader exploration of the group in connection with like-minded writers and reformers in the United States and Europe. While this study begins with a discrete place and time—late nineteenth-century Lima and the writers who gathered there—it strives to understand that place and time not as an anomaly or a facet of Peruvian literary history, but as part of a hemispheric intellectual movement that undertook pedagogical publishing projects, often international in scope, and imagined them as intellectual tools for continuing the political work of independence. I will argue that a historical period in which careers in letters included professional writing and professional teaching, with a great deal of crossover occurring between these spheres, demands a method of reading that takes this relationship into account. A long line of American authors, from Cabello and Matto to Aurora Cáceres, Soledad Acosta, Domingo Faustino Sarmiento, and Mary Peabody Mann, saw the publication of books and journals as a form of intervention capable of shaping the historical memory and civic life of the Western Hemisphere, and so thought in terms of the most efficient transmission of content useful to these ends.

*Moral Electricity* proposes, then, an alternate reading of nineteenth-century intellectual history, one in which the burning literary question is pedagogical: How to create the new generation of reader-citizens who will sustain stable democratic republics? What happens to writing when it seeks at once to be pedagogical and beautiful? What happens to literary aesthetics when they are enlisted in the challenge of transmitting civically impactful content? The result, I will argue, is an integrated approach to publishing, writing, and reading that crosses the borders of genre and nationality.

## *Moral Electricity—Magic and Persuasion*

The phrase "moral electricity" appears in an 1856 article by the US transcendentalist and common school advocate Charles Brooks. Brooks is speaking of an inherent quality of transmission that he believes the products of the nascent US publishing industry should demonstrate going forward. The term itself came into prominence during the French Revolution to describe the mutual political influence among individuals gathered in an assembly (Rosanvallon 44). Early nineteenth-century uses of the term in English and Spanish described influence exercised either by crowds or by individuals.[6] Decades after Brooks's invocation of "moral electricity," the Puerto Rican philosopher and educational reformer Eugenia María de Hostos mentioned *electricidad moral* in an essay proposing that women might be better receptors than men for positive moral influences implanted in books. Both constructions (and neither author cites anyone else on electricity as a metaphor) echo a sentiment expressed by Germaine de Staël's 1799 treatise on the social influence of literature; part of the author's task, she asserted, was to tap into an "electrical commotion" (*commotion électrique*) by which moral messages were transmitted and maintained (*De la littérature* 381).

This metaphor for invisible or insensible transmission—electricity moves from one object to another, creating changes that are visible to the eye even though the process of transmission is not—loops around through time and space to the very circle of writers, many of them feminist women, who kept the Lima literary scene alive on the page and in public life through books, journals, and Gorriti's *veladas*. Charles Brooks, for example, makes an appearance as "Cárlos Brookts" (*La ley* 100–101) in Serrano's *La ley del progreso* (Quito, 1880), a book very much modeled on Domingo Faustino Sarmiento's *Las escuelas: base de la prosperidad y de la república en los Estados Unidos* (New York, 1866), a fact that Serrano readily acknowledged. Serrano would also follow Sarmiento's lead in championing Horace Mann and Brooks, reformers who made investigative trips to Europe in search of positive educational examples. These US intellectuals were, Serrano attested, exemplary figures for Spanish American educational reform. Sarmiento and Mann had met during the Argentine's educational tour of Europe and the United States, while Serrano had left her native Spain to travel and write extensively of, in, and about the Western Hemisphere. Their textual convergence underscores the global, cosmopolitan nature of educational discourse in the nineteenth century, a discourse that resists analysis confined to a single nation or a single language.

Inherent to this literary cosmopolitanism is the effort of communication and the question of how best to reach a wide readership. Electricity as a metaphor for connection and transmission leads a life to some degree parallel with the role planned for sentiment in a number of nineteenth-century novels.[7] Early on in *Lágrimas andinas*, her comprehensive study of Matto's literary aesthetic, Ana Peluffo points to the author's use of sentiment as an expressive technique. This antiquated literary device, systematically debunked by the priests of high modernism, is, Peluffo proposes, the primary cause of her disappearance from the canon in the decades following her death in 1909 (49). Asking, in essence, what would happen if we were to view sentimentality as an expressive tool rather than an aesthetic (and even moral) weakness, Peluffo suggests that sentimentality's purpose could be the creation of a national community in which emotion transcends differences of language, race, and social class (50).[8]

In Peluffo's analysis, sentiment serves a pragmatic, aesthetic purpose. She argues, for example, that while Matto's dramatization of the lives of indigenous characters for an audience of Creole elites invites the charge of exploitation and lack of authenticity, *some* sort of manipulation is necessary to make the world the novel creates portable and decipherable to its audience (74). Peluffo is asserting that indigenous suffering must become an "aesthetic artifact" (74) in order to reach its Lima audience, or, to put the argument another way, that Matto needed to simplify and underline the injustices faced by the country's Andean indigenous population in order to make them convincing to coastal, urban readers.

The technique Peluffo describes runs counter to at least one commonly held belief about the nature of teaching: the belief handed down from Rousseau that it is the teacher's task to push the student toward the unadorned world itself rather than an expression of it. The Rousseauian directive is deconstructive in that it requires the teacher and student to mistrust and dismantle those expressions rather than be moved by them. Peluffo proposes the opposite, positing the novelist's art as a pedagogical form of adornment calculated to take the reader's biases into account and thus to render as accurate a *perception* of reality as possible. In her view, education performs the sort of presentation that Rousseau's ideal tutor would teach his student to distrust.

Kate Jenckes and Patrick Dove have identified this contradiction between the making and unraveling of myths as a central problem for Latin American cultural studies, as its pedagogical agenda of demystification chooses between a posture that is "either too aestheticist or not aestheticist enough" (16). That is to say, a field that aspires both to "affirm materiality—even within language—as a necessary condition for any relation between subject and world" and "to critique aesthetic ideology and its complicity with structures of domination and normativity" will find itself simultaneously engaged in the dismantling and the construction of aesthetic objects.

The "subject-world" connection to which Jenckes and Dove allude becomes a web of connections when we take into account the world-author-reader-world relationship in which an author such as Matto seeks to deliver a new world to her readers with the expectation that they will be capable of receiving this fictional world and will, in turn, behave differently in the real world they inhabit throughout their everyday lives. As Víctor Goldgel has pointed out, the aesthetic serves, in the context of nineteenth-century Latin American letters, as a category that unites what contemporary observers tend to classify as the scientific and the literary. Far from being a rarified pursuit defined by its distance from everyday life, the aesthetic, which Goldgel defines as the means of perceiving the world, was an essential element of any intellectual community (173). An author who, like Charles Brooks or Eugenio María de Hostos, *believes* in the transformative powers of the book is therefore trusting the medium not only to deliver a world to its readers but also to deliver those readers back to the world with their perspectives and behavior fundamentally changed. Believing in the book the way Matto, Serrano, Cabello, and González de Fanning believe in the book means giving the book a supernatural task. Electricity comes onstage as the mystical force capable of carrying it out.

The omnipresence of the word "electricity" in all manner of nineteenth-century discourse, from Mary Shelley's *Frankenstein* to Whitman's "I Sing the Body Electric," demonstrates just how deeply it had ingrained itself in public consciousness. Spanish America was no exception. The February 8, 1890, edition of Matto's *El Perú Ilustrado* (no. 141) would tell its readers that reality had become stranger than fiction by offering as "news" the story of "Jusuah Electricman," the North American inventor of devices such as the *escribógrafo*, the *medicófero*, and the *galvinopater*, devices that used electricity to perform the human offices of writer, doctor, and father. Electricity thus described is an invisible, dangerous, and progressive force that accelerates social change and disrupts tradition while saving labor—a compressed and exaggerated figure for the industrial revolution.

Along with this penchant for disruption, electricity also carried with it connotations of speed. Just as steam travel had effectively shrunk the world and profoundly altered public consciousness of space and time in the first half of the nineteenth century, electricity, by way of the telegraph and the telephone, was creating new networks for the lightning-fast distribution of information in the years surrounding those Lima *veladas*. The "nineteenth-century pan-Hispanic women's network," as coined by Martin, necessitated both the publication and transport of journals and books, and a surge in international travel and conferences. The press release was born in this era, as was the web of correspondents sending dispatches back and forth between American and European capitals. All of these trends made it possible for a relatively modest gathering in Gorriti's classroom annex to reverberate far beyond the experience of those actually present.

On a broader scale, one of the factors that connects the diverse writers and contexts I will be addressing is the consciousness of being part of a newly networked world and the belief that this sense of connection creates new opportunities for the printed word to multiply the civic influence of a single intellectual. Scholars trace the Spanish American faith in the saving power of book publishing at least as far back as 1797, when Pablo de Olavide's *El evangelio en triunfo* proposed the novelistic delivery of enlightened Christian content as an antidote to the French Revolution while aiming at a Spanish and Spanish American readership.

Half a century later, commentators like Charles Brooks urged the rapid creation of an American publishing industry as a countermeasure against the arrival of European books and their dubious political influence.[9]

## *Pedagogical Americanism*

The wide temporal and geographical sweep of the title phrase "Moral Electricity" alludes to the hemispheric dimension of this project. Since it examines the Lima group as an intellectual network in connection with other networks across space and time, the project cannot be neatly contained by national borders. The legacy of book anxiety in the United States and in Spanish America—the sense that the New World must at once create a book market and the means of supplying it—is bound up, I will argue, with moral and political aspirations that cannot be easily untangled. The New World's will to write and will to publish is therefore both commercial and ideological, fueled by a fear of European authority via European imports on the one hand, and by a future-centered belief in the moral superiority of republicanism over monarchy and empire on the other.

The particular hemispheric approach I will be taking also depends on the vitally important connections established by the intellectuals themselves. Most of the Lima writers had at least some familiarity with British, French, and US books, and all of them worked to create a regional Spanish American sensibility that defied boundaries and incorporated allusions to US reformers such as Brooks and Mann, Harriet Beecher Stowe, and Abraham Lincoln, as well as writers from Europe whose works were embraced by US and Spanish American readerships—most notably Samuel Smiles, the British author of inspirational biographical collections. In the paradigm of the *veladas*, being hemispheric is a basic qualification for becoming a competent reader in Spanish America. The hemispheric was a historical *condition* of the nineteenth century, not simply a construct imposed by scholars from the twenty-first century.

My use of the term "hemispheric" also references the now-established field of Hemispheric American Studies. In a recent collection of the same title, Caroline Field Levander and Robert S. Levine introduce a series of essays dealing with case studies from the colonial era to the present in which reading hemispherically shifts the critical ground for practitioners of the US-centric field of American studies. Declaring their intent as that of disrupting the national framework in temporal and geographical terms and "putting different national histories and cultural formations into dialogue" (2), Levander and Levine argue that one of the advantages of this transnational approach is the new lens it provides for observing the nation state: "We are able to see the nation as a relational identity that emerges through constant collaboration, dialogue, and dissension" (5). In their view, hemispheric approaches serve to reopen and reconsider rather than to reify the national categories that have long governed literary and cultural history. The result they describe is "a heuristic rather than content- or theory-driven method" and one that "allows for the discovery of new configurations rather than confirmation of what we think we already know" (9). Levander and Levine's formulation might appear modest on first reading, but by focusing on the disruptive potential of new comparative configurations, they effectively equate being hemispheric with questioning the boundaries and structures upon which cultural and literary studies have been conducted, whether from the perspective of American Studies (their chosen bailiwick) or from that of Latin American Studies.

Levander and Levine cite Walter Mignolo's *Local Histories/Global Designs: Coloniality, Subaltern Knowledges, and Border Thinking* as a work performing hemispheric thinking from the Latin American perspective. Mignolo speaks not from a self-identified center of cultural production, but from a space that US-centric nationalism has tended to define away as an exotic periphery. Noting that cultural authority tends to translate into the ability to make local ideas pass for universals, he argues that "today it is urgent to confront 'absolute knowledge' with its own 'geopolitics of knowledge,' to focus on the enunciation rather than the enunciated" (Mignolo xiii). For the intellectuals of Lima, for whom gender and geography could be doubly marginalizing categories, print culture served as a great leveling ground from which they could critique and integrate European and US authors and ideas into a literary and educational philosophy that billed itself both as a response to local conditions and as a projection of regional and hemispheric promise. The social reform they hoped to inspire in books would make Peru and other American republics into moral and political prototypes at the vanguard of a long narrative of progress rather than copies of a real or imagined Western Europe. The transnational print network they composed not only served to expose the contingency of the nation-state but also sought to generate a positive corrective of its own, articulating a particularly American aesthetic that would synthesize what they saw as the unrealized promises of independence.

Gretchen Murphy has pointed out the inherent problem that a hemispheric approach faces when it attempts to posit itself as the neutral eraser of national boundaries. Since the hemispheric concept is itself defined by a boundary between the New World and the Old, it is, she argues, "an unlikely divide for challenging border effects in literary studies" ("The Hemispheric" 566). Murphy suggests that the scholar who wishes to take a hemispheric approach might ask whether the construction serves as "an end in itself or an intermediate step toward a moral globalized literary study" ("The Hemispheric" 567). This study opts for the latter approach—the hemispheric as a step toward the global—by focusing on the process by which nineteenth-century intellectuals shaped themselves as members of global networks. As a conservative national capital that was also a thriving global port, late nineteenth-century Lima was the pinnacle of the hemispheric-to-global sensibility. It is no accident that the reform-minded intellectuals who participated in the *veladas* subscribed to the first-person-plural construct. The "we" of the *veladas* could effortlessly expand from a localized cosmopolitan group in the city to the broader shared consciousness—regional, even global—with which they came to identify themselves. In this paradigm, the youthful intellectual from the provinces arrives in Lima and feels herself entitled to its smorgasbord of European intellectuals and best-selling US authors. Such intellectual freedom of movement, I will argue, was in fact an essential component of an American consciousness that viewed the New World as a political and educational vanguard free to construct its future from a wide array of readings and appropriations.

This consciousness, which I call pedagogical Americanism, functions as one of a trio of concepts—the others being gender emancipation and a belief in the pedagogical utility of literature—that held the Lima group together and sustained its faith in its own publishing program. My hemispheric approach is both circumstantial and ideological, to borrow a distinction Anne Garland Mahler made in her recent article on the Global South. Arguing for the Global South as a more useful interpretive category than postcolonialism in the context of the Civil Rights movement, Mahler distinguishes between categories defined by "trait-based and circumstantial conditions" and those with "ideological grounds for inclusion," in her case a particular antagonism toward the Global North (113).

In my study the ideological glue that holds the American hemisphere together is a hope for the New World as a grand educational project combined with an anxiety about the baleful influence of a politically and morally decadent Old World that dominated literary output through its powerful publishing interests. The pedagogical Americanists thus coupled their idealism with a keen attention to the literary marketplace. The development of a New World publishing industry and the requisite system of distributors, editors, and writers would necessarily accompany the project to produce a better sort of book, a book produced to educate and attract republican readers.

This spillover between the pedagogical and the literary among the Lima writers is analogous to the shared vocation of literary author and newspaper writer that has come to be identified with the Latin American participants in modernism, a movement that was gathering momentum at roughly the same time. Andrew Reynolds has pointed out that the expanding nature of print journalism "provided them with the necessary networking abilities to form strong ties with literary figures and other agents in the literary field" (15). I argue that the combination of a global press, an expansion in book publishing, and a global discourse on educational reform provided similar opportunities for the Lima group in a historical moment Reynolds associates with "the expansion from a national to a transnational literary perspective" (145).

## *American Imperatives of Infrastructure and Distribution*

Any exploration of the role of pedagogy in nineteenth-century Spanish American letters must contend with a global literary market and a community that crosses national boundaries. The question of what "arrives" on the Spanish American literary scene is, at the final stage, very much in the hands of Spanish American intellectuals. "Influence" obeys a chronology that depends both on publication and on the later acts of reading and being cited. The central argument I will be making is that the emerging discourse of Latin American feminism typified by (though not restricted to) the Lima circle is inseparable from a discourse on pedagogy and publishing traceable across time and space.[10] On a temporal axis, it engages with decades of republican discourse on intellectual independence from Europe; on a spatial one, it forms itself in dialogue with a rich conversation on publishing, literary aesthetics, and educational reform underway throughout the Americas and Western Europe. Mary Louise Pratt's essay "'Don't Interrupt Me': The Gender Essay as Conversation and Countercanon," neatly sums up the difficulty faced by aspiring Latin American women of letters as that of breaking into "the male monologue that has been canonized as the Latin American essay" (13). In Pratt's analysis, Latin American women who wished to be public intellectuals faced even greater obstacles than those who wished only to be influential writers within an extant literary sphere. Arguing persuasively that what has come to be the canon of the nineteenth-century essay is centered almost exclusively on texts "whose topic is the nature of criollo identity and culture, particularly in relation to Europe and North America," a subgenre she classifies as the "criollo identity essay" (14), Pratt attests that female intellectuals, who were actively excluded from the identity project, justifiably responded by creating a parallel genre, "a tradition that could accurately be called the *gender essay*" (15).[11]

Pratt identifies a number of characteristics of the "gender essay," among them the use of "the form of a historical catalogue" and a lack of dependence on national categories (17). She also notes the relationship between the historical project of emancipation—"Historically, it can be read as the woman's side of an ongoing negotiation as to what women's social and political settlements are and ought to be in the postindependence era"—and a certain ideological iconoclasm that by turns argues against and makes pragmatic use of societal expectations and prejudices: "Ideologically, its discussions of womanhood are eclectic, operating both within and against patriarchal gender ideologies" (16). This analysis has much to recommend it, not least being the widely expressed consciousness among nineteenth-century Latin American feminists that they were indeed inhabiting a world parallel but separate from a dominant male monologue. On the other hand, the possibility of overlap between the gender essay (which also invokes identity) and the Creole identity essay (which tends to employ and sometimes abuse the Enlightenment association with emancipation) suggests a larger project, the identity essay in the Americas, written from differing individual perspectives. One of the advantages of pedagogy as a hermeneutic lens on the output of Spanish American feminists who saw themselves as novelists, educators, and women of letters is the degree to which it acts as a bridge between the parallel discourses of gender emancipation and Creole identity.

Almost a century before the writers of the Lima group were coming into prominence, Germaine de Staël had suggested that literature might serve as a path to greater political influence for women who were systematically excluded from the formal political process. While lamenting that the French Revolution had failed to advance the cause of female emancipation, and had in fact fallen into the throes of a patriarchal backlash, Staël argued that women writers would need to destroy the arbitrary boundary between the literary and the "real" world in order to bring their writings to bear on the dominant discussions from which they were excluded. Staël's question was, in effect, what's the point of a woman's writing literature if it does not intersect with politics? "Certainly, there is no career so limited, so confined, as that of Literature, if we view it in the light in which it is frequently considered,—as detached from all philosophy" (*The Influence* 139).

Staël's approach to the bearing of literature on politics and society would be heartily echoed by the writers of the Lima group, who spoke unapologetically of producing "social" novels. Frequently cited in Spanish-language periodicals throughout the nineteenth century, Staël also garnered mention in the biographical collections of two of Matto's contemporaries, Soledad Acosta and Aurora Cáceres. Like Harriet Beecher Stowe, she remained a polestar for Spanish American feminists seeking to link literary production and political power.

The political-influence test for literature's artistic merits was a cultural phenomenon that by the end of the century stretched from Buenos Aires to New York. In an 1891 issue of *La Revista Ilustrada de Nueva York*, José Ignacio Rodríguez invoked *Uncle Tom's Cabin* in a review of Helen Hunt Jackson's *Ramona*, remembering Stowe's work as an omnipresent classic—"Everyone can say, without exaggeration, that he or she has read this book" (138).[12] Moreover, the Stowe-Jackson comparison led him to summon a Victor Hugo quote on the power of sentiment—"Sentiment awakens the love of the truth very tear erases something" (143)[13]—before concluding that Stowe's and Jackson's novels had helped change public opinion on slavery and the rights of Native Americans. Rodríguez is likely quoting from Hugo's volume of poetry

*Le rayons et les ombres* (1840) in which the speaker holds forth on the utility of crying, concluding with a pair of lines that might be translated as "Every tear, child, / Washes something away" (n. pag.).[14] His careful framing and elliptical translation manages to turn the poem's endorsement of sentiment into an aesthetic that calls on the power of emotion to invoke real political action rather than empty cathartic release.[15]

On the other hand, an aesthetic based on sentiment suggested the question of just how effective emotion could be as a tool for reaching across large social divides. In the twentieth century, US critic James Baldwin critiqued *Uncle Tom's Cabin*, in particular its continuing vogue as "Everybody's Favorite Protest Novel." Baldwin saw the book as an aesthetic and political failure. Arguing that it provoked sentimental emotional connection with the reader in lieu of real political change, he effectively dismissed the affective dimension that served as the formal bedrock for the social novel.[16] Baldwin attacks sentiment as a sign of simulated rather than genuine connection between human beings: "Sentimentality, the ostentatious parading of excessive and spurious emotion, is the mark of dishonesty, the inability to feel" (14). As far as the reader's reaction to the book is concerned, Baldwin mistrusts the emotional effect of sympathy. He suggests that the "protest novel" pretends to inspire genuine political action but in reality provides an aesthetic experience that stands in for such action: "We receive a very definite thrill of virtue from the fact that we are reading such a book at all" (19).

Baldwin's critique looms large over the twentieth- and twenty-first-century reception of *Uncle Tom's Cabin*. Henry Louis Gates Jr. and Hollis Robbins devote much of the introduction to their 2007 edition, *The Annotated Uncle Tom's Cabin*, to the value of reconsidering Stowe's novel a half-century later. Gates and Robbins argue that Stowe needed sentimentality and melodrama to perform what they see as her great political reframing act: she managed "to remove the question of slavery from the male discourse of Jeffersonian individualism, which had not had much success in ending slavery by 1852, and to resituate it squarely in the heart of the family circle" (xiv). Sentimentality, as they see it, proved a necessary tool for the task of bringing its readers in touch with the domestic reality of slavery, with all of its underlying sexual energy (xx). Where Baldwin sees the use of sentiment as an aesthetic defect and a sign of an author's infelicitous connection with her characters, Gates and Robbins see a pedagogical technique necessary for a readership obstructed by a web of prejudice and social taboos.

For the writers of the Lima group and for feminist scholars such as their younger contemporary Elvira García y García, sentiment functions as an essential force for an aesthetic experience designed to spur the reader toward political action rather than to substitute for it. García y García makes this vision of the empowered reader an essential aspect of her aesthetic vision. Art, she argues, gives readers and spectators an artificial world that convinces them to act differently in the real one "when it tends to strengthen this calm, beneficent and royal power, that we exercise at first over ourselves, and, secondly, through ourselves, over the environment that surrounds us" (64).[17] Here the aesthetic experience depends on three vectors, the last two stated and the first implied: the ability to be influenced by a reading, the ability to exercise influence over oneself in response to the reading, and the ability to bring that influence to bear on everyone else. Literary value comes about because of influence, and influence is effected through a series of "teaching moments."

## *Chapter by Chapter*

This study is organized into five chapters, dealing respectively with different conceptual manifestations of the teaching book: the republican ideal of the book and publishing industry of the future; the autodidact as exemplary citizen; the biographical collection as a frame for rethinking history through networks; the aesthetics of the classroom narrative; and the theory of the social novel. While most of the primary source materials were published in a period we could define broadly as that of national consolidation—roughly 1830–1898—the textual relationships I will be analyzing often present alliances that stretch the bounds of chronology, as biographical collections blur time and space to create a textual community of heroic figures, and certain reformist moments become touchstones capable of transcending their immediate context. By tracing the intellectual history of the pedagogical imperative in Spanish American letters through a few key examples, I will be dealing with "influences" not so much as the unconscious effects of one writer's work on another, but as narratives of reading. The chronology that governs this study is characterized not by publication dates (the first moment something *could* have been read), but by the contexts in which influences are acknowledged, quoted, and appealed to as sources of authority.

Chapter 1, "Independence and the Book in Subjunctive," takes its title from the well-known passage in *Recuerdos de provincia* in which Sarmiento recounts his "discovery" of Ackermann's catechisms, educational texts published in London for distribution throughout the Americas. As Sarmiento tells the story, his surprise encounter with the catechisms served as physical confirmation of an imaginative "invention" he had already made, that such books should be available for youths like himself who found themselves deprived by circumstances of the voice of a teacher. The book, he believed, could serve as the autodidact's tutor and pedagogue. This chapter discusses the recurrence of this idea among Spanish American and North American intellectuals in the period immediately after independence as a response to the postrevolutionary anxiety over the lack of domestically published books, the dangers of European ones, and the desire to make the products of print culture match the promise of the rhetoric of the independence movement.

Chapter 2, "Exemplary Autodidacts," deals with the American construction of the heroic autodidact, focusing on Benjamin Franklin, Sarmiento, Abraham Lincoln, and Sor Juana Inés de la Cruz. It argues that the frame of the self-taught hero forces a narrative approach on education and imagines the student-reader as a single category.

Chapter 3, "Collective Feminist Biography," takes the intellectual ramifications of the exemplary life further as it focuses on the surge in production of feminist biographical collections in Spanish America during the last decades of the 1800s. By focusing on a paradoxical American anxiety—the fear, on the one hand, that the story of independence and its positive moral content would be forgotten if not transmitted to future generations and, on the other hand, that traditional historiographic approaches would glorify violence and military virtues above all others—these chapters argue that biography takes on a special importance in the context of postindependence as a kind of "virtuous history" in which heroic figures serve as moral examples to children. This chapter also traces the collective biography's ability to create virtual intellectual communities, a special concern for the writers of the Lima group.

In Chapter 4, "Novelistic Education, or The Making of the Pan-American Reader," I analyze the interplay between pedagogy and literary aesthetics, with a particular focus on how the classroom or the perception of the classroom shapes the book. This sort of encounter happened literally in book projects by US reformer Bronson Alcott, Acosta, and Serrano, as these writers attempted to recreate classroom dialogue on the page, a leitmotif that served as a backdrop to a number of textbooks and textbook anthologies by authors such as José Martí, William Holmes McGuffey, Juana Manso, and Clorinda Matto. For these textbook/anthology projects, literary or historical merit comes to mean the ability to communicate specific moral content, as the authors justify their selections based on how the texts are expected to influence their readers. This chapter will argue that a form of "pedagogical reading" emerges from these discussions of how texts should be received. Owing a great deal to the connection between beauty and transmissibility explored in Friedrich Schiller's *On the Aesthetic Education of Man* (1794), the pedagogical aesthetic defines beauty as effective literary pedagogy and literary technique as the writer's toolbox for making a message graspable to readers.

The final chapter, "Educational Aesthetics and the Social Novel," takes this notion of the pedagogical aesthetic and applies it to the theoretical discussion of the novel transpiring throughout the Western world in the last decades of the nineteenth century, with special attention to the fervor of the discussion in Lima, where so many threads intersected in person and on the printed page. The international bylines of a publication such as *El Perú Ilustrado* illustrate the global dimension of this debate, as does the interest in explaining and comparing the work of contemporary (and contemporarily read) novelists such as Victor Hugo, Émile Zola, Harriet Beecher Stowe, and Leo Tolstoy. The circle of Lima novelists that included Matto and Cabello and that counted Acosta as at least an honorary member, was characterized by feminism (with varying degrees of radicalism), professional experience (as teachers and editors), and ambition (for the political and aesthetic possibilities of the social novel). I will argue that what emerges is an original vision of the novel as a prose form shaped by common, though often contentious, notions of civic empathy and the public good.[18] For novelists such as Matto, Cabello, and Acosta, literary creativity cannot be separated from a very clear notion of public perception and need. Accordingly, their literary aesthetic equates with the responsibility to make the printed page a moral force that, like educational narratives and biographies, connects individual and collective morality in a circuit of perpetual reform.

# 1

# Independence and the Book in Subjunctive

### *"Moral Electricity," or Writing and Reading Virtue*

Charles Brooks's 1856 essay "Moral Education: The Best Methods of Teaching Morality in the Common Schools," appeared in Henry Barnard's *American Journal of Education* as part of an ongoing conversation on the role of books and reading in education. In a twenty-first century climate of educational debate centered on skills such as literacy, arithmetic, and problem solving, Brooks's easy link between reading and morality underlines just how much the grounds of educational debate have shifted in the century and a half since his essay was published. A staunch proponent of the common school movement and the notion of public education as a stay against political corruption, Brooks had, ten years before, asked the rhetorical question "What have the United States to fear from the kingdoms of Europe?" and answered it himself: "Little from their navies; less from their armies; little from their commercial competition; less from their political creeds." With nearly every measure of contemporary state power exhausted, Brooks concluded that it was only by bad moral influence—"their moral and political corruptions"—that the great European powers could ever threaten the United States (*Remarks* 38).

Having established the United States as a world power with nothing to fear from conventional statecraft (a line of argument Abraham Lincoln would take to great rhetorical effect in his declaration, in the years leading up to the US Civil War, that only internal disagreement could wreck the project of independence), the Brooks of 1856 nonetheless finds the US moral identity to be very much a work in progress. Asking himself another broad question—What kind of literature should the new nation be producing?—he rattles off an equally snappy and provocative answer: "We need books charged with moral electricity, which will flow by an insensible stream into the student's open soul" ("Moral" n. pag.).

Brooks's use of a electricity as a metaphor for a powerful but invisible form of transmission carries particular weight in a century whose early days had been enlivened by Michael Faraday's experiments designed to render electricity's effects visible to observers and by the macabre craze for galvanic experiments that attached electrodes to the corpses of animals and jolted them into lifelike motion. Brooks also highlights the reader/student's receptivity—"open soul"—and emphasizes the stealthy means by which the book's undefined moral message will reach it. The use of "student" rather than "reader" to describe the moral receiver suggests the book as a teacher, an anthropomorphized description that makes the book-reader relationship a personal one and that harkens back to the pre-print era when such a relationship would have been the only efficient means for communicating moral messages. The new book, by Brooks's lights, should not only be capable of transmitting morality and more of it than is apparent at any given moment, it should also be thought of as a teacher in search of students, a teacher whose worth depends on a moral message and the ability to transmit that message. Finally, by choosing to direct the electrical impulse toward the student's "soul" rather than a more prosaic "brain," Brooks suggests that the book will offer what he and his contemporaries called "education" and took to mean the learning of ways of being in the world, rather than "instruction" or the learning of useful skills.

Brooks's choice of metaphor united the vocabulary of empirical science with that of morality. Electricity's invisibility was an inconvenience to Faraday's experiments, one that prompted a number of innovations, as David Gooding has noted, designed to make the force visible to a not necessarily theoretically grounded public.[1] For Brooks it was this invisibility that made electricity the perfect metaphor for the transmission of moral content sufficiently influential to effect real world changes in readers and societies. Germaine de Staël's 1799 treatise on the social import of the literary, *De la littérature considérée dans ses rapports avec les institutions sociales*, had already defined the usefulness of "eloquence" as a connecting force that united a shared sense of virtue, a force writers could tap "if you know how to give that electrical commotion in which the moral being thus contains the principle" (381).[2] Suzanne Guerlac has noted that Staël's argument emphasizes the synthetic quality of eloquence as a force that "touches both reason and the passions" and thus helps to bring about "the social affections of admiration and enthusiasm required for love of the nation" (48).

Staël, whose work had been translated into English by 1812, was above all intent on creating a revolutionary ideology that would replace the mythology and rhetoric of the preexisting order.[3] For Brooks the occasion for taking up virtue and its invisible transmission is, in a practical sense, a moment of industrial development in which large-scale publishing is becoming part of the US reality. Any urge to wax triumphant on the young nation's rapidly developing industrial infrastructure is tempered by the fear that material prosperity has been accompanied by moral decline, a sentiment that runs through the discourse of US transcendentalism and is crystallized in Emerson's "The American Scholar" (1837). Spanish American thinkers such as Andrés Bello pronounced a similar need for moral and intellectual revival, not because they felt that too much prosperity had left their societies morally bereft, but because they believed public morality would be a cornerstone for republican stability.[4]

Staël, writing from post-Revolution France and soon to be exiled from it forever, was putting to literary use a metaphor that had first come to life as a description of the psychological effects of crowds on individual voters. As detailed by Pierre Rosanvallon, moral electricity referred to a special civic influence believed to reside in the physical presence of a crowd. Rosanvallon cites a commentator from the 1790s who referred to the capacity of a crowd, in the moment, to transcend individual selfishness: "By way of I know not what moral electricity compounded of elements of all sorts, the majority experiences a shock against which it is helpless" (44). He also notes a 1789 law requiring that public gatherings be held the evening before important votes in the presumable hope that the electric effect would carry over into the next day. The phrase cropped up repeatedly in the US and Spanish press of the early nineteenth century. In 1842 the *Journal of the American Temperance Union* looked toward the future and concluded that "the world has neither seen nor felt the strength and power of the moral electricity it will yet see and feel" ("Journal" 88).[5] Six years later the Spanish progressive newspaper *El Espectador* translated the words of a social reformer in France who referred to "that moral electricity that is released in contact with associated men" ("Luis Blanc" 2). In the first case the effect is generalized. The temperance narrator believes in a chain of influence in which the work of a single reformer multiplies as "one heart kindled with a great moral idea, imparts it in a moment to a thousand, and that thousand to other thousands, and society is revolutionized" ("Journal" 88). For the French speaker, it was a group dynamic that produced the effect. In both cases the invisible electrical force became visible as a large-scale shift in public opinion. Here was an instrument of influence perfectly fitted for a republic and easily multiplied if the printed page could be turned into a conductor.

On the Western side of the Atlantic, the Puerto-Rican intellectual Eugenio María de Hostos employed electricity as a metaphor decades after Brooks, tying it to a stereotypical notion of sentiment as the female-gendered pairing of the emotion-reason binary, and arguing that female students might be the best possible conductors of "moral electricity": "Sentiment awakens the love of the truth in populations unaccustomed to thinking about it, because there is a moral electricity and sentiment is the best conductor of that electricity" (*Ensayos* 37).[6] Paired with traditionally gendered notions of sentiment, this link between emotion and transmission becomes an argument for increased educational opportunities for women: "Sentiment is an unstable, transitory and inconstant faculty in our sex; it is a permanent and constant faculty in women" (37).[7]

This particular spin on the relationships between reason, sentiment, and public morality would also appear in the writings of fin-de-siècle Latin American feminists of both sexes as an argument for why the Spanish American republics needed more women writers and intellectuals. Finding in Staël's sense of postrevolutionary crisis a connection with the reality of Spanish American political and social life a century later, women of letters such as Soledad Acosta and Aurora Cáceres would give Staël a prominent place in their own chronologies of noteworthy literary women while proclaiming the works of women writers as an antidote for a corrupt political culture. In 1895 Acosta, a Colombian novelist, critic, and editor, would acclaim her contemporary, the Peruvian novelist Mercedes Cabello de Carbonera, not on the basis of her successful novel *Blanca Sol*, which had already run to several editions, but because she believed the success of *Blanca Sol* meant that Cabello was capable of writing another sort of book: "No one better than her to give birth to beautiful books, *distinctly American*, that were not sad pictures of very sad uncontrolled passions" (*La mujer* 410).[8] Acosta includes this text in a collective biography that we will explore in more detail in later chapters, and early on she declares a sense of Spanish American crisis, referring to the "cataclysm of immorality, of impiety, of corruption that threatens it" (xi).[9] Against this backdrop, it is to Spanish American women that Acosta entrusts "the great work of regeneration" (xi).[10]

And while Acosta does not focus on books alone as the vehicles of this regeneration, she expects women to contribute, among other roles, "as writers who should broadcast good ideas in society" (386) and so evaluates Cabello de Carbonera as a writer who "could write very noble literary works that filled her readers with enthusiasm for the good and the desire to imitate the examples that she should write" (406).[11] Acosta's elegant grammatical construction is difficult to reproduce in English. The books she describes and their effects on readers all take place in the imperfect subjunctive. They are hypothetical books depending on the condition that Cabello de Carbonera should choose to write them. Where Hostos envisions women as electrical readers, predisposed to receive moral content more reliably than men, Acosta asks her readers to see women authors as particularly electrical writers, writers capable of producing these hypothetical works that will have such clear and far-reaching moral influence. Against a moment of perceived crisis, Staël, Brooks, Hostos, and Acosta coincide in looking for resolution in a morally influential yet-to-be-carried-out act of writing, publishing, and reading. In Acosta's case this hypothetical moral influence serves as linchpin for a feminist argument based as much on practical necessity— the need for moral regeneration throughout the region—as on narrative of emancipation. She argues for the expanded education of women at least in part on the basis of the educational books these emancipated women will produce.

## *Book Scarcity and the Book in Subjunctive*

At roughly the same moment that Brooks was contemplating the United States' need for moral electricity, the Argentine politico and writer, Domingo Faustino Sarmiento, one of Spanish America's most assiduous readers of the educational press, had mentioned his own boyhood debt to Ackermann's catechisms, published in Spanish in London and distributed widely throughout Spanish America in the 1820s, with peak production falling between 1823 and 1828 (Roldán Vera, *The British* 24).[12] Generally written by learned Spaniards or exiled Spanish Americans, Ackermann's catechisms covered everything from arithmetic to Greek mythology. Along with pure basic content—the nineteenth-century version of a MOOC with no active link—some catechisms also offered meta-reflections on the state of life and letters, as in Joaquín Lorenzo de Villanueva's *Catechism of the Literatos* (Catecismo de los literatos).

A humanist and priest by trade, like Brooks, who was himself a Protestant clergyman, Villanueva assessed the promise and dangers of literature in strikingly similar terms. In both cases the positive moral potential of books colors and is colored by a desired kind of reading. Villanueva, for example, notes the common critique of realistic works of fiction and theater as mimetic reproductions of life that thus risk glorifying the evils they wish to condemn because their formal structure forces them to represent those evils convincingly. While not discounting this danger altogether, Villanueva shifts the focus to the intentions of the reader rather than those of the writer. When the catechism's examiner asks "Can the truth be read out of pure curiosity?" the scripted reply distinguishes between superficial and morally directed readings, or to use Brooks's terminology, between brain readings and soul readings: "The truth deserves to be read to be engraved on the spirit: to be sought not for the pleasure of novelty, but rather the fruit" (Villanueva 96).[13]

Villanueva makes it clear that he is writing from a position of knowledge about the contemporary book market and not as a reactionary opponent of progress. His questioner posits the morally positive novel as a concession to contemporary tastes and a product not of some moralistic cabal of reformers but of the market itself. As he puts it—"The masses want to learn morality in novels"—and if this condition is accepted as the novelist's point of departure, the only solution is to meet the public where it can be found: "Give it to them pure, and not corrupted: not in a ridiculous way, but rather with the decorum that society's most important science demands" (60).[14] The aesthetic imperative to make morality reasonable and to present it within an aura of social importance becomes, in Villanueva's vision, the modest moral scope of the novelist's art. Here the task is not formal innovation as an expressive goal but taste and decorum, as a means of conserving morality as a topic of "serious" discussion even while presenting it as mass entertainment. Villanueva is framing the Aristotelian challenge to please and instruct in the context of what a perceived mass audience already desires.

There is an important difference between where Villanueva and Brooks place their own perspectives on the moral novel. For Villanueva, the Spaniard, writing several decades *earlier*, the literary market is a given, a condition of the novelist's world, and not something an individual novelist or theorist of the novel would presume to shape. Brooks, on the other hand, writes from a rhetorical point zero, calling, in effect, for a new industry that will make a new kind of product and with it a new buying public whose habits and expectations will presumably be molded by the hypothetical authors to come. Where they agree is in their identification of the book as medium defined by its ability to transmit moral messages to the reader even when the reader is not aware of receiving them. Villanueva's focus on purity, the injunction that novelists should give the public "pure" the morality it wants or thinks it wants, suggests the possibility of an "impure" delivery or a confused marketplace in which books are essentially "moral" but offer false and true versions of morality. Brooks's use of the term "electricity" renders morality, which he does not feel the need to define, as a content that can become not only transmissible but completely intermingled with the vehicle of the transmission. He speaks not of content rendered transmissible—that would be "electric morality"—but of a means of transmission rendered moral.

Perhaps the excessive "futurity," to borrow Carlos Alonso's term, of Brooks's vision of the literary industry and marketplace to come should not surprise us. Villanueva is, via Ackermann, effectively writing from a London that is not only the undisputed center of the English-language publishing world of the nineteenth-century, but a center of Spanish-language publishing as well, home to established communities of interlocking (and sometimes opposing) Spanish and Spanish American intellectuals in exile.[15] Brooks's vision of a new continent in need of new books is colored by his own reflections on the intellectual relationship between the United States and Europe.

Ironically, Brooks, like his fellow common school proponent Horace Mann and Mann's self-declared Argentine disciple Sarmiento, had made a European tour motivated at least in part by the desire to bring some of the continent's intellectual perspective on education into the US common school movement. In his 1846 reflections on Europe's moral influence, Brooks had floridly condemned the office of letters in terms that merged morality and politics. Along with the general fear that literary imports could become the mode of transmission of "moral and political corruptions," Brooks also made his fear apply to the character of European writers themselves. Noting how much harm could be done by "the second-rate writers of Europe," he identified them as "These legislators in the republic of letters, or rather these submarshals in the intellectual empire," in a twist on Percy Shelley's oft-cited description of poets as "the unacknowledged legislators of mankind" (*Remarks* 39). Brooks attacks the very skillfulness of European writers when he decries the dangers of rhetoric put to immoral ends. They had produced "the boldest defenses of immorality and revolution," and their sensibility was invading the Edenic New World: "Many of them find their way into our own country, where they perform the part which the serpent did in Paradise" (39).

There is a lot to unpack in Brooks's thicket of metaphors, but two points are of special interest. First, by identifying European writers as "submarshals of intellectual empire," Brooks both recalls and revises Shelley, and the echo serves to emphasize an intractable political difference between US and European sensibility, a binary in which the United States equates to the republic and Europe to monarchy and empire. Brooks's comparison could well extend to the rest of the New World as a much more republican continent than Europe, a political avant-garde by comparison. Next, with the curious attack on "immorality and revolution," a charge calculated to bring up associations with the French Revolution and the more recent events of 1830, Brooks manages to levy the paradoxical charge that Europe sports antiquated governments combined with rebellious and immoral publics. On one hand, the continent is too revolutionary, and on the other hand, it has not been revolutionary enough.

Brooks's critique does not single out France, but it gives clear voice to the complicated US perspective on the destruction of the monarchy that did more than any other to support its independence in the first place. Refracted through Anglophone histories of the French Revolution such as Carlyle's and the position in the US zeitgeist of Burke's critique of revolutionary terror, Brooks's evaluation of Europe carries an almost scolding moral edge and finds empirical proof that Americans need not envy the old metropolis or look back to it as an authority. A parallel Spanish American example would be the Mexican clergyman and revolutionary Fray Servando Teresa de Mier, whose action-packed memoirs of travels through Spain, France, and Italy took pains to point out the relative poverty of the population and backwardness of the clergy in comparison with Mexico.

Brooks's combination of pedagogical sensibility and interest in the publishing industry also finds its share of Spanish American counterparts. Where he and his contemporaries, Horace Mann among them, worried about local production of the right sort of books as an economic and intellectual defense mechanism against a perceived flood of European imports, Spanish American intellectuals such as Sarmiento, José del Valle of Central America, and even the rapidly aging Simón Bolívar, who ruled Gran Colombia in the 1820s, would urge the development of local print production more as a matter of desperation than choice. Printing books at home would be the only way to ensure a steady supply of suitable materials.[16]

Two decades after Charles Brooks and Horace Mann lamented the limitations of the US publishing industry, Sarmiento would publish *Las escuelas: base de la prosperidad i la república en los Estados Unidos* (New York, 1866), a treatise intended for Spanish American readers that offered up US progress in public education as an example for the Spanish American republics to follow. In it he would cite Mann's complaint about the insufficient availability of books in his native Massachusetts as a jumping off point to illustrate the severer book scarcity of Spanish America. Noting that Mann "had made the discomforting and alarming discovery that in that republic of then almost a million inhabitants there were no more than THREE HUNDRED LIBRARIES," Sarmiento can only compare the expectations the number implies in terms of book-wealth with those of the fabulously rich in terms of money: "Nothing more than three hundred sixty libraries! What misery? It's like what the bankers always say when some new venture is proposed. 'It won't even leave me with a million!'" (*Las escuelas* 251–52).[17]

Sarmiento's ironic tone is clearly intended to ridicule the Spanish American situation rather than that of the United States, and just in case the point should be lost, he goes on to give his message in more straightforward terms: "Three hundred sixty public libraries would be the glory of South America, with 20 million inhabitants and the world as a dwelling-place" (251–52).[18] The numerical leap his calculations presuppose—a twentyfold difference between the US reality of book distribution and the Spanish American *hope* for it—underscores the shock Sarmiento is hoping to produce in a Spanish American readership that will necessarily be transnational and scattered, given that his words are published and distributed from New York. His ironic sense of a special Spanish American book crisis feeds into a historical reading of US and Spanish difference. What sums up the experience of being a subject of Spanish colonialism, Sarmiento argues, is an intellectual reality in which "The work in twelve volumes containing the list of forbidden books is the alpha and omega of Spanish knowledge of the era. To know what it was not permitted to know!" (250).[19] Here Sarmiento's indictment of Spanish colonial history intends something other than an essential difference between Spanish American and US culture. Having posited public enlightenment as a condition necessarily tied to availability of printed material, he presents the United States as a country in which a large-scale project to develop a publishing industry has been underway for decades and as proof that public consciousness can be the great infrastructure project of the nineteenth century in South America, too.[20]

This sentiment and the desire for national comparison it demonstrates were staples of educational discourse throughout the Americas, from the fact-finding foreign tours carried out respectively by Mann, Brooks, and Sarmiento, to Miguel Luis and Gregorio Víctor Amunátegui's 1856 treatise *De la instrucción primaria en Chile; lo que es, lo que debe ser* (On primary instruction in Chile; what it is, what it should be). The Messrs. Amunátegui argued that the populations of more technologically advanced nations were aided by education as though by a mechanical or industrial breakthrough precisely because of the universality of human intellect: "The Yankees, the English, the French, the Germans, not only see, hear, smell, taste, and touch as we do, they also almost all know how to read, write, and do arithmetic, and this helps them to be more industrious, more moral, more religious" (4).[21]

What is more interesting for our purposes is the shared anxiety about books that seems capable of transcending even categorical differences in production and availability. Mann and Sarmiento have in common a penchant for using publishing and distribution as shorthand for an anxiety about the book that betrays a corresponding belief. This belief is the persistent almost nagging sense of the untapped potential of the form. Both thinkers continually imagine print media as the site of an advance always just around the corner, which will communicate encyclopedic content effortlessly or at least to a degree that surpasses the reader's conscious awareness and effort. Like electricity, this communicability of the written world will be a force whose power is visible only in its effects.

Sarmiento's recounting of his "discovery" of Ackermann's catechisms—and his description isn't specific enough to show if Villanueva's was among them—had sprung from a double sense of scarcity. Writing in 1850 of his teenage self in 1826, Sarmiento remembers finding himself removed from the priest who had been his teacher and mentor. His desire to hear again the lost pedagogical voice of a teacher who taught more by speaking than with books leads him to imagine that there should be a textual substitute for the pedagogue. When he comes across Ackermann's catechisms, a set of publications calculated to fill just the market niche he has intuited, his enthusiastic reaction elevates reflection to invention: "I have found them! I could exclaim like Archimedes, because I had predicted, invented, and looked for those catechisms" (*Recuerdos* 147).[22]

The use of the verb *invent* suggests an equation between imagining an object and creating it, and with it a progression in which the notion of the teaching book as an educational tool that ought to exist leads to the vision of a finished project that in fact already exists, having been invented by someone else. He had remembered himself as wandering and "dreaming congresses, war, glory, liberty, in sum the Republic," and deciding that students in his situation should not have to live completely in their heads: "But there should be books, I said to myself, that deal especially with these things, to teach them to children" (147).[23] Here the youthful Sarmiento calls, as Acosta would call decades later, for a book in subjunctive, a book that in fact existed, but that he could claim to have dreamed into existence himself because of the limits of his own experience.

Sarmiento's emphasis on the particular moment in which the book could still be predicted in subjunctive, at least from interior Argentina, finds echo with a more broadly shared Spanish American anxiety about the book. Where Brooks and Sarmiento's sensibilities meet is precisely around the question of the book in subjunctive. Both Brooks's idealism—"We need books charged with moral electricity"—and Sarmiento's (at least remembered) inventiveness in the face of scarcity—"But there should be books"—find their vision of futurity, in terms of both social change and government reforms, summed up in a vision of the book still to come. As believers in the moral influence of literature, they also count on this book to help bring about the new social and/or moral order they represent.

It isn't difficult to find other examples of the rhetoric of the book in subjunctive in a Spanish American context. In Central America the Honduran-born José del Valle (1780–1834), a jurist and essayist closer to Simón Bolívar's generation than to Sarmiento's, founded and edited *El Amigo de la Patria*, a newspaper that offered a moderate, Enlightenment-tinged take on Spanish American futurity. One of the founding voices of the Federal Republic of Central America (1821–1841), del Valle has been described as a "citizen of Central America and would-be citizen of all America" (Parker 528–29) and as a master political pragmatist in an unstable environment, able "to think like a liberal and act like a conservative, in order to keep his position" (McCallister 129).[24]

Del Valle's 1829 *Memoria sobre la educación* employed the language of the Bourbon reforms, imperial Spain's last failed reform project in the Americas, to sketch out the necessary scope of a Spanish American educational program. With an implicit nod to the long tradition of Hispanic voices on the theme of agricultural reform, del Valle sees a gap in education, which he defines as another form of cultivation: "There should be another system of *hominis cultura* to develop all of the faculties of man" (*Memoria* 36).[25] He goes on to explain that his own text had begun as an attempt at a much larger project: "a dictionary dedicated to the sciences that would offer, in the sum total of its articles, a system of methods to facilitate their acquisition" (38).[26] Clearly echoing Diderot and D'Alembert's eighteenth-century encyclopedia, the work they insisted could be completed only by a team of intellectuals, del Valle's proposal adds the dimension of knowledge acquisition. Targeting an unlearned audience, it would provide methods for learning the very information it contains. Like Sarmiento's imagined catechism, del Valle's book proposes to fill a supply and demand gap by producing an encyclopedia whose job, in part, it will be to create a public capable of actually reading it. Del Valle has not gone so far as to suggest a book that will actually teach the public literacy, but one that will make literate but unscientific readers competent in the use of empirical methods.

Unlike Sarmiento's moment of discovery, however, del Valle's perceived gap does not lead to a breakthrough publication. He confesses that his own inadequacy—"the inferiority of my knowledge" (*Memoria* 39)—has made the project an impossible one to complete.[27] Instead he will develop a collection of articles on education, something that we might describe now as a forerunner to Sarmiento's *Educación popular* or Mann's *Common School Journal*, projects that saw print decades later. But again, in less than the space of a page, del Valle finds himself stymied, this time not by his own limitations but by those of the Spanish American market. As a profit-making or even a break-even proposition, it strikes him that the article collection would be doomed: "It would be costly to publish it in a country where printing is expensive and where the buyers of books are few" (39).[28] Del Valle's thought experiment thus falls into a conceptual vapor lock: the educational project that would turn the Spanish American public into a readership is of course not feasible until a certain percentage of that public can be defined already as book-buying readers. In order to exist in the market, the teaching book must, at least to some degree, already be unnecessary. Del Valle concludes that what he will in fact publish is this single *memoria* in the pages of *El Amigo de la Patria* with the implicit hope that it will create the conditions for the teaching book and/or the encyclopedia that remain in subjunctive limbo.[29]

## *Sagas of the "Biblioteca Americana"*

Del Valle's hopeless desire to write an encyclopedia from early nineteenth-century Central America does become something more than a mere dead end. He uses the failed or never attempted project as the inspiration for an insightful journal article on education and thus exemplifies the fluid relationship between books and magazines as venues and imaginary places in Spanish American letters. In a literary world in which novels frequently made their first appearance on the pages of a newspaper and in which the books themselves would be printed on a printing press owned by a newspaper, the worlds of periodicals and books were conceptually and physically intertwined.[30] Along with the encyclopedia, the encyclopedic and in some cases transnational periodical served as another kind of publishing dream. And if del Valle despaired of the difficulty of reaching a literary marketplace from within the confines of a provincial capital in Central America, the attempt to capture a spirit of Spanish America from the safer distance of a metropolis like London or New York carried its own perils. Andrés Bello's London-based publishing projects, *Biblioteca Americana* and *El Repertorio Americano*, exemplified the close relationship between book dreams and the periodical press. And while they do not provide a concrete link between European thought and Gorriti's Lima salon, they did introduce Staël's writings on the social influence of literature to a Spanish-speaking, pan-American audience of the sort envisioned in those *veladas*.

Bello, a delegate from Venezuela's first independent government, had stayed in London, while his even younger colleague Simón Bolívar returned home to eventual fame and glory, and in the years preceding his own return to Spanish America and subsequent fame as founder of the University of Chile, Bello participated in a number of publishing projects directed at an imagined pan-Hispanic readership. For Bello, as for many others in the pluralistic Hispanic exile community, London afforded the transatlantic distance in which to imagine and communicate with a readership spanning all of Spanish America. *Biblioteca Americana*, as noted by Gómez García, included a translated fragment of Staël's treatise on the social effects of literature, a text translated into Spanish and annotated by Bello's coeditor, Juan García del Río. Gómez García identifies the publication of Bello and García del Río's *Biblioteca* and the transatlantic publication that followed, *El Repertorio Americano*, as steps that helped create "the opening of an unknown creative horizon" (22–23).[31] He also traces a progression between those early (and unsuccessful) magazines and projects such as Sarmiento's *Recuerdos de provincia*. This is one way of parsing what Mary Pratt has identified as the "European-American creole logic" of a publishing project by expatriates writing from England and seeking to define their work as essentially American (*Imperial* 170).[32]

García del Río's specific comments on Staël underline his (and we may assume, Bello's) belief in a number of pedagogical assumptions. He quotes George Washington on the benefits of free circulation of information (and merchandise) and sees in Staël's work the articulation of how human motivation at the individual level becomes the lever of widespread social and political change. Staël, he asserts, "has shown with great exactness just how powerful an influence literature has on the virtue, happiness, glory and liberty of nations, and the immense power it exercises over these great sentiments, prime movers of man" (García del Río 20).[33] García del Río's seemingly simple progression is worth breaking down. Beginning with the large argument of literature as an influence over abstract "national" emotions scattered over the experiences of countless individuals, García del Río works backward to the universal notion of these emotions as primary motivators for human behavior. Some pages later, he will credit Staël with a diagnosis for Spanish American political instability. Her writings speak of the dangers of "the selfishness of a state of nature combined with the active multiplication of social interests" along with those of "corruption without culture," and in these warnings, García del Río sees the need for a grand project of group education: "It's absolutely necessary, then, Americans, for us to dedicate ourselves to self-improvement, and to advancing our intellectual faculties" (35).[34] The crisis of independence is a crisis of education, and therefore a crisis of culture, best remedied by writing and reading. *Biblioteca Americana* presents itself as annunciator of and solution to the problem.

Three years later, penning the prospectus for another transatlantic project titled *El Repertorio Americano* (1826), Bello posited both projects as the fruits of deeply felt need for "a periodical that would defend, as a cause close to its heart, the independence and freedom" of the Spanish American republics, and one that, among other tasks, would serve as a real-time archive for summaries of domestic and foreign writings on the Americas as well as for the collection of previously unpublished materials (Bello 3). Speaking of those "unpublished works," Bello asks the archivist's timeless question about oblivion, a question sharpened by the patent lack of a Spanish American publishing industry: "How many of these lie buried in the coffers of collectors for lack of resources to publish them in America? How many perish in the hands of ignorance and apathy, defrauding their countries of useful information and their authors of public praise and gratitude?" (3) These questions make a nod both to a set of material limitations— "lack of resources"—and intellectual or even moral ones—"ignorance and apathy"—to paint a Spanish American reality in which circumstances work against the printed word.

Bello's shift to the new project acknowledges this Spanish American deficiency as an obvious reality. He dismisses *Biblioteca Americana*'s failure as the result of "obstacles impossible for us to foresee or overcome" despite a demand for the publication that exceeded the number of printed copies (4). The new venture, he argues, will succeed because of "a better organized system in the distribution and circulation of the journal," and because of its being published (as was the first) in London, which he characterizes as an absolute necessity, given its position at the center of a web of transatlantic trade. Connection, Bello seems to be asserting, means more than location, so he can frankly declare, speaking of the British capital: "Its commercial relations with the countries on the other side of the Atlantic make it, in a sense, the center of them all" (3).[35] For much of the early independence era in Spanish America, Europe functions as one of the only possible platforms for the region-wide distribution of ideas.

Bello designates his own journal as a rapid remedy for the lack of Spanish American book production and the resulting gap in popular and academic knowledge on Spanish American topics among the Spanish Americans themselves. When he outlines the goals for his new magazine proposal, he includes among them the diffusion of historical information: "We propose to illustrate some of the most interesting events of our revolution, unknown to much of the world and even to Americans themselves" (5–6). Along with the task of bearing witness to events that have been forgotten, Bello also characterizes this historical imperative as a moral one. History, and recent history (at least in the American context), becomes for Bello a natural point of convergence between the attractiveness of narrative and the moral influence that narrative can exert on its readers, as the task of circulating "any number of interesting anecdotes in which the talents and virtues of our immortal readers stand revealed, as well as the sufferings and sacrifices of a heroic people" folds into the larger goal "to establish the cult of morality on the indestructible basis of education" (5–6). While Bello is careful to classify this history as popular *and* heroic, he includes the virtues of the Spanish American public along with those of its heroes and praises "the clemency of some, the generosity of others, and the patriotism of almost all." His phrase reaches a rhetorical climax on an unattributed citation linking individual heroism and national identity: "We believe that the heritage of every free country lies in the glory of its great men," a phrase Bello credits to "a distinguished writer" (5–6).

Bello is arguing at once for the intrinsic aesthetic and historical value of the "anecdotes" of the struggle for independence, but also for their collective role in developing a national and regional identity—in this case, a shared Spanish American republican consciousness. This problem, the narrative task of constructing a shared American mythology, is one area of national development where Spanish American concerns echoed those of US thinkers. In the waning days of the US struggle for political independence from the British Empire, the US journalist, schoolteacher, and lexicographer Noah Webster, who would publish the first American dictionary of English in 1828, had argued that a narrative history of the American Revolution should be written and distributed widely as a text for the new republic's schools. In his 1790 work, *A Collection of Essays and Fugitiv Writings* (the spelling "Fugitiv" is an example of Webster's experiments toward a more phonographic English), Webster complains of "the want of proper books" a few pages after he had acknowledged his own belief that "vice always spreads by being published" (23, 21).

The ideal schoolbook for the new republic as Webster imagines it would include the following components: "A selection of essays, reflecting the settlement and geography of America; the history of the late revolution and of the most remarkable events and characters that distinguished it, and a compendium of the principles of the federal and provincial governments" (23). Webster's catalog includes both factual content and the "good principles" that he argues are essential for "The great art of correcting mankind" (22). On the one hand, his proposed book will make students conversant with the factual and biographical details of the foundation of the republic and its physical landscape. Here we might say his plan echoes the emphasis on geography and natural resources so prominent among educational texts of the Bourbon reformers, Jovellanos and Campomanes, and with it an Americanization of the colonial problem of mapping and exploiting New World nature. The "good principles" his plan offers are those of the existing governmental structure—his book appeared just three years after the 1787 Constitution of the United States of America—as well as whatever political and/or moral lessons could be gleaned from the narration of the "remarkable events and characters" of the independence struggle.

Like the Spanish American commentators who followed him, Webster saw in the printed book a way to render permanent and pedagogical the events of the revolution itself as well as the lively debates in which he had himself participated in the US pedagogical press. This formulation of "progress" from periodical press to book publishing frames a narrative of development in which the presence of a newspaper industry confirms a certain level of modernity, while the vision of the book in subjunctive wraps up a combination of practical and mystical notions of the yet-to-be-tapped potential of the printing press for reproducing and advancing that modernity.[36]

The notion of national or collective progress toward a book in subjunctive is far from being an exclusively American idea. Maurice Blanchot's phrase, "*the book to come*," describes a remarkably similar phenomenon not necessarily connected to the New World pursuit of independence. This future book, he argues, is "the book written in nature," and he describes it as a mystical whole that, like the natural world under the taxonomy of Enlightenment observers, could only be brought to light in pieces: "hidden and venerable book that shines in fragments hidden here and there" (Blanchot 228). Blanchot's phrasing brings to mind Enlightenment notions of the New World as a natural reservoir awaiting its catalogers, but he writes with the French fin de siècle poet Stéphane Mallarmé in mind, with particular emphasis on his debt to the German Romantics, and he quotes Novalis on the dream of future books as a necessary precondition for the intellect that seeks to investigate the world: "To write a Bible, said Novalis—that is the madness that every knower must welcome in order to be complete" (228).

One New World version of this totalizing desire would be the kinds of projects announced by Brooks and Webster—the creation of a publishing industry designed to incorporate moral lessons based on a perceived US distance from European corruption and the imperative to include New World material, historical narratives, place-names, and spellings in the printed textbooks used in US schools. This vision of the US publishing industry sees it both as a pedagogical tool that will raise awareness of the struggle for independence and the events leading up to it, and also as print validation for US customs and modes of speech. Andrés Bello's *Gramática de la lengua castellana destinada al uso de los americanos* (1847) and his later writings on the importance of narrative history are parallel examples that combine the desire for a codified American language and an American historical narrative written in it. Just as Webster proclaimed the events of the independence struggle itself as fit material for the foundational narrative textbook for the republic's schools, so Andrés Bello, in his inaugural address at the University of

Chile, would challenge his listeners, the writers of the future, to "write about subjects that are worthy of your country and posterity" before offering his own patriotic assessment of what those subjects might be: "And has not our young republic already presented you with magnificent themes? Celebrate its great days; weave garlands for its heroes, consecrate the shroud of the country's martyrs" (Bello 136). For Bello as for Webster, the project of making new American books benefits from the distinct advantage of the narrative at hand, the stuff of myth in the sense that the independence struggle is an origin story, at least in political terms, and one that can still be composed and distributed before the generation that witnessed it has passed.

In the years after the 1836 founding of the University of Chile, Bello would continue to wrestle with the question of what sort of influence historical narrative can and should seek to visit on its readers, especially when those readers are the citizens of a relatively young republic. One of his first claims is that independence should be recognized as a singular historical event. The present moment from which Bello writes is marked, as he sees it, by both an abundance of accessible sources for historical narrative and an urgent need to get those narratives down on paper: "There is no lack of materials to consult, if they are sought intelligently and patiently in private collections, in archives, and in trustworthy traditions, and we must hasten to publish them before they become completely obscure and forgotten" (157). The notion that future historians will recalibrate any immediate historical verdicts strikes Bello as an argument for writing as many narratives as quickly as possible so as to give those future historians more material to work with (158–59). Part of the business of being a young Spanish American republic, Bello argues, is the need to create a written historical tradition: "The first step is to get the facts straight, then to explore their spirit, demonstrate their connections, reduce them to broad and comprehensive generalizations" (171).

Ever anxious about the power of a written record and the pernicious influence of its absence, Bello imagines a historiographical future rife with chaos and distortion if attempts at historical narrative are not made immediately. "If history is not written by contemporaries, then future generations will have to write it by following adulterated oral traditions (for nothing deforms and falsifies as quickly as oral traditions), newspaper articles, impassioned speeches by political parties, the product of first impressions, and arid official documents whose veracity is frequently suspect" (158–59). Here Bello, like Webster before him, offers a tacit definition of America as the focal point of a crucial instant in historiography, the forefront of a Western narrative of progress. The task is twofold, though not two-stage, as the public must be convinced simultaneously that the hemisphere's narrative is worthy of being written and of being read.

### *Olavide's Unwritten Gospel*

Bello and Webster's emphasis on the moral writing and rewriting of history finds a precursor in the Peruvian-born courtier and educational reformer Pablo de Olavide (1725–1803). A popular author and intellectual in his own time, and the host of lively gatherings of the sort that Gorriti would revive in her own day, he was undergoing at least a minor revival in the final decades of the nineteenth century. While he spent most of his life and all of his writing career in Europe, Olavide straddled a geographical and political divide that allowed Spain, Peru, and France to claim (or dismiss) him as part of their literary history. A brilliant administrator, he was named *Oidor* and auditor general of the Viceroyalty before he turned thirty—a meteoric rise that at least one Spanish reviewer would cite as proof that Creole claims of colonial unfairness in appointments and promotions were greatly exaggerated (Barrantes 42).[37] In Spain he wrote a treatise on education, a number of plays and essays on theater, and directed the royal program that brought European colonists to Sierra Morena. When he ran afoul of the still-powerful authorities of the Inquisition, France seemed a logical enough place of refuge for an intellectual whom one contemporary called "the target on which the Inquisitors (may they rest forever in peace) fired their perfidious shots" ("Una proeza" 123–24).[38] In France, "The precursory lightning bolts of the Revolution managed also to illuminate Olavide's soul" (Barrantes 61), and it was only when he found himself threatened by the guillotine that he escaped once more, in the spring of 1794, to "a friendly roof in Chaverny, near Blois" (62), where he wrote the work that would become a kind of masterpiece, a multivolume epistolary novel that would see print in Valencia in 1797 and in subsequent editions under the title *El evangelio en triunfo*.[39]

Written at a (barely) safe remove from the tumult of the revolu-

Cover page of *El Perú Ilustrado* featuring a tribute to early Peruvian networker and moral novelist Pablo de Olavide (1725–1803). Courtesy of the Library of the University of California, Berkeley.

tion by a one-time supporter driven to disillusionment with the cause (P. P. M. Vélez has referred to the book as having been composed "almost at the foot of the scaffold of the unfortunate Louis XVI" [Vélez 159]),[40] *El evangelio en triunfo* is nevertheless the work of a dedicated social reformer whose educational writings had served as precursors to more famous texts by Pedro Rodríguez, Conde de Campomanes, and Gaspar Melchor de Jovellanos. Too radical to remain in Spain and too conservative for the Jacobins, Olavide spent his days in the country villa of a friend weaving the autobiographically tinged tale of a secular philosopher's conversion to Christianity,[41] a book that served as a kind of passport back into Spain, where he wrote poetry and a series of short didactic novels that would be published in New York two decades after his death and only added to his oeuvre in the late twentieth century by the Peruvian critic Estuardo Núñez.[42]

While Olavide does not choose the term *desengaño*, which we could translate as "disillusionment," in his title, his work serves as an early example of an argumentative tack that would become popular among Spanish conservatives in the decades after the Napoleonic invasion of Spain and the explosion of independence movements in Spanish America.[43] Placed in an exiled limbo in which the complexities of geopolitics to some degree mirrored the contradictions of his own position—too much of an orthodox Christian for revolutionary France, too liberal and too enlightened for Spanish Catholicism—he painstakingly frames *El evangelio en triunfo* as an attempt at another impossible book project, the presentation of Christian doctrine in a form palatable to enlightened readers. Striking a tone that would remind Spanish readers (if not Spanish censors) of Feijoo's *Teatro crítico universal*, he presents Voltaire as the literary villain of the age by likening his widely circulated texts to "poisoned arrows" let fly on an unsuspecting public (*El evangelio* 4:296).

Lest the critique of Voltaire lead his readers to assume that a particularly manipulative *writer* is the cause of the era's loss of religious faith, he also provides a critique of public taste that very much serves as precursor to the laments of nineteenth-century educators focusing their critique on the popularity of the novel. The problem with the reading public, as Olavide sees it, is that its palate has been ruined. In his own historical moment, the era of the French Revolution, readers will only sample ideas seasoned with "the salt of jokes and the pepper of gossip"

(4:302).⁴⁴ Amid such a distortion, taste itself, which might have led the literary marketplace to reward virtue and punish subversion, sends false signals as "The poison is sweet and the antidote seems bitter to them" (4:307).⁴⁵

Against this grim vision of the writer-reader relationship in which the old charms no longer work, at least as incentives to Christian notions of virtue, Olavide expresses the Christian book in subjunctive that the Enlightenment needs to read and produce, a work that will appeal to public taste such as it is while at the same time shaping the popular notion of virtue—a book that will meet the public in its place and move it somewhere else. These reflections, it should be noted, come at the end of a four-volume chronicle of one philosopher's conversion from secularist to enlightened Christian. Thus a weary reader survives Olavide's twisting journey back to Christian orthodoxy only to meet his appeal for a new book that would combine the clearest arguments for the Christian faith into a single narrative and thus serve, like the historical narratives imagined by Noah Webster and Andrés Bello, as both a record and a pedagogical tool (4:317). Such a useful work, Olavide continues, would be the ultimate publishing project, a no-brainer for the conservative governments that have already shown their willingness to amass armies to fight the French Revolution.

Olavide's interest in the book project of the future relates directly to his own sense of print technology as a revolutionary force for shaping public opinion. In volume three of *El evangelio*, he had observed that "in our time the art of printing has reached, in our hands, a level of perfection it never had before" (3:377)—and new technology translates into new opportunities for enlightened evangelism via the printed page.⁴⁶ These observations do not come out of nowhere. In fact, Olavide alludes to his notion of the book to come as early as the prologue to *El evangelio* when he speaks of the pedagogical utility of "a concise book, with a clear method, and a style proportional to its intelligence" (1:vi).⁴⁷ The "electrical," as Brooks would put it, or effortless and invisible delivery of the message, will happen by way of narrative, as the events of the story occupy the reader's attention: "A story that pretends to nothing more than storytelling, sustained by actions and animated by dialogues, could perhaps awaken curiosity, make itself of interest to readers, and give them a fondness for doctrine" (1:ix–x).⁴⁸ Olavide is particularly vague on just how this collateral effect will occur. Does the "doctrine" in question mean religious doctrine in general, as a subject of debate, a new interest that will be the first path on the way to Christian awakening, or does it mean orthodox Christianity itself? What comes through clearly is the inherently deceptive nature of the project, since the narrative cannot at once seek to interest readers in Christian doctrine while at the same time "pretending to nothing more than storytelling." Here storytelling is akin to rhetoric in its original sense, a technical use of language to achieve a desired result. And here, of course, the very limits of public taste work for rather than against the hypothetical Christian author. The public that wants only poison will receive an antidote disguised to taste like poison.[49]

Olavide died in Jaen, Spain, in 1803, two decades before Ackermann's catechism project would put moral literature into the hands of Spanish American youths who would one day become influential leaders.[50] In 1828, however, a handful of moral novels appeared in Spanish in New York City, published by the house of Lanuza, Mendia and Company, all listed as either anonymous or written by "el autor de *El evangelio en triunfo*." Olavide scholar Estuardo Núñez would classify these works as latter-day versions of the *novela exemplar* of Cervantes on the one hand (100), and as a Spanish outgrowth of the moralism of eighteenth-century British fiction on the other (86).[51] Noting that Lanuza's New York-based, Spanish-language catalog included translations of Voltaire and biographies of George Washington and Benjamin Franklin, Núñez describes Olavide's posthumous novels as books that fit in by dint of their hybrid nature as "a genre mixed between the novel and the didactic text" (102), and identifies Olavide, who never returned to his native Peru, as "the first American novel in time although not in themes" (109).[52]

Olavide enjoyed and suffered the combination of celebration and oblivion not uncommon for unorthodox thinkers of his generation, sharing the distinction of appearing in Marcelino Menéndez y Pelayo's *Historia de los heterodoxos españoles* (1880–1881). Providing the literary equivalent of damnation with faint praise, Menéndez y Pelayo classifies Olavide as "a philanthropic dreamer, but with a certain naïve good faith that at times makes him agreeable" (*Historia* 3:207).[53] Writing in the same time period as Pardo Bazán, Acosta, and Cabello de Carbonera, Menéndez y Pelayo also goes to some lengths to affirm the sincerity of Olavide's religious conversion and of *Evangelio en triunfo*, as well as the book's success: "Published in Valencia in 1798 without the author's name, it was reprinted four times in one year, and reached every corner of Spain, provoking a favorable reaction for Olavide" (3:215).[54] If we combine this evaluation with Gerard Dufour's assessment that "it was a widely purchased book, a *best seller*, as we would say nowadays," but that on the other hand "those who had the patience to read it until the end were very few" (164), the picture that emerges is of a book that at least succeeded in turning the figure of Olavide into a household word.[55]

Olavide's fame extended beyond the Spanish-speaking world, too, showing up as it did in the correspondence of Diderot and Voltaire, among others. This cosmopolitanism, of course, serves as at best a double-edged form of virtue in the eyes of commentators such as Barrantes and Lavalle, who are prepared to celebrate Olavide precisely because of his eventual rejection of the ideals of the French Revolution.[56]

Lavalle has nothing but praise for *El evangelio en triunfo*, which he refers to as "an edifying book" and which he credits with possessing "vigorous logic and a vast and profound erudition both theological and philosophical" (Lavalle 116).[57] Identifying him as a part of a catalog of literary defenders of the faith that begins with Chateaubriand and ends with Donoso Cortés (116), Lavalle argues that one of Olavide's singular attributes is his narrative of conversion: "Like the fierce Sicambrian, he burned down what he had once adored and adored what he had once burned down" (117).[58] Despite the sarcasm and condescension of Barrantes's and Lavalle's portrayal of Olavide and especially of his relationship with Enlightenment philosophy, their ultimately positive verdict reveals the degree to which Olavide's twisting allegiances, which served to produce so many enemies in the present tense of his lifetime, could make him a rallying point for all sorts of readings of the French Revolution from the safer space of the late nineteenth century.

Lavalle, it should be added, is convinced that his book is doing Peru a great service by bringing back the legacy of an enlightened/Christian hero who had largely been subsumed into the historical memory of the mother country. His 1885 edition (the original was published in 1859) recounts the author's experience of finding a street called "calle de Olavide" during an 1880 visit to Madrid. He notes the contrast with the Lima, ca. 1880, in which "there is nothing that recalls that here a man who was called an *honor to his country* was born, educated and lived up until the age of 24" (135).[59] One thing Lavalle is sure of, in 1859 as well as 1885, is that Olavide represents a "severe and eloquent moral lesson" (xvi), a sentiment only magnified by the War of the Pacific (1881–1883)—which he admits delayed preparation of the second edition—and the ensuing sense of crisis and political instability in Lima (x).[60] The writer who planned a publishing project as a response, indeed an antidote, to the excesses of the French Revolution, would thus enjoy a kind of twilight afterlife as a morally conservative hero to brandish against nineteenth-century positivism. The book itself, remembered as a beautiful coffee-table piece encountered in childhood, ironically becomes the tool for Lavalle's exploration of the "real" Olavide and thus a backward-pointing marker to his time-bound future-mindedness.

### *Exemplarity: The Case for a Universal Lima*

There is little evidence that Olavide served directly as a fount of inspiration for the circle of feminist writers and intellectuals who gathered at Juana Manuela Gorriti's Lima *veladas* of 1876 or 1877, or even for the subsequent moral and political theories of the novel that Mercedes Cabello de Carbonera, Clorinda Matto, and other members of that generation would formulate. One late nineteenth-century commentator disturbed by the rising materialism of Peruvian society in the wake of the defeat in the War of the Pacific would decry "the dizzying whirlwind of material interests in which our young society finds itself enveloped" (Orbegosa 3), and then invoke Olavide in her plea for a national sense of history, remembering "our beloved *patria*, illustrious cradle of Olavide and Pardo" (4).[61] It was during the run-up to the war that Gorriti convened her literary salons very much in the tradition of Olavide, which came to be known as the *veladas literarias*, a phrase that served as a title for an 1892 collection of talks given at those events.

That publication, when read alongside the accounts of observers and participants such as Serrano, crystallized the *veladas* as international literary events linking not only Lima and Buenos Aires but also the various home countries and countries of residence of the participants, as they included talks given by authors and talks sent from abroad by authors and read by someone else. While the talks preserved in Gorriti's volume make no mention of the word "electricity," in terms moral or otherwise, they do repeat the synthesis between moral idealism and scientific terminology. Taking up the same topic that prompted Eugenio María de Hostos to speak of moral electricity, Benicio Alamos González's talk, titled "Enseñanza superior de la mujer" (Higher education for women), lamented the fact that "up until now she has been used at half-steam," and suggested that "we work so that she is given the full steam of science and art, so that she can help the man to pull more rapidly the carriage of human progress" (Gorriti, *Veladas* 348).[62]

In Alamos González's case, the industrial metaphor of scientific and technological progress as a train car being pulled forward by the efforts of women and men creates a doubling effect as the metaphor of "steam"—a more visible form of energy than electricity—describes both the new impulse that should be given to Spanish American women and the force behind the larger narrative of progress already underway. Women must go "full steam" as part of a metaphorical locomotive made up of both women and men that will presumably be operating at "fuller steam" with both halves of the region's population supporting it. Alamos González's proposal stops short of being revolutionary, despite his introductory phrase—"The revolution that I'm going to propose to you will not be violent" (348).[63] Soon after the locomotive metaphor, he returns to the Pestalozzian notion of motherhood as the basis of female education. And his proposal sits alongside a talk given by Mercedes Cabello de Carbonera arguing for women's education and the importance of women writers.

The metaphors that bring this network together and that link it with broader networks of writers and educational reformers—steam, electricity, the promise of a book in subjunctive—all point toward the book as a project capable of shaping the future on an industrial scale via personal connection. Edmundo Bendezu Aibar, for example, would point to the idea of "exemplarity" (*ejemplaridad*) in his attempt to link Cabello de Carbonera all the way back to Olavide (82–83).[64] Indeed the promise of a book to come remains an attractive ideal across a century in which the landscape of publishing and writing in Spanish America changed utterly. As Roldán Vera has noted, the century's narrative is one of large if inadequate expansion of the region's literacy rate, from "less than 10% in 1800, increasing to 15% in 1850, and reaching around 27% by 1900" (*The British* 34), and the subjunctive book would be just as attractive an idea at the beginning of the twentieth century as it had been at the end of the eighteenth. In the next two chapters we will explore the hemisphere-wide obsession with biography, the genre that most straightforwardly sought to harness exemplarity for its readership, and another possible but always sufficiently doubtful means of attempting the mythical teaching book to come.

# 2

# Exemplary Autodidacts

## *The Autodidact Mystique*

One window into the power of the heroic learner as narrator is the posthumous fame of Sor Juana Inés de la Cruz, the poet in life who went on to become an exemplary autodidact generations later. Her reappearance in the writings of generations of feminists who followed the Lima group also speaks to the power of the autodidact as a symbol and spur to gender emancipation. When the twentieth-century Mexican poet and person of letters Rosario Castellanos took up the question of the book she would like to take with her to a desert island, one of the authors she had trouble dismissing was the seventeenth-century Mexican poet and person of letters Sor Juana Inés de la Cruz. A nun whose poems were published to great acclaim in Madrid during her lifetime but whose confessor eventually ordered her to abandon all literary pursuits, Sor Juana is a canonical writer whose career was to some degree defined by marginality. When a contemporary writing under a pseudonym challenged her right to publish on theological topics, the poet became an autobiographer and traced her own intellectual history in her "Response to Sor Filotea."

Looking backward three hundred years, Castellanos is struck by the secular tone of Sor Juana's epistemology—"If she wants to arrive at God, she wants to arrive by the use of reason and not illumination" (164), and when she takes up the question of women autobiographers, Castellanos places Sor Juana in the company of Saint Teresa of Avila and Virginia Woolf.[1] The latter, Castellanos imagines, "would have found in this figure an antecedent for her archetypal Judith, possible sister of Shakespeare, possibly gifted with genius like his but sacrificed for the patriarchal organization of society" (34).[2]

Castellanos is recounting Woolf's thought experiment: what would happen if Shakespeare had a sister, Judith, with all of her brother's literary gifts? Rather than finding literary stardom and historical transcendence, she argues, this hypothetical sister would have come to an unhappy end completely determined by the prejudices of her historical moment, an end that her talents would only serve to magnify. Woolf imagines "that any woman born with a great gift in the sixteenth century would certainly have gone crazed, shot herself, or ended her days in some lonely cottage outside the village, half witch, half wizard, feared and mocked at" (*A Room* 51). Sor Juana's life story confirms or debunks the rhetorical certainty of Woolf's conclusion depending on how much we choose to weigh her successful career as a poet against her decision to abandon writing late in life at the orders of her confessor.

By considering Woolf and Sor Juana together, Castellanos makes Sor Juana a real-life example of Woolf's hypothetical construction and implicitly argues for women's life writing as historical necessity. Woolf's book is structured as a search for successful, exemplary women writers on the one hand and, on the other, as an attempt to map just how much literary achievement has been prevented or forgotten by a conspiracy of opposing social and historical forces, some conscious, some not. When Woolf opines, thinking of a nameless face at the counter of a shop, that "I would as soon have her true history as the hundred and fiftieth life of Napoleon or seventieth study of Keats and his use of Miltonic inversion" (94), she indicts the larger world of publishing for leaving out the stories of ordinary women in favor of the repetition of a male-dominated canon. She also suggests women's life writing as a necessary condition for political progress. The fact that she must invent a Judith Shakespeare serves as evidence not only of the patriarchal false memory she wishes to map but also of a need for such biographies and the existence of a potential readership.

Woolf shares with John Henry Newman an academic reverence for literary tradition as the precondition for any present notion of literary potential—the belief that mediocre talent in a tradition has at her fingertips more tools for reaching a readership than the transcendent talent outside a tradition—and so the question of what has been written, read, or forgotten in the past takes on a more than hypothetical importance as a producer of the literary and intellectual present. Woolf's

Venezuelan contemporary Teresa de la Parra would take a similar tack, finding solace in Sor Juana as proof that real intellectual culture lurked inside the network of colonial convents. The surviving works of the poet and autobiographer thus speak for an unnamed legion of forgotten or would-be writers. By Parra's lights the figure of Sor Juana stands out as "prototype of the intellectual mystic that so abounded in the colonial convents" (2:42).[3] By this reasoning, it is not historical circumstances alone but historical circumstances plus centuries of forgetting that have made it possible to frame Sor Juana as one of Woolf's literary freaks.

The convent itself serves as a convenient metaphor for the paradoxical relationship between expression and formal confines, and so Castellanos celebrates Sor Juana's ability to contain multitudes within a small space—"Sor Juana, who takes advantage of her confinement in the punishment cell to discover some principle of geometry [ . . . ] who in the kitchen probes the fundamental principles of chemistry [ . . . ] who in children's songs perceived the rhythm that orders the universe" (164).[4] In this sense, Sor Juana's confinement in the convent becomes the setting for what we might call "a cell of one's own" or an institutional variation of the "room of one's own" that Woolf would identify as a literal and figurative requirement for a writer's development—and in British and Western society in general, a space denied even to educated women. Castellanos invokes Sor Juana's precursor, Saint Teresa of Avila, as an example whose life embodied intellectual freedom born of physical confinement: "Behind the bars of enclosure it becomes apparent to her what Valéry would formulate centuries later: that from the greatest rigor is born the greatest freedom" (Castellanos 33).[5]

The image of a hypothetical universe of reading in which Woolf's Judith Shakespeare might communicate with Sor Juana underlines the degree to which life writing—biography and autobiography—depends on a circuit of readership. When Castellanos champions women's life writing as a reality check that represents "the rejection of those false images that false mirrors offer the woman in the closed gallery in which she lives out her life" (18), she acknowledges the existence of a community of readers and potential imitators of exemplary lives, a community whose underrepresentation on the printed page only increases the importance of each individual written life.[6]

Sor Juana would also be adopted as an early symbol of independent American thought, a precursor of independence avant la lettre, a national symbol of "the deed of *becoming what one is*" (18).[7] By this lens the heroic autodidact has in common with the independent republic the metaphorical arc toward knowledge and autonomy, the arc in which the narrative of the student serves both as a metaphor and as a guide. The circuit of readers makes each written life the tale of one education enacted on the page and innumerable educations inspired among future readers. In this sense, the autobiography of intellectual awakening is the ultimate book in subjunctive for the republic that is a metaphorical student and that identifies with the educations of its founders, precursors, and representatives. Two hundred years after Sor Juana's death, the North American diplomat, intellectual, and republican aristocrat Henry Adams would define his own life story as an attempt to resolve a persistent "problem of education" (Adams 4).

For the independence-minded audience, whether independence means national or personal emancipation, the struggles and triumph of the autodidact prove the exigency of knowledge under difficulty while painting a personal and national example of the learner who never stops learning. In this chapter I will examine three exemplary autodidacts with particular resonance in Spanish America—Benjamin Franklin, Domingo Faustino Sarmiento, and Abraham Lincoln. Like Sor Juana, these figures came to life as textual creations acknowledged for exercising a moral influence on readers. While the veneration of these figures no doubt contributed to the patriarchal power structures against which the Lima circle would argue, the repetitions and variations of their stories established habits of reading that the Lima circle's own biographical projects would seek to redirect. Just as all three of these figures became associated by analogy with larger historical processes, so the feminist biographies I will analyze in the following chapter make exemplary women models of the narrative progression of the cause of women's rights. Biography as a genre raises questions about the historiographical limits of narrative prose and the barriers between fictional and nonfictional narratives, as the biographical or autobiographical frame became a common one for novels of education, including those of the Lima group. Despite the national and even local identities of the heroic autodidact's origins, the arc of eventual triumph invariably ends with his or her ascension to an international stage. Biography comes to serve as a particularly portable form of history capable of making its subjects move in space and time to serve as powerful examples in the reader's present tense.

## *Narrative and Schooling*

The use of the exceptional autodidact as proof of the cultural value of his or her entire society takes on particular significance when viewed through the prism of political independence. Sor Juana as validation of Mexican colonial (and therefore Creole) society is a perspective shaped by the political events of independence, the events that rendered Mexican society a political entity in need of its own validation. Benjamin Franklin and Domingo Faustino Sarmiento, the former a colonial subject who participated in the independence struggle and the latter a barely post-independent citizen who ties his own birth to that of independent Argentina, are cases in point. On the one hand, the need to be an autodidact implies insufficient educational infrastructure, even as the autodidact is made to serve as an example of cultural vitality.

The metaphorical question of what we might call "what we talk about when we talk about education" becomes even more fraught when we consider the distance between the individual anecdote and the statistical implications of an educational system.[8] One point of commonality between post-independence Spanish America and the United States is the simultaneous discussion of education as a general, systemic priority and of the heroic autodidact, the system-less learner, as the embodiment of a vaguely defined republican educational spirit. While nineteenth-century observers such as Sarmiento would marvel at the progress of the US common school movement and the contrasting lack of public education in Spanish America, and while a general consensus has emerged categorizing the *Spanish American* era of independence as a time marked by "the crisis of almost all possible sources of legitimacy" (Caruso 278), both continents approached and achieved independence even as broad discussions of systemic educational reform were well under way.

Independence-era Spanish America was awash in the sentiment championed by Bourbon reformers such as Olavide, Campomanes, and Jovellanos that traditional models offered ornamental rather than practical skills and thus produced the wrong sort of professionals. Jovellanos, for example, lamented in the last decade of the eighteenth century the existence of "so many professorships, in sum, that only serve to make an overabundance of chaplains, friars, doctors, people of letters, scribes and sacristans, while what are lacking are mule-drivers, sailors, artisans and workers" (Jovellanos 399).[9] The distinction between the first list and the last separated "sterile classes" from "productive" ones (399). Along with this division between producers and transporters of tangible economic commodities on the one hand and the professional members of a bureaucratic service economy on the other, Jovellanos also breaks down scientific investigation into two categories—learning for its own sake and learning as a kind of office seeking: "The sciences have ceased to be for us a means of seeking the truth and have become a resource for seeking a living" (394).[10] Here Jovellanos is interested not so much in "practical" versus "impractical" scientific knowledge as in judging whether the investigation in question counts as a real or false encounter with the world. Just as the narrator of Rousseau's *Émile* would stress the importance of an education based on things rather than the words that name them, so Jovellanos and his Spanish and Spanish American contemporaries would celebrate the need for a new kind of professional who would work not with words and documents but with plants, livestock, and machinery.

This reformist sensibility that stressed practical over theoretical knowledge, things over words, as Rousseau's formulation had it, would find echo in North American writers who stressed an empirical approach to science as a way of proposing republican class sensibility as an alternative to the British class system. Thus Benjamin Franklin's 1784 pamphlet "Advice to Such as Would Remove to America" (also published under the title "Information to Those Who Would Remove to America") worked to temper the hopes of Europeans who expected to find easy prosperity in the New World. In North America, Franklin argues, "It is rather a general happy mediocrity that prevails" (459), and productive economic activity is more the norm than accumulating rents with the result that "paintings, statues, architecture, and the other works of art, that are more curious than useful" (460) have trouble finding buyers or patrons. Franklin's word, "curious," is the same one used by Caldas to condemn the "aerial systems" that he argued took the place of useful knowledge in colonial schools (269).

Along with contempt for the merely "curious" object of production, Franklin shares the Bourbon reformers' fascination with the physical processes of agriculture, manufacture, and distribution. He expresses the popular cult of the mechanic aphoristically: "The people have a saying that God Almighty is Himself a mechanic, the greatest in the universe; and He is respected and admired more for the variety, ingenuity and utility of his handiworks, than for the antiquity of his family" (460). This philosophy of honoring physical labor serves, in Franklin's formulation, as a natural consequence of life in a country with more arable land than accumulated capital. Franklin also argues that these material conditions produce moral influence, too, that the broadly shared need to make a living has an overall positive social effect: "Industry and constant employment are great preservatives of the morals and virtue of a nation" (464). This formulation suggests a vision of the New World as a kind of moral asylum, on the one hand, from the vices and corruption of Europe, but also as a special kind of moral school in which a different relationship to labor and production serves as a counter to class prejudice. In Franklin's description, monarchy and aristocracy are counter to the material circumstances of North America, and the moral effect of these circumstances serves only to bring popular wisdom and prejudice against them, too.

The confluence of geography and schooling is another commonplace of late eighteenth-century thought. Just as Rousseau's *Émile* had presented ideal education as a retreat from society that concluded only with the student's successful reintegration, so Montengón's *Eusebio* narrated the education of a Spanish boy shipwrecked on the Delaware coast and placed under the guidance of a Quaker artisan, with whom he eventually makes an educational journey back to the European continent, a trip that Clara O'Hagan has called "a parodic reversal of eighteenth-century New World travel" (84).[11] Eusebio's saga and Rousseau's revival of *Robinson Crusoe* as one of very few recommended texts for his Émile showcases the degree to which the eighteenth-century educational narrative was an Atlantic project: it could create fictional worlds of experience-based education in which that experience took the form of a transatlantic voyage. By making firsthand knowledge of ocean transport such an important component of their educations, narratives such as Eusebio's or Rousseau's use of *Crusoe* also provide their own commentary on this world defined by trade.

And it would also be a mistake to identify the eighteenth-century educational universe as a strictly Atlantic one. The period saw widespread translation into Latin and English of Ibn Tufayl's *Hay Benyocdán*, often given the Latin title of *Philosophus Autodidactus*. Originally composed in Arabic by the twelfth-century, Córdoba-born philosopher, it was available in Latin, English, Dutch, and German by the end of the eighteenth century.[12] Tufayl's story narrates the education of a young man miraculously born on a desert island and ends with his integration into the society of a populated island nearby. His education, conducted in isolation like Émile's, serves the counterintuitive purpose of making him fit for society. The English translation of Tufayl's text is sometimes cited as one of the inspirations for *Robinson Crusoe* (see Baroud). What both texts have in common, along with the narrative of the shipwreck, is the use of an isolated setting to produce a temporal interruption—a space in which the education of the isolated student literally skips ahead of whatever progress continues in the society left behind.[13] Like Schiller's metaphor of aesthetic education as the "skilled watchmaker who can fix a broken watch while its hands keep moving," the island becomes the safe space where a single part in the social machine can be altered and refined away from the movement and influence of the rest (Tauber 34).

It is against this backdrop and in the wake of the military success of the North American revolution that Benjamin Franklin undertakes his own autobiography, the project that would have such an influence on the young Argentine Domingo Faustino Sarmiento a few decades later. For Sarmiento the encounter with Franklin's autobiography provided a moment of epiphany that matches the intensity of his "discovery" of Ackermann's catechisms.[14] Remembering the moment in *Recuerdos de provincia*, Sarmiento recounts an emotional, visceral identification—"I felt myself to be Franklin" (162)—that led him to a series of striking conclusions about his own potential: "And why not? I was poor like him, studious like him, and putting my mind to it and following his footsteps I could one day train myself like him, be a doctor *ad honorem* like him, and make myself a place in American politics and letters" (162).[15] Sarmiento's list of markers for fame and success is telling. From shared circumstances and traits—poverty, studiousness—could spring the two markers of intellectual success, the *honorary* degree, a symbol of a symbol of academic achievement, and the more abstract and slippery honor of "a place in American politics and letters" (162). What's obviously missing from the list is any sort of political or intellectual content for these markers to represent. Sarmiento's construction says nothing about what he will study or write or from what political or literary perspective he will make himself known to readers. His first intellectual identification is as the object rather than the source of influence, and the only concrete quality that emerges is the ability to be influenced by another autobiography.[16]

This elevation of fame and influence over content is by no means accidental. Sarmiento remembers Franklin's autobiography as the second book to affect him deeply, after Cicero, and he offers up a veritable genealogy of biographical influence, explaining that "Franklin's life was for me what Plutarch's lives was for him, what Henry IV, Madame Roland and so many others were for Rousseau" (*Recuerdos* 151).[17] The act of recounting this circuit of influence again leads Sarmiento not to any concrete conclusions about the writers or the books themselves but to the idea for yet another publishing project to keep the circuit going. He argues that "The life of Franklin should be among the primary school texts" with the goal of forming a society profoundly affected by the influence of Franklin's example—"that there wouldn't be a single child with any inclination towards the good, who was not tempted to be a little Franklin, by way of that beautiful tendency of the human spirit to imitate the models of perfection it conceives" (151).[18]

Franklin also serves Sarmiento as a way to link contemporary biography to the familiar genre of the lives of the saints. He notes that the very saintliness of the church-sanctioned biographies makes it difficult for young readers to relate to them, especially given the fact that no one is seriously encouraging them to imitate the miracles that saints have performed: "But however well-intentioned the child might be, from the beginning he renounces any pretention to perform miracles, for the simple reason that those who counsel it abstain from performing them themselves" (152).[19] What Sarmiento suggests instead is a kind of secular sainthood based not on supernatural events but on the practical application of reason. The autodidact who becomes a political and scientific innovator, he argues, "should be on the altars of humanity, should be greater than Santa Barbara, advocate against lightning, and should be called the saint of the people" (152).[20] By opening up the category of the "saint of the people" for the autodidact who becomes a revered public servant, Sarmiento is of course making an argument not only for Franklin's sainthood but also for his own.

At the same time, his argument against the efficacy of miracle-performing and long-dead saints articulates the pedagogical principle of example and imitation—that something in the human spirit naturally strives to become the convincing example of excellence once that example has been presented—and it makes the principle the basis for a publication project. The Mignet text he mentions, *Vie de Franklin: à l'usage de tout le monde* (Mignet, 1848), had made its own poetic argument for the power of example. Intuiting that some readers might object to making such an exceptional individual into a general example, Mignet argues at the beginning of the book that "if Franklin was a man of genius he was also a man of good sense" (10), and then goes on to present *his* theory for the general power of exceptional examples, arguing that the striving of the many, over time, to imitate the wise and the heroic works as a motor of gradual progress.[21] The imitation of outliers causes a shift in averages and norms that Mignet sums up aphoristically: "The genius of one man becomes the good sense of the human species, and a hardy novelty changes into a universal norm" (12).[22] For Sarmiento, who elsewhere goes to great lengths to posit himself as just the sort of untouchable genius that some readers might be afraid to imitate (see Haberly, "Francis" 289–90; Molloy; and Altamirano and Sarlo on Sarmiento's hyperbolic descriptions of his own translations and reading), the universal teachability of biography becomes the larger frame not only for his admiration of Franklin but also for his presentation of himself.

It's also worth pointing out that Sarmiento's notion of a Spanish-language accessible Franklin had already taken physical form on the printed page by the time he published *Recuerdos de provincia*. An 1843 edition entitled *El libro del hombre de bien, Opúsculos morales, económicos y políticos estractados de Benjamin Franklin* (The good man's book, moral, economic, and political treatises extracted from Benjamin Franklin) had been published by Don Antonio Bergnes and Co. in Barcelona. Sarmiento's recounting keeps this edition from predating his own wish for a portable Franklin, since he traces that reaction back to his initial youthful encounter with Franklin's autobiography. The Bergnes edition, unlike that of Mignet, took the form of an anthology of Franklin's writings rather than a reconstruction of his autobiography. The author of the collection's preface (signed "P.F.M.") defined his project as one of "service to popular and public education" and suggests its usefulness for teachers and parents who wish to impart Franklin's lessons to their charges as well as for "heads of families."[23] What all will find, he argues, are "important advice and ingenious rules of conduct for every stage of life" (*El libro* 4).[24] Like Mignet this author sees a collective form of progress from individual encounters with Franklin and declares his final purpose to be an overall improvement in public morality that will render his own social world more rather than less stable: "It is hoped that the publication of this BOOK will contribute to the moralization of the youth and the moderation of the masses, without which there would be no social order!" (4).[25]

The Bergnes edition did devote significant space to Franklin's life, offering a forty-six-page biographical summary with a monarchist slant that characterized the American Revolution as a colonial dispute with Parliament rather than King George III (34). Bergnes's Franklin, like that of Mignet and Sarmiento, stands out above all as an exemplary autodidact marked by traits that could presumably also serve the legions of students enrolled in schools who did not find it necessary to be teachers to themselves: "the perseverance and the energy of his initiative to cultivate his reason and perfect himself. He himself was his teacher" (21).[26]

However much he may or may not have read from the Mignet and Bergnes versions of the portable, teachable Franklin, Sarmiento self-consciously fits his admiration of Franklin into a notion of biography as above all a pedagogical tool, a means of both creating the exemplary life and delivering it to general readers. This perspective isn't original either, of course, and Franklin's own autobiography (a problematic text that was still not widely available in its complete form in the middle of the nineteenth century) invites a reading that considers life as a series of publishing products and the exemplary American as a developmental editor, a fountain of inspiration, and an answer to the question of what sort of book the world needs now.

## *"Discovery" and the Pedagogy of Example*

Franklin's text and his own vision of its construction intertwine with the theme of publication in a number of complicated ways. First there is the matter of language. The earliest (1791) editions of part of the autobiography circulated in French. So prevalent was this French edition, which could well have been Sarmiento's introduction to Franklin, that the first English edition (London, 1793) frankly acknowledged itself as not an original document but rather as an attempt to intuit how Franklin's text *might* have read in the original English.[27] Having already argued for the importance of Franklin's life as an example to youthful readers, a theme Franklin himself glosses early in the autobiography, the London editor includes a letter from Dr. Richard Price commending the text as "a striking example, how a man, by talents, industry, and integrity, may rise from obscurity to the first eminence and consequence in the world" (*Works* vii). Franklin's text (in the original English) expresses freely what the author sees as the value of a publishing project in which "the conducting Means I made use of, which, with the Blessing of God, so well succeeded" are made available to "my Posterity." Whatever the book's merits as entertainment, Franklin is convinced that his descendants will be interested to know those "conducting Means" since "they may find some of them suitable to their own Situations, and therefore fit to be imitated" ("The Autobiography" 488).

Consummately aware of the metaphorical possibilities of life considered as text, Franklin also uses the opening pages of his autobiography to pose to himself the proverbial question of whether he would choose to live the same life over again. He answers in the affirmative, "only asking the Advantage Authors have in a second Edition to correct some Faults of the first" ("The Autobiography" 488). Books play an important role in Franklin's narrative, as in those of Sarmiento, Sor Juana, and Santa Teresa. He recounts reading Defoe's *Essay on Projects* and Cotton Mather's *Essays to Do Good*, concluding that these two volumes "perhaps gave me a Turn of Thinking that had an Influence on some of the principal future Events of my Life" (495). He also remembers Plutarch's *Lives*, and with a more melancholy tone, the fact that as a child of few means he was as often forced to make do with his father's "Books in polemic Divinity." Here his regret is "that at a time when I had such a Thirst for Knowledge, more proper Books had not fallen in my Way" (494).

Just as young Sor Juana was willing to give up cheese for learning because she believed "it made one slow of wits" (15), Franklin is willing to give up sleep when his own circumstances demand it. Having befriended a bookseller's apprentice while an apprentice himself, Franklin convinces his friend to let him borrow books overnight on the condition that he return them before the shop opens the next morning. Franklin remembers those energetic days this way: "Often I sat up in my Room reading the greatest Part of the Night, when the Book was borrow'd in the Evening and to be return'd early in the Morning lest it should be miss'd or wanted" ("The Autobiography" 495). If Sor Juana is willing to give up cheese in return for learning, Franklin is willing to sacrifice the better part of a night's sleep.[28] Sarmiento recounts similar feats of sleepless reading, remembering his time as a young man under house arrest—"In San Juan I had my house for a prison and the study of French for my recreation."[29] Eating, sleeping, and reading/translating French with a dictionary converge in Sarmiento's narrative, in a daily discipline marking the obsessive pursuit of knowledge: "I had my books on the dining room table and I parted them so they could serve breakfast, then after that for lunch, and at night for supper: the candle went out at two in the morning and when I was excited about a reading I could spend three days sitting down, checking the dictionary."[30] Even with this heroic attention and dedication to reading, Sarmiento concludes that he would classify himself as an auditory learner—"Always active was the organ of information and instruction that I had most at the ready, which was my ear" (*Recuerdos* 156).[31] Giving a list of the persons whose words and conversations had served as a sort of poor man's university lecture, Sarmiento remembers that in many cases the instruction was given unwittingly ("sin saberlo") (156). Like Sor Juana before him, he finds that obstacles only provide further opportunities for comprehension and that the world functions as a pedagogical device whatever its intentions may be. Sor Juana, for her part, remembers engaging "many subjects, seeing that each augments the other" and doing so "without benefit of teacher, or fellow students with whom to confer and discuss, having for a master no other than a mute book, and for a colleague, an insentient inkwell" (*Poems* 25).

Sor Juana's circumstances made it impossible for her to posit herself as a teacher or any sort of example to the younger generation—one of the ostensible purposes of her autobiographical sketch was to prove her humility—but she does mark herself as a lifelong student and counts books as important above all because they offer such examples, "many and illustrious women" who have inspired her own learning (45). In this sense her tone differs markedly from that of Sarmiento and Franklin, for whom the act of teaching clearly overlaps with that of student. Where Sor Juana and Franklin and Sarmiento do overlap is in the validation all three take in referring to their public, published selves. Sor Juana, for example, makes it clear that her questionable protestations of modesty and moral inadequacy need not extend to her poetry: "I confess openly my own baseness and meanness, but I judge that no couplet of mine has been deemed indecent" (65). Here the praise she offers for her own verse is of the lightest sort possible, but it does emphasize the validation of public life—others have read her verses, they therefore exist outside of her, and these others have not found them indecent. Sarmiento and Franklin narrate scenes of literary "discovery" in which their texts survive on their own and reflect glory back on them, likewise showing just how important the public identity as writer is to their own development into the exemplary autobiographical persona narrating the tale. Paul Giles has argued that this Franklin comes forward "not so much with any Machiavellian strategy" but rather with the frank acknowledgement of his own desire "to harness the new technologies of the eighteenth century in order to transliterate himself into a man made out of words" (Giles 84).

Sor Juana's autobiography-under-duress recalls her written critique of a well-known priest's sermon that started the whole controversy. She remembers her text as a sort of abandoned intellectual child, "For like a second Moses I had set it adrift, naked, on the waters of the Nile of silence" (67) that only came to take on a life of its own in the hand of a reader, the "Sor Filotea" to whom her autobiography makes reply. In this description, which on one level is a bald attempt to escape being associated with her own words, Sor Juana narrates a nightmare version of the relationship between author and text. An incidental piece of writing comes back to haunt the writer, and so she protests "that had I known, the very hands of which it was born would have drowned it" (67), letting the Moses metaphor take a macabre turn.

Franklin and Sarmiento write not only in an age of easier and more widespread print distribution, but also on the fringes of established newspaper cultures in which the writings of a male author, even one from a marginal social class, will not necessarily be ignored or attacked. In Franklin's case, the writing career begins when he is apprenticed to his brother's printing house, publisher of *The New England Courant*. Wishing to see his own writing on the *Courant*'s pages "But being still a Boy, and suspecting that my Brother would object to printing any Thing of mine in his Paper if he knew it to be mine" ("The Autobiography" 499), Franklin remembers the ruse that allowed the text to precede the author: "I contriv'd to disguise my Hand, and writing an anonymous Paper I put it in at Night under the Door of the Printing-House" (499). The article appeared and Franklin felt the very welcome *frisson* of listening to the praise and speculation of readers who did not know they were in the author's presence: "I had the exquisite Pleasure, of finding it met with their Approbation, and that in their different Guesses at the Author none were named but Men of some Character among us for Learning and Ingenuity" (499). Franklin's scheme eventually comes to grief when his brother finds out he is authoring anonymous pieces, and his writing becomes the source of a genuine family rift when a controversial article draws government censure and causes his brother to be briefly imprisoned.

What is remarkable about the retelling is how Franklin remembers the episode not only as a validation of his ability as a writer but also as a moment in which readers' reactions serve literally to place him among "Men of some Character among us for Learning and Ingenuity." Writing as the triumphant national figure rather than on the defensive, Franklin can claim the reflected glory of his writing self as part of his larger identity, the exact opposite move from the one Sor Juana is forced into by her circumstances. Franklin's scene draws its dramatic tension from the impossibility that an apprentice could really be a writer on the one hand, and the secure reputation of Franklin the writer who remembers it on the other. Thus the remembered moment is not an aberration but an early validation.

Sarmiento narrates his own arrival onto the printed page as a similar act of subterfuge that produces a similar pleasure, the dramatic irony of hearing himself discussed by learned and esteemed figures who see before them Sarmiento the person without knowing he has become Sarmiento the author. Remembering that his first article appeared in *El Mercurio* on February 11, 1841, Sarmiento recounts awaiting news of its reception and hearing the reports of approval pour in like telegraphs over the course of the day, first from the community of Argentine exiles and eventually from two of the most important arbiters of mainstream intellectual opinion: "The next day I found out that don Andrés Bello and Egaña had read it together and found it good. God be Praised I said to myself; I'm saved!" (*Recuerdos* 177).[32] His tale of spreading approval thus includes a reenaction of what Sylvia Malloy has called a "scene of reading"—that image of Bello and Egaña reading together—and a rhetorical version of salvation via the printed page plus critical approval. Next comes the reenactment of Franklin's scene as Sarmiento goes to a party in disguise and baits his listeners with a critique of the article that provokes an acerbic response and thus "convinces" him of the merits of his own work: "I finally had to assent that the article was irreproachable in terms of style, pure in its language, brilliant in images and nourished with healthy ideas buffed by the smooth varnish of sentiment" (178).[33]

In Sarmiento's universe the virtues of the text take on extra-textual importance as well. He compares his success to that of "those French writers, who from a ramshackle fifth-floor garret, launch a book out into the streets and receive in return a name in the literary world and a fortune" (178).[34] This narrative of redemption—self-worth as a function of reader-response to the text—depends on more than simply producing a popular or well-respected body of writing. Sarmiento and Franklin's tradition is that of the public intellectual as public teacher and the production of texts as the highest and most universal form of pedagogy, so as each tells the story of becoming important, he also tells the story of becoming a teacher. In keeping with the American obsession of the book in subjunctive, each offers a litany of unfinished projects of didactic intent. Sarmiento's project is the life of Franklin and later on a realized life of Abraham Lincoln. Franklin remembers his newspaper as a kind of public pedagogy—"another Means of communicating Instruction" ("The Autobiography" 550)—and he also recounts his youthful notion of "the bold and arduous Project of arriving at moral Perfection" (540).

This project led him to divide moral performance into thirteen virtues ranging from "Temperance" to "Humility" and to create a chart for marking each day's performance, organized so that one of the thirteen would be emphasized. Franklin also includes a daily schedule (filed under the virtue of "Order") that divided the day into one-hour blocks and set aside seven for sleeping, eight for working, and so on. He notes that he managed to keep any sectarian notion of religion out of his program and imagined how it could thus have become a universal textbook of virtue—"I should have called my Book the ART *of Virtue*, because it would have shown the *Means and Manner* of obtaining Virtue; which would have distinguish'd it from the mere Exhortation to be good" (546). His book, like Olavide's dreamed-of volume, would have employed reason to win converts, though in Franklin's case the creed converted to would be a secular notion of virtue rather than Christianity. Franklin's own memory treats the project as a failure on two counts. First, he did not manage to achieve perfection in the thirteen virtues and so argues that the system functioned more as an ideal than as a set of instructions to produce a desired result: "As those who aim at perfect Writing by imitating the engraved Copies, tho' the never reach the wish'd for Excellence of those Copies, their Hand is mended by the Endeavor, and is tolerable while it continues fair and legible" (546). The plan also failed as a publishing project, and here Franklin blames "the necessary close Attention to private Business in the earlier part of Life, and public Business since" (547). In a sense, it is the creation of his own life that has turned the didactic manual of virtue into a perpetually postponed book. What Franklin has instead is material for an autobiography.

And as his handwriting metaphor suggests, Franklin's failure at the grand magnum opus of the didactic publisher nonetheless stoked his ambition for didactic publishing, for his newspaper work and the creation of *Poor Richard's Almanac* (549).[35] He also remembers that his father used to quote a verse from the book of Proverbs: "Seest thou a Man diligent in his Calling, he shall stand before Kings, he shall not stand before mean Men." This mantra he can claim to have filled after a fashion, even if he never literally believed it would come true: "for I have stood before five, and even had the honor of sitting down with one, the King of Denmark, to Dinner" (538).

It probably should not come as a surprise that Sarmiento also rehearses this last rhetorical move, the irony of unexpected elevation, on more than one occasion in his memoir. Remembering his time as a self-directed student in Copiapó, Sarmiento paints in lustrous detail the miner's garb he had taken to wearing "for economy, entertainment and mischief" and imagines that even years later the juxtaposed figure he cut must live on in the imagination of the town's inhabitants: "Many people in Copiapó still retain the memory of the miner who could always be found reading" (*Recuerdos* 153).[36] This vision of himself as the elevated "saint of the people" brought to the point of standing before kings or at least presidents and congresses by dint of his own diligence and intellectual prowess manages to draw strength from its own precariousness.

Just as Franklin can marvel in mock modesty about how a poor boy from Boston has come so far, so Sarmiento can employ the lingering suspicion of his lack of proper credentials as proof that he is something more than a run-of-the-mill university graduate.

Recalling an incident in which "there arose in Santiago a feeling of scorn about my inferiority, in which even schoolchildren participated," Sarmiento counters with his present elevated state in a reply that makes a virtue out of his irregular education: "Today I would ask all those youngsters from the newspaper if it was really necessary. Had their studies been more serious than mine? Would they want to try to fool me, too, with their six years at the National Institute?" (156).[37] This is the same Sarmiento who a page later would remember himself as a brash young man fueled in self-confidence by biography, citing "my daily contact with Caesar, Cicero and my favorite characters" (157).[38] Given the meta-dimension in which he effectively posits his younger self as a test case for the effects of biography on an interested and diligent reader, Sarmiento's boast doubles as an argument for the pedagogy of imitable example. By repeating Franklin's scenes of autodidactic empowerment and the not-so-perceptive observers who are surprised by it, Sarmiento provides a slow-motion demonstration of the autobiographical-autodidact circuit.

## *Plagiarism and Pedagogical Reading*

The autodidact's self-conscious emphasis on circuits of reading and therefore on writing as a process validated by influence exercised on the reader and not by commentary from outside the circuit makes plagiarism a hot-button topic, particularly in an era where print technology made the theft of words and ideas an easier crime to commit. Franklin and Sarmiento each detail examples of plagiarism committed by people they admire and in each case justify the act as a utilitarian one. The New World condition of operating under book scarcity makes the distribution of information a more vital concern than authorship.

Remembering one of his own revered teachers, the historian Gregorio Funes, Sarmiento recounts how the master's mixture of broad erudition and carelessness about sources meant that one of the effects of his prose on the erudite reader was a creeping sense of déjà vu: "And so the reader began to perceive that in many of his works there were sentences, passages, that had already sounded graceful to his ears, and pages that his eyes remembered seeing" (*Recuerdos* 100).[39]

Sarmiento is quick to defend Funes, while noting that the clergyman and intellectual had been accused of plagiarism, by describing this particular charge as one that resonates altogether differently in the context of Spanish America: "which for us becomes rather a clear sign of merit than a reproach" (100).[40] The repetition of a good idea has pedagogic value, Sarmiento, insists, that far exceeds that of the claim to originality of a mediocre one: "That which we now call plagiarism was called richness and erudition back then; and I would prefer to hear for a second time an author worthy of being read a hundred times" (100).[41] If development means the creation of bibliographic resources sufficient to detect the plagiarist, it also means that the plagiarist has in a sense become less necessary. Sarmiento remembered Funes as a teacher rather than as an author, and his project is the distribution rather than the creation of quotable sources.

This story echoes Franklin's memory of a particularly eloquent Presbyterian minister who managed, for a time, to entice him into attending weekly worship services. Franklin remembers that the man's career was put in jeopardy when a parishioner remembered having heard one of his sermons preached somewhere else and was able to track down a written source, "in one of the British Reviews" from a sermon of the Baptist minister James Foster ("The Autobiography" 551). When the incident rose to the level of a scandal, Franklin remembers having taken the futile position of supporting the minister using a pedagogical defense much like that of Sarmiento: "I rather approv'd his giving us good Sermons compos'd by others, than bad ones of his own Manufacture; tho' the latter was the Practice of our common Teachers" (551–52). Franklin also notes the minister's singular talent for plagiarism: "His Memory was such as enabled him to retain and repeat any Sermon after one Reading only" (552). Franklin emphasizes his own commitment to the minister as an effective social influence not despite but *because* of his plagiarized sermons when he recounts that the incident marked his break with the congregation, at least as far as attendance at worship services was concerned (552).

The argument that Sarmiento makes directly and Franklin obliquely is for a pedagogical notion of authorship in which the role of the author is to distribute information as efficiently as possible to a public with few options for informing itself. Implied is a critique of American development, as Franklin's nod to "our common Teachers" producing "bad ones of their own Manufacture" and Sarmiento's "which for us" suggest an especially deprived American public for whom the normal rules of originality may not reasonably be applied. In both cases the "originals" being plagiarized are clearly European, and the pedagogical reading that Franklin and Sarmiento propose transforms this from a sign of cultural subservience to a practical use of the materials at hand. Funes and the nameless preacher have in a sense delivered the European intellectual goods to their audience without in any way fomenting the idea of Europe as a cultural authority. In much the same way that Turgot credits Franklin with "stealing God's thunder and the king's scepter," the preacher and teacher/historian have stolen the substantive elements of European intellectual culture and repackaged them as American.[42]

## *"Look at Lincoln"*

The need for portability, for making ideas travel, effectively creates the circumstances under which a plagiarist can be said to add value rather than to steal it. The universality of the autodidact's narrative transcends space and time as well, making it possible for a deceased North American writer to become the closest possible intellectual companion to an ambitious youth like Sarmiento, who identifies with the circumstances of the story and is, even without realizing it, looking for anecdotal clues that will help him to surmount them. Sarmiento's great international publishing project turned out not to be a life of Franklin, however, but a life of Abraham Lincoln who became, like Stowe, a symbol for the eradication of slavery. Lincoln's humble class background also helped transform him into a symbol of New World opportunity. Eliminating monarchy was one thing, but elevating a farm boy born of illiterate parents to the presidency of a republic was quite another.

Lincoln's resonance as a transcendental New World symbol and Sarmiento's attempt to harness it into a hemispheric biography demonstrate the naturally close relationship between the autodidact and the burgeoning publishing and distribution industry of the mid-nineteenth century. Sarmiento's 1866 *Vida de Abrán Lincoln* (Life of Lincoln), published in New York City for a Spanish American readership, billed itself as a compilation, an act of distribution rather than writing. In the prologue, Sarmiento described his task in terms very similar to his defense of Funes: "Rather than doing it, we have directed the work of adapting, in the language spoken in South America, a Life of President Lincoln, pieced together from the various ones already in print" (*Vida* xi).[43] He also argues that Lincoln's fame makes it absurd to suggest that his biography could in any sense "belong" to a single writer—"The truth is that no one can with any propriety call himself the author of the biography of men who have arrived amid the agitations of public life to positions as esteemed as Lincoln" (xi).[44]

Lincoln, like Franklin, functions in the narrative mold of the autodidact who comes from humble origins to occupy a visible position on the world's historical stage, and so Sarmiento can revel in the portrait of the rustic come to occupy a position before and even above that of kings: "Look at Lincoln coming with an axe over his shoulder, the emblem of the work that conquered the land, from the bosom of the Kentucky forests, pioneer of the desert, gifted with that moral science of the Law, that forms the beauty of that character that Cooper parades through all of his novels" (xxvii).[45] This Lincoln is a literary character, a walking noble savage on the one hand, and a walking symbol (with his axe) of industrial progress on the other—a perfect synthesis of all the benefits of civilization and barbarism.

And this triumph, the education or elevation of Lincoln, remains a pedagogical narrative in Sarmiento's telling, and one that makes Lincoln less an autodidact deprived of organized educational structures and more the logical product of a society Sarmiento views as one gigantic educational institution:

> He has become a lawyer, orator and legislator; absorbing in his sponge-like nature the essences of civilization, government and liberty, that are floating and diffused in the atmosphere of the United States, and that are re-concentrated daily in four thousand newspapers, in millions of books and pamphlets, that popularize one person's knowledge, another's experience, the results of science or of its application, throughout the land. (*Vida* xxviii)[46]

Here, in a nutshell, is the portrait of the pedagogical reader in a state of near Platonic ideal. Sarmiento's Lincoln steps forth as an unusually gifted learner—"sponge-like nature"—and one who has the good fortune to come of age surrounded by an echo chamber of what Sarmiento identifies as political virtues: civilization, government, liberty. What Sarmiento is really trying to praise is the society that could produce a Lincoln; a few pages later he will baldly declare that "South America's political school is in the United States" (xlvii).[47] Here, as in his description of Funes or Franklin's reconstruction of the nameless minister, content takes precedence over authorship. The United States as he constructs it functions pedagogically precisely because it systematically reproduces and repeats ideas. The sponge-like Lincoln can scarcely avoid hearing and seeing "civilization, government and liberty" at all registers of social discourse.[48]

When Sarmiento gets down to listing the individual pedagogical influences he believes to be decisive in forming Lincoln's character, what he comes up with is a collection of environmental factors and social interactions: "forest" and "life as an ordinary person" respectively yield "the sense of harmony of the laws of the universe" and "his knowledge of the nature of the masses" (xxviii–xxix). Among the institutional influences Sarmiento also counts "the Illinois Legislature" as the source of Lincoln's acquaintance with "the habit of parliamentary debate" and using the English words "jury" and "meeting" as the places where he learned "the practical knowledge of the laws" and "the inspirations of politics" (xxviii–xxix).

At the same time that Sarmiento's Lincoln emerges as the product of a specific environment of everyday democratic pedagogy, he also stands forth as another example in the biographical circuit, an exemplary figure created by his own readings of the lives of other exemplary figures.[49] So Sarmiento imagines Lincoln reading Weems's *Life of Washington* by firelight after a hard day's work and suggests that this book "should have effected in his spirit an influence like that attributed to Plutarch's Lives on the public conduct of others figures" (*Vida* 5–6).[50] Here, as in Sarmiento's own admiration of Franklin's autobiography, the circuit becomes wholly American.

During the year or so before the publication of his life of Lincoln, Sarmiento struck up a correspondence and friendship with Mary Peabody Mann, a well-known US writer and the widow of Horace Mann. Mann served as a de facto agent and publicist for the Lincoln biography and other projects along with organizing a program to send US teachers south to Buenos Aires. Sympathetic to Sarmiento's vision of a

North-South circuit of exemplary lives, she enthusiastically plugged the biography. Her favorable review in the *Christian Examiner* went so far as to suggest that the book, obviously cobbled together from English-language sources, be translated *back* into English. Along with offering "all the points in Mr. Lincoln's character, from the beginning, which have a bearing upon the greatest interests of humanity" (M. Mann 133) the book served, Mann points out, as a working anthology of Lincoln himself, providing copious quotations of "the noble words, the matchless reasoning and argument, that always distinguished him in public life" (137).

While admitting that "we have all Lincoln's words preserved somewhere," Mann goes on to point out that the particular circumstances of Sarmiento's work make it an altogether differently framed and therefore vital presentation of Lincoln: "Here they are brought together for the instruction of a nascent nation, and it may be hoped that the book will be translated word for word, for our own youth to read; for it is little likely that in the hurry and skurry of our fast American life they will hunt them out of Congressional Globes, and other old newspapers" (137). As in Franklin and Sarmiento's pedagogical plagiarism defense, Mann's case for what would seem to be a redundant act of translation, almost a parody of translation, rests on a perceived need for diffusion. Pedagogy is deeply important not only as a reason for wanting to distribute the book to US readers but also as an argument for why *this* re-edition of Lincoln's words is so vital. Sarmiento's Lincoln is organized with pedagogical intent and aimed at a "nascent nation," and it therefore follows that it would be a vital reimagining of words that are otherwise resting in diverse archives and perceived to be all the safer and more stable for it. Mann imagines a US youth complacent in the possession and comprehension of its Lincoln and thus in need of being awakened to the essential role he might play in a context of existential republican struggle.

Mann's plea for the translatability of Sarmiento's Spanish-language Lincoln might also be viewed as a self-serving move. She was, after all, the translator for the English version of *Facundo*, which she mentions early in the review, and she writes as one invested in a notion of the applicability of one American example to another American place.[51] Later in the piece, she will suggest a parallel between Sarmiento and Lincoln as writers of a special sort, whose words themselves can be expected to reverberate within and beyond their own countries of origin. Just as she hopes that Lincoln refracted back to the United States through Sarmiento's lens may one day influence new generations of US students, so she imagines that Sarmiento's own words might produce a renewed sympathy between the United States and Argentina, a sense of shared American destiny:

> It is to be hoped that they will all be translated into English, and that the two Republics will go hand in hand to a noble destiny, such as the eye hath not seen, nor the heart of man conceived, but in glimpses obtained from time to time from that mount of vision to which the thought of untrammelled freedom for all mankind sometimes lifts the exalted soul. (138)

In Mann's almost mystical vision of political progress toward "untrammelled freedom," it is the translated words that take the lead. Sarmiento's rhetoric will produce sympathy in US readers and that sympathy will bring the republics together as each reading public comes to understand and cherish the words of one of the other republic's statesmen. While this vision is remarkably egalitarian in its rendering, Mann's hopes for Lincoln's effects on Argentine readers makes it clear that she agrees with Sarmiento in placing the United States in a leading role. She praises Sarmiento's pedagogical Lincoln not only as one that could serve US students, too, but also as a means of pointing out lessons she sees as particularly necessary for Spanish America: "not only that labor is honorable, but that free institutions and education give every man, however humbly born, a chance to be a benefactor to his country and mankind" (136).[52] Lincoln serves as an example of class mobility and the utility of physical labor to a society Mann sees as too aristocratic. Lincoln presents a paradox, too, since on the one hand Sarmiento intends him to represent US society and on the other his progress as an autodidact makes him a *sui generis* educational example and not necessarily the product of a specific system or social structure. Mann's review touches on this contradiction when she refers to his self-directed education "as the highest education, possible only to a man of native genius" (136). Genius, as Mann is defining it, functions as a pedagogical shortcut that allows the young Lincoln accelerated progress in the knowledge of "precisely what one wants for the unfolding of the mind," a kind of knowledge, she adds, "that is only gained ordinarily by experience, and often by a great deal of fruitless experience" (136). So this Lincoln, like Sarmiento and Franklin, occupies a flexible textual position, on one hand serving as an example to ordinary readers, and on the other hand demonstrating just how much his singular progress necessarily separates his life from theirs.

## *Conclusion: Biographical Use and Abuse*

Nietzsche's well-known phrase and title—*The Use and Abuse of History*—sums up an argument highlighting the limits and attractiveness of historical analogy as a rhetorical device. In the case of Franklin, Sarmiento, and Sor Juana, we might well speak of the use and abuse of the exemplary life as conveyed either by autobiography or biography. Sylvia Molloy has described Sarmiento's autobiography as "an exemplary piece, quite in keeping with the principles of nineteenth-century biography, a model endowed with moral and national value" (Molloy, "The Unquiet" 196).[53]

And the question of motive takes on similar importance when the autobiographer becomes a biographer. Barry Velleman has described Sarmiento's Lincoln biography as "a self-benefitting text" ("Introduction" 38), and Sarmiento himself recounted in an 1866 letter to Mann how he believed that Lincoln's example served to vindicate the controversial executive decisions he made while governor of San Juan, especially the suspension of habeas corpus and the use of military tribunals that "were based on practices in the United States, and Lincoln and Johnson served as my supporters" (Ard 221). He adds that "my *Life of Lincoln* now stands as my defense, as you, who understand very well the spirit of that book, well know" (221). Carrying the argument of self-defense even a step further, Sarmiento goes on to claim that what his critics most resent is his ability to command the attention of a large reading public in both the United States and South America: "I write for an illustrious public with the same assurance as if I were in some small republic" (221). Part of the larger effect of the Lincoln project, then, is to bathe a single Argentine politician in a hemispheric glow of the heroic executive. On the one hand, Sarmiento the biographer is making the case for US presidents as governmental exemplars on Spanish America, while on the other hand, those presidents are making the case for a particular kind of executive and a central government willing to take extreme measures to quell internal rebellion.

The question of Lincoln's international appeal assumes center stage in "Interchange: The Global Lincoln," a conversation among a group of eleven scholars conducted online and assembled by the *Journal of American History* in 2009. One of the participants, Nicola Miller, sums up the portable Lincoln that interested Sarmiento and other Spanish American politicians as one in which emancipation was de-emphasized in favor of strong central leadership: "Lincoln as a nationalist, successfully prevailing over the forces of disunity" ("Interchange" 470). Identifying the preferred Latin American Lincoln as "an institution builder rather than an emancipator" ("Interchange" 470), Miller also identifies the elevation of Lincoln's biographical example as part of a larger current in political and pedagogical thought, the creation of "a pantheon of heroes from Latin America's fight for liberation and republicanism, heroes who were all acclaimed for having transcended narrow, local interests in order to promote the modern values of the New World, *Americanismo*" (470–71). This Lincoln, Miller concludes, was conceived not as a product of the United States "but rather as quintessentially American in a far broader way" (471).[54]

Miller also concurs with Carolyn P. Boyd in identifying Lincoln's rise as a transcendent biographical subject with a broader movement toward a secular cult of biography in the late nineteenth century. Boyd points out the ubiquity of "collections of brief biographies, written with moral and political intent, that were published for both adults and children in the late nineteenth and early twentieth centuries" (466). Describing these works as "similar to the books of martyrs and saints," Boyd sees them as evidence of "the expansion of schooling and of a literate public as well as efforts by progressives to mobilize the masses in opposition to the status quo" (466). Just as this *Americanismo* could appeal to Spanish liberals despite obvious circumstantial differences, so the transcendent power of secular saints such as Lincoln managed to blur the North-South divide within the hemisphere. Miller suggests that *Americanismo* functioned as a flexible mindset, one that "sometimes included the United States and sometimes didn't," but in which Lincoln and other secular US saints retained a permanent moral power. This moral power could be kept on retainer to provide rhetorical leverage against "whichever 'imperialist exploiter' was being attacked at the time" (479), even or perhaps especially if that exploiter was from the United States.

Sarmiento's project therefore represents an early attempt to harness the life of Lincoln for hemispheric and national use, and his collaboration with Mann demonstrates the degree to which his use of Lincoln was self-conscious and calculated. In this case the construction of the mythological Lincoln almost overlaps the living one, and Sarmiento and Mann measure the immediate memory of Lincoln the living president against their own projections and predictions of the useful effects a textual Lincoln will have on future generations. We might say that pedagogical publishing mirrors actual pedagogy in the sense of being an activity that weighs the present as a step toward a desired future. Sarmiento's Lincoln is helpful in the short term as a frame for executive action within a republic while serving in the long term as the link to an ideal of hemispheric cooperation.

# 3

# Collective Feminist Biography

## *Biography as Useful History*

Sarmiento's attempts to make Spanish-language publishing events out of the lives of Franklin and Lincoln underscored the larger nineteenth-century traffic in useful lives as political and pedagogical tools. In her summation of Lincoln's rhetorical power as an exemplary autodidact for all seasons and climates, Boyd points out the example of one Spanish biographer, Rafael M. de Labra, whose 1887 collection of biographies compared Lincoln to Haitian leader Toussaint L'Ouverture in terms both moral and political as "products of Nature and History, destined to correct the injustices and evils produced by human malice" ("Interchange" 490). Labra also echoes Sarmiento in defining Lincoln as a reader of biography and thus a cause for celebrating an affinity for the pedagogical use of the genre particular to the United States (Labra 118). Exemplary biography distributed to the masses accomplishes, he argues, two tasks at once. It provides individual inspiration "because the most humble man recognizes himself" in the obstacles and triumphs of the exemplary figure, while at the same time presenting a general picture of national history (118).[1]

Labra's formulation is, in 1887, far from an original pedagogical principle. The usefulness of biography for historical study was a truism that extended backward at least to the occidental fascination with Plutarch's *Parallel Lives*, but the climate of educational reform among nineteenth-century reformers such as Horace Mann had given it a new urgency. We have already noted the degree to which the "subjunctive book" of the eighteenth-century imaginary, the book that would solve social and political problems all at once, often revealed autobiographical or biographical tendencies, in Olavide's desire to turn his own disillusionment over the French Revolution into a great work of Christian evangelism, or José Cecilio del Valle's dream of a collection of the lives of *sabios* as a basis for formulating a general pedagogical plan (del Valle, *Escritos inéditos* 42). James Simpson's argument (ca. 1834) that suitably pedagogical histories still needed to be written would become a galvanizing idea for Horace Mann (131). In his 1841 report on the state of education in Massachusetts, Mann complained that histories focused unduly on warfare and other violent acts: "How little do they record but the destruction of human life" (H. Mann n. pag.). What the history curriculum should emphasize, he argued, was "the biography of great and good men," since the narrative attraction of the story would serve as an agreeable gilding for the pill of moral virtue, "as they are prone to imitate what they admire, it unconsciously directs, while it delights them" (H. Mann n. pag.). By 1843, the publication year of the Barcelona edition of Franklin's writings and life, Mann's *Common School Journal* would reprint an endorsement of George S. Craik's *The Pursuit of Knowledge Under Difficulties* (1841–1843), a biographical collection of the stories of autodidacts. Charles Brooks would sound a similar note in 1856, recommending that lessons be drawn from "biography of good men and women who have resisted temptation, and attained eminence by their moral force of character," on the one hand, and "biography of bad persons who have come to poverty, disgrace and ruin by yielding to temptation" on the other (Brooks 336).

This belief in the essential value of biography as a better way of teaching history would inspire a flood of biographical compilations in the last decades of the nineteenth century. Linked by themes, time periods, nationality, or geographical region, the group of individuals collected in a given compilation would effectively transcend whatever other categorical axes might otherwise have divided them. Together they also added numerical force to the lone example, proving by sheer volume that the lessons provided in each anecdote applied not only to one but to many. The trend also included feminist compilations—Acosta and the Peruvian writer Aurora Cáceres published two of the better-known Spanish American examples. Here the compilation format allowed the editor to produce a work that provided strength in numbers, empirical evidence that gender emancipation was a historical narrative that had already been long under development. The narrative of the autodidact proves as attractive for compilations as for individual biographies, and the geographical sweep that many compilations offered provided an international dimension far beyond that of a single narrated life.

The books themselves crossed international boundaries, as exemplified by the worldwide and multilingual success of British compiler Samuel Smiles, whose biographical anthologies were widely read and cited in Spanish America. For the feminist compilers, this dimension was particularly important. Collections that included well-known women from many nations could employ examples of progress elsewhere as a call for change in Spanish America even as they developed large virtual communities of influential women to which Spanish Americans, too, could claim to belong. Compilations also encouraged a professional sense of belonging, as the collected figures included could become a virtual guild if categorized by profession and because, if literature or letters were among the listed professions, the compilers could claim implicit membership status of their own. In this chapter I will look at the tradition of the reciprocal biography among educational reformers and at the work of Smiles, who served as an inspiration for the Lima group. From there I will shift to an examination of the feminist collective autobiography and the virtual international networks constructed from Lima. I will be arguing that the autobiographical compilation serves to create and nourish the idea of an international community of readers, an essential concept for educational reformers and aspiring novelists alike, and that it serves the feminist compilers in particular as a tool for legitimizing education and letters as professional fields in which they can locate themselves. Behind the compiler's zeal, I will argue, is the desire and need to create the figurative and literal space for her own career in letters.

### *Making Education Heroic*

Henry Barnard's *American Journal of Education* reprinted arguments for the usefulness of biography in general, for example the aphorism from Raumer's *History of Pedagogy* that "the history of the world is the biography of the human species" ("Aphorisms" 101), while also taking on the specific biographical project of memorializing great teachers. Barnard's journal published Zalmon Richards's "The Teacher as Artist" in 1864, two years before Sarmiento's Lincoln would hit the presses. Addressing himself to teachers and the teachers of teachers, Richards made the case for creating a pantheon of great teachers in the hopes of inspiring a circuit of influence among educators: "The names of the educational heroes whose history this Journal has given will be handed down from generation to generation, to encourage other artist-teachers in their toil, *whose names* may be forgotten, but whose *works* will remain, and whose *record* will be on high" (Richards 69). This formulation employs the idea of the autobiographical circuit to promote a parallel hall of fame for pedagogues and a notion of teachers as producers of "works" whose stories, like those of writers and students and artists, will serve to inspire future generations of imitators.

Richards was celebrating a regular feature of the journal, which offered short biographies of teachers and educational reformers, contemporary or long deceased, from the Americas and Europe. Sarmiento's own biography would run in December 1866—"His moral influence was of the highest kind. The office of Schoolmaster was a very humble one in S. America, until he exalted it by his example and his eloquent word for it" ("Educational Biography" 595)—and in that same year the journal printed Sarmiento's own reflections on "The Dignity of the Schoolmaster's Work." Here the Argentine educator and biographer praised the US historical landscape as one that offered the particular advantage of many models worthy of imitation—Washington, Franklin, Penn, Winthrop, Williams—"and so many others, without a conqueror among them, nor a successful villain, nor a tyrant, nor a glorious criminal" ("The Dignity" 65).

Sarmiento's insistence on the virtuous nature of the US pantheon of heroes, heroes exempt from Mann's critique of the historiographical tendency to glorify warfare, echoed George Craik's formulation, in *The Pursuit of Knowledge Under Difficulties*, that equated scholarly ambition as a special kind of ambition and the biographies of great autodidacts as necessarily virtuous examples, since intellectual ambition "never excites in us an interest dangerous to feel, nor holds up to us an example criminal to follow; because its conquests have been a blessing and not a curse to humanity" (Craik 18). For Craik the autodidactic circuit is perfectly suited to the nineteenth-century explosion in book publishing. As he puts it, "books, and especially elementary books, have, in our day, been multiplied to an extent that puts them within the reach almost of the poorest student," and since by Craik's lights books are "the best teachers" ("at least to the more mature understanding, and in regard to such subjects as they are fitted to explain") (16), the age of mass publishing invokes the possibility of a golden age for autodidacts in which more information and more encouraging stories of other autodidacts are readily available in places where they would once have been impossible to find.

Along with the morality and morale-building nature of the autodidact's narrative, Craik also extolls self-teaching in epistemological terms, by arguing that knowledge itself is in general created without teachers: "Everything that is actually known has been found out by some person or other, without the aid of an instructor" (16). This assertion, at best a debatable summation of the autodidact's history in Western culture (it elides, for example, the penchant that even self-conscious autodidacts such as Franklin have for creating scenes of school-like instruction in the absence of a formal school), serves the purpose of giving inspiration to those readers who find themselves without the means for formal schooling or facing other educational obstacles. Craik suggests that wide exposure to the life stories of autodidacts can only lead to the conclusion "that no difficulties, however great, are any reason for despair" (55). This property that a Spanish-speaking reader might call *ánimo* forms an important part of Samuel Smiles's argument for *Self-Help*, his own compilation of heroic autodidacts.

Like Craik, Smiles directs his text to a readership he believes to be in need of encouragement above all else. He calls attention to his own work as one that seeks to teach "the lessons of industry, perseverance, and self-culture" (*Self-Help* vi). Smiles also speaks in the spirit of moral education, and he stresses that as far as "the worth and strength of a state" are concerned, success depends "far less upon the form of its institutions than upon the character of its men" (14). First published in London in 1859, Smiles's text, a compilation of largely British biographies, reveals the national chauvinism of its compiler, as Smiles concludes early on that "The spirit of self-help" can be categorized as "a marked feature in the English character" and one that "furnishes the true measure of our power as a nation" (16). George Craik's volume was similarly marked by geography, and a contemporary review from *Parker's Philosophy of Arithmetic* (reprinted in *Common School Journal*) makes note of the editor's intention to bring out "a volume of American characters" to provide a hemispheric complement to Craik's originals ("Pursuit" 44).

Smiles does manage to boil down the many anecdotal successes of his volume into a kind of epistemology of learning. He prizes energy and cheerfulness—"an excellent working quality, imparting great elasticity to the character"—above natural ability, and he makes statement on difficulty and victimhood that echoes Craik: "Necessity, oftener than facility, has been the mother of invention" (*Self-Help* 92). Smiles, like Craik, has little patience for reformist arguments focused on inequalities of race or social class, and he defines learning as a meritocracy: "The road into knowledge is free to all who will give the labor and study requisite to gather it" (281). The focus on the last pair of terms, "labor and study," glosses over the question of nature versus nurture, or genius versus hard work. Is the great autodidact a Mozart of comprehension or an example of what hard work can accomplish for similarly industrious citizens regardless of social class or intellectual talent?

### *Right and Wrong Reading*

For Smiles "labor and study" means that diffusion alone can never really define the modern age. The simple availability of books will not necessarily translate into moral advancement if the right sort of books are not available and if they are not read with the "right" sort of spirit. As far as books are concerned, Smiles's definition of the "right" sort is less clear than his definition of the "wrong" sort, and he singles out novels and novel reading for special opprobrium. Far from seeing the increased circulation of books as necessarily a boon for the autodidact, Smiles laments that "never, perhaps, were books more extensively read or less studied," and defines the accompanying risk to be that of producing a society of dilettantes rather than *sabios* (*Self-Help* 283). At the same time that his proposal seems to popularize learning by arguing that limitations of income and social class need not be barriers to the exceptional individual, Smiles makes it clear that he is not proposing populism: "We may not believe that there is a royal road to learning, but we seem to believe very firmly in a 'popular' one" (286). His critique of mid-nineteenth-century material progress extends to the application of industrial thought to learning. He thus notes his disapproval of "labor-saving processes" for education, arguing that "we often imagine we are being educated while we are only being amused" (286).[2]

Smiles also intertwines this critique of industrial progress as a model for learning with a healthy suspicion of the book itself, a wariness that echoes Emerson's famous directive from the "The American Scholar" that much depends not on the reading materials themselves but on the creative impulse provided by the reader. Smiles's principle is a link between labor and the ownership of knowledge, an echo of Locke's explanation of labor and property: "Knowledge conquered by labor becomes a possession, a property entirely our own" (288). Reading itself, Smiles argues, can easily devolve into "a mere passive reception of other men's thoughts" and a sensory experience he likens to "gazing through the shifting forms in a kaleidoscope" (291–92). Smiles's metaphors become more judgmental the longer he contemplates the question. He asks rhetorically "how much of our reading is but the indulgence of a sort of literary epicurism, or intellectual dram-drinking" (291–92). The pleasure of reading, the very element that makes a book a perfect gilding for the moral message contained inside, also suggests the possibility that reading could become a vice like any other. Speaking of this entertainment reading and its effect on republican citizens, Smiles concludes that "about the best that can be said is that it merely keeps them from doing worse things" (291–92).

Smiles makes a distinction between knowledge and moral virtue, worrying that "knowledge of itself, unless wisely directed, might merely make bad men more dangerous, and the society in which it was regarded as the highest good little better than a pandemonium" (290). Here his sentiments strike echo with those of Antonio José de Irisarri, the Guatemalan-born revolutionary who stepped onto the world stage as Chile's representative in London during the early years of independence. Decades later Irisarri would contemplate what he saw as the moral and educational failures of the independence project, and his frustrations would blossom into a polemical investigation of the assassination of Antonio José de Sucre—*Historia crítica del asesinato cometido en la persona del Mariscal de Ayacucho* (1845)—and a pair of what might be called picaresque novels set in Independence-era Spanish America, *El cristiano errante* (1847) and *Historia del perínclito Epaminondas del Cauca* (1863). Having come late in life to play the role of disillusioned skeptic, Irisarri would ridicule the progressive mentality as a kind of magical thinking in his last book, turning a popular refrain on its head: "One of our wisest adages says that you can't make the sun rise sooner by getting up early. You can't achieve useful progress just by wanting to progress more rapidly" (*Historia del perínclito* 38).[3] Irisarri would look back on the post-Independence history of Spanish America as a narrative of political corruption and so begin to wonder if the historical evidence supported the notion of an increasingly literate public as an increasingly virtuous one. So Irisarri would ask in 1839 whether the readers of his newspaper, *La verdad desnuda*, really felt that a lack of literary acumen was at the root of the region's political problems: "Is it by chance those who don't know how to read and write who have put us in this situation? Surely not; it's those who know how to read and write very well" ("Próspecto" 3).[4] This is the anxiety about the printed word that runs as a kind of counterbalance to the enthusiasm for the possibility of the printed page. Horace Mann, whose commitment to the diffusion of the printed word cannot be questioned, nevertheless warned his readers that "*light reading makes light minds*" ("Third Annual Report" n. pag.).[5]

Smiles was not only writing on the cusp of a transatlantic interest in the possibilities of book publishing for mass pedagogy, he was also writing at a moment of increased transatlantic circulation, and he achieved an international appeal comparable if not greater than that of Craik. Widely translated into Spanish, Smiles's work appeared in a number of short editions in Madrid, Barcelona, and Paris between 1875 and 1910, while attracting favorable reviews in the Spanish press. The Madrid newspaper, *El Solfeo*, for example, gave notice in December 1876 of the arrival of the Madrid edition of *Los hombres de energía y coraje*, a translation of a portion of *Self-Help*. Identifying the author's central premise this way, "The primary human virtue is the will to rely on oneself" (La primera virtud del hombre es la voluntad de bastarse á si propio) (4), *El Solfeo* went on to clarify that Smiles was presenting "a doctrine that is contrary to the Spanish character; by which I mean, at least, that of the Spaniards," before concluding that his entire book as well as this excerpt deserved to be read (4).[6] The *Revista de Andalucía* would agree with *El Solfeo*'s assessment, and would go out of its way to identify the new Spanish edition's ties to Labra, whose comparison of Lincoln and Toussaint L'Ouverture has already been discussed. Printed by Aurelio J. Alaria, the work had appeared, both reviews concluded, thanks to the support of Labra's abolitionist society (the *Revista de Andalucía* refers to "the activity of that untiring propagandist against slavery, our enlightened friend D. Rafael de Labra") (*Revista* 192).[7]

This Madrid edition was the first of many, as Smiles's biographical collections appeared in editions published in Barcelona with such titles as *Vida y trabajo, o caracteres peculiares de hombres según su laboriosidad*, *cultura y su genio* (1887); *Inventores é industriales* (1884); and *El caracter* (1900). Garnier Brothers editions followed as well, including an 1892 edition titled *El deber*. In 1895 the same Paris publishing house would release an edition of *El caráracter* as well as a translation carrying the title of Smiles's original compilation: *Ayúdate (Self-Help) con ejemplos sobre el character, la conducta y la perseverancia*.[8] Like the London in which intellectuals like Blanco White, Andrés Bello, Antonio José de Irisarri, and many others disputed the cause of Spanish American independence in the first quarter of the nineteenth century, fin de siècle Paris represented a clearinghouse for Spanish-language publishing, a physical location where the manuscripts of Spanish and Spanish American writers often coincided.

## *Collective Biography and Spanish American Crisis*

In the same year that these Paris editions of Smiles's work appeared, the Columbian novelist and essayist Soledad Acosta invoked *Self-Help* as a model for her own frankly didactic work of bibliographic compilation, *La mujer en la sociedad moderna* (Acosto, *La mujer*), declaring her intention to "follow Smiles's idea in his wonderful book called *Self-Help*" (viii).[9] Offering what she calls "a reasoned combination of biographies" (vii), Acosta seeks the magnetic power of the imitable example, "because the good is also as contagious as the bad" (68).[10]

Acosta agreed in broad strokes with the emphasis on moral education espoused by Horace Mann, Charles Brooks, and other US reformers of half a century before, and like them she devoted a good deal of worry to the fear of what bad written examples would produce in readers. Where Brooks and Mann worked in a US context in which slavery loomed as the great continuing injustice, Acosta wrote from Colombia, and on behalf of a South American contingent that had in her view become endangered by the political repercussions of the immorality of its people. Speaking, as she puts it, from "our Republics, in which the normal state is that of revolution and the exceptional one that of peace and concord" (20), Acosta advocates for what she calls "the moralization of the lower classes" (137–38).[11] With this at the very least questionable diagnosis of the continent's political illness—Acosta's contemporary, the Peruvian novelist Mercedes Cabello de Carbonera, for example, would find the "lower classes" to be a reservoir of moral firmness relative to the high-society Lima—Acosta appointed what she called "la mujer moralizadora" as the necessary literary example. Identifying this exemplary woman as "she who with her virtues and good works gives an example worthy of being followed by others" (171), Acosta argues that this sort of figure has particular significance given what she sees as the natural pedagogical efficacy of example, which she calls "one of the most powerful weapons that God has given us" (189).[12]

Acosta's proposal clearly followed the trend established by Craik and Smiles with an added Spanish American emphasis on political instability as the sign of a need for moral correction. At the same time that her collection invoked an overtly feminist goal of depicting the lives of women who served as moral *and* economic examples—"women who have lived for their own work" (ix)—it also emphasized a moral role identified with the feminine.[13] In a line of reasoning that would become commonplace among the Lima group, who often differed on other points, Acosta pinpointed feminine moral virtue as the antidote for masculine moral corruption, both at the personal and the national level.

The late nineteenth-century proliferation of feminist biographical compilations follows a larger interest in biography as a key to reimagining Spanish American history as a source of inspiration. In 1883 Acosta had published a more traditional collection, *Biografías de hombres ilustres ó notables* with the Bogotá publisher of *La Luz*. Giving her reasons for writing the book as the educational need to make heroes of some of the early founders of Colombia whose temporal distance made them easier to evaluate objectively than the leaders of Independence, Acosta reveals that early on she decided a comprehensive history was beyond her talents. What she discovered, however, was the essentially expressive nature of biography:[14] "The life bare of all novelistic intrigue, without adding anything or taking anything away, of each of these personalities, was enough to interest the reader and supplied all of the effects of an historical-novelistic scene" (*Biografías* 2). By alluding to the "cuadro histórico-novelesco," the genre par excellence for costumbrista writers such as herself who sought to capture details of Creole life with a particular appeal to the nostalgia and pride of their Creole readership, Acosta makes a link between the historiography of colonial heroes and the very specific form of realistic fiction popular among Spanish American writers of her time.

Acosta takes care in her prologue to cite the Manuel José Quintana's prologue to his classic biographical collection *Vidas de los españoles célebres* (3). In the original, Quintana explains that he wishes to produce "a work of agreeable reading and moral utility," an aim very much in keeping with Acosta's, and he goes on to explain that he will occasionally need to offer harsh judgments of well-known historical figures.[15] Quintana justifies this by making a distinction between the living and the dead. If "the living are owed in presence or in absence the contemplation and attentions that the world of social relations prescribes," the case of the dead is different: "The dead are owed only justice and truth" (Quintana 6).[16] As far as Quintana is concerned, his history deals with the dead, to whom no emotional debts can be owed. Acosta draws a different conclusion for her collection. While her subjects are as distant as Quintana's in temporal terms, she chooses to frame them by proximity rather than distance "because they live in their children and grandchildren, in the laws they made and parties they founded" (*Biografías* 3).[17] For Acosta knowledge of the biographies of famous players in Colombian history is an absolute requirement for anyone who seeks to understand the Colombian present, not so much because she views the early conquistadors as participants in an unbroken chain of events that leads to and determines the present (in this work, at least, Acosta avoids taking on the question of the continuity of history), but rather because she sees a kind of cultural heredity linking present-day Creole civilization with that of the early European founders. In line with the long-standing Creole practice of attempting to control and spin, if not minimize, the degree of connection to indigenous American culture, Acosta devotes an entire paragraph to the argument that Creole civilization should be viewed as a European one, *regardless* of what its racial makeup might be.

Insisting that the study of indigenous culture has value to contemporary Creoles "more as an ethnographic curiosity than as useful knowledge," Acosta acknowledges the existence of indigenous communities as well as "the great mixture of the indigenous race with the white that exists in Colombia," but she dismisses this influence as one that is on its way to vanishing—"is tending to disappear"—before the advance of what she defines as an overwhelmingly European society perched on the South American continent (*Biografías* 2).[18] Here Acosta makes use of an eloquent tautology and one that depends, as so many of the historical and biographical arguments of her contemporaries do, on a pedagogical notion of reading. She defends a European reading of Creole society as a pedagogical necessity:[19] "The civilization that we enjoy comes to us from Europe, and the Spanish are the spiritual progenitors of the entire population. Therefore it is to them that we should pay attention, if we wish to know the character of our civilization" (2). The argument is simple. Beginning with a notion of "spiritual" heredity capable of transcending racial and historical reality, Acosta posits that the spiritual present can be understood only by an investigation of the spiritual past, which she has defined as European. Part of what makes the construction so striking at a rhetorical level is the use of the terminology of race (progenitors) in the service of an ostensibly nonracial formulation (the spiritual rather than the physical) to reinforce the racial exclusion of the indigenous population. The whole construction rests not only on the unchallenged assumption that the status of "spiritual progenitor" only be accorded to Europeans, but also on Acosta's insistence that this spiritual legacy is the only sort of knowledge that will be valuable in understanding the spiritual present tense. The story of the conquerors is all of the story, she is arguing, because Creoles have decided to make it so.

Acosta's choice of a framework, a history constructed of biographies, many of figures who lived centuries before but whom she contextualized with the Spanish America of her own time, was part of another regional trend. Five years earlier Clorinda Matto had published her history-by-biography, *Bocetos al lapis de Americanos célebres* (Lima, 1890), and fifteen years later Z. Aurora Cáceres's *Mujeres de ayer y de hoy* (Paris, 1910) would appear. In each case the author/editor—and all three writers were known for their original works, too—framed the collection as a necessary tool for creating a revival of public morality in Spanish America or, in Acosta's case, for obtaining deeper knowledge of a perceived moral essence. While all three are conscious of a national context, Peru for Matto and Cáceres, Colombia for Acosta, their compilations and the reasoning they provide for them cross national boundaries and invoke a sense of shared regional crisis.

Matto, for example, introduces *Bocetos al lápiz de Americanos célebres* as the manifestation of her desire to foment "sacred memories and deserved respect" in a reading public she identifies as "American youth" (*Bocetos* 15).[20] Answering, in effect, the same sort of "call" for pedagogical biography that had animated US reformers in the first half of the century, Matto expresses her belief in the power of the details of an exemplary life that focuses on imitable virtue rather than the avoidance of vice "by taking the important points in the life of an individual from the cradle, exploiting his good actions as examples, with more satisfaction than his vices for anathema" (13–14).[21] Along with the positive notion of biographical study based on exemplary rather than cautionary tales, Matto also fashions a rhetorical relationship between past and future that manages to weave nationalist and regionalist sensibilities into the same argument. She finds that a present sense of moral crisis makes a certain kind of historical recovery vital and useful as "the sons of men that walked the earth leaving virtues and glories as the footprints of their transit, remain as a good element of the social regeneration to which we aspire" (14–15).[22] To the logical questions of "Which crisis?" and "Whose crisis?" Matto suggests varied but related answers. It is after all to the "youth of America" that she has directed the collection, and she declares her optimism that her book is participating in a national narrative of regeneration: "I count myself among the believers. I have faith in the future good destinies of Peru" (15).[23] Matto's introduction to her biographical collection also follows the convention of esteeming history as an almost impossible art and so positing biography as a less impossible book in subjunctive.[24]

Where US reformers in the first half of the nineteenth century worried that too many histories glorified war and concluded that the teaching of history would have to wait until a generation of historians produced works in praise of civil process, Matto invoked the supreme difficulty of the historians' task as that of rendering facts teachable without compromising the level of detail on offer. The historian, she says, must at once wield "the scalpel of the anatomist" in order to produce a detailed and accurate analysis of events, before turning his or her attention to the problem of communicating them to the classroom, a transition she sees as requiring "the scrupulous attention of the alchemist" (13).[25] What she offers, she argues, is something more distilled because it is by nature easier to formulate a coherent moral narrative from the life of a single person rather than the combination of characters and circumstances that would necessarily occupy the narrative of a series of events. The biographical frame supplies a narrative arc of its own.

## Tradition and Innovation: Collective Feminist Biography

Acosta and Aurora Cáceres's feminist compilations combine the arguments for biography as a pedagogical genre with a particular vision of the female gender role in the process of moral regeneration. Here again it is possible to read the justifications that Acosta and Cáceres give for a focus on female biography as a gendered version of the division between biography and traditional historiography proclaimed by Horace Mann half a century before.

Solangii Gallego has also noted the peculiarity of Acosta's decision to list Smiles as an important influence and, in fact, a model, while neglecting to mention any of a number of collective biographies of women that had been published in the nineteenth century (158). Among the texts Gallego lists are Serrano's *América y sus mujeres* (1890) and *El mundo literario americano* (1903) (both published under her pen name, La Baronesa de Wilson), along with earlier works such as Diego Ignacio Parada's *Escritoras y eruditas españolas* (1881) and Gertrudis Gómez de Avellaneda's *Albúm cubano de lo Bueno y lo Bello* (1860) (155n31, 155n32). Gallego notes that Acosta's years as a magazine editor also gave her an ample background to write the lives of her contemporaries and immediate predecessors; she had, as Gallego puts it, been cultivating the project for decades: "She had been planting the field of her work for decades" (Gallego 158).[26] It also bears pointing out that Bello and García del Río's 1823 *Biblioteca Americana* included not only a translation of Madame de Staël, but later on a biographical catalog of notable women. The catalog quoted French sources on Staël's literary importance and also produced a definition of the female role as that of "mediator between the natural harshness and sentimental capacity of humankind" (García del Río 368).[27]

The collective biography as a literary and/or historical genre has attracted recent attention among English-language scholars, who trace it to Renaissance writers such as Boccaccio and Christine de Pizan. Alison Booth's study of the British and US tradition of women's collective biography uses the term "prosopography" to describe the art of writing collective biography, and she details a number of rhetorical advantages that accrue with the accumulation of examples, among them a tendency "to resist the preeminence of a heroic individual" (9), even while fomenting in the reader the art of "comparative judgment of personality" and "the encouraging view that noteworthy lives differ enough from each other to leave space for others to join them" (10). Another advantage that the collective biography offers its readers, beyond traditional, individual biography, is the organizing power of the "the category or principle of selection," which Booth defines as an essential "rhetorical frame," and one that ties the form to public pedagogy: "The anthology of the great teaches greatness, of women womanhood, of writers what it takes to make a writer" (10). Selection criteria function therefore as a kind of pedagogical shorthand for what the reader can expect the book to do through the power of example.

Booth focuses her study exclusively on British and US examples, arguing that the English-language press has produced the "largest body of such works" since 1830, even as she laments the lack of "an international Genome Project that would synthesize the prosopographies of women in all languages and eras" (7). Glenda Mcleod employs another term, the "catalog of women," in her 1991 study of collective female biography and focuses on earlier texts, among them Christine de Pizan's *Cité des dames* (1405), but Mcleod notes that early on her impetus, too, comes from the post-1830 English-language press: "One point of departure for this study could be Virginia Woolf's striking insight that women dominate poetry but are all but absent in history" (4). Here Booth would certainly object, since she notes that the production of collective biography itself makes Woolf's lament for missing women's history read like a denial of what was already available—"For Woolf, it seems, the lost biography is much more desirable than the one ready to hand" (232). Woolf and Booth converge in their emphasis on scarcity—real or perceived—as an essential condition underlying the production and consumption of the collective female biography. The genre is itself a specific kind of book in subjunctive.

If Spanish America is largely left out of the Anglophone debate on collective biography, its prototype of female autobiography, Sor Juana's *Respuesta a Sor Filotea* is also an early example of a sort of collective biography, as it includes a "catalog of women" designed to produce the effect of legitimacy and normality through the accretion of individual examples (see Peraita, esp. 75–76). Nina Scott echoes Peraita's view of the catalog as a virtual club to which the catalog's author or compiler is essentially applying for membership. For Scott the biographer as writer functions from within a double frame because the catalog of her book reflects and creates the literary space into which the biography itself and all of her other books will be received: "Their principal motive was to insert themselves into an ongoing tradition of illustrious women in order to legitimize their own writing" (207–8). Scott cites this clear self-interest as a deviation from the traditional emphasis on piety and moral purity above all other qualities in the life stories of influential women.

The writers of the Lima group took a different tack, choosing to manipulate rather than to dismiss the traditional view that marginalized women while at the same time endowing them with a certain moral authority. Here the notion of republican political crisis and a desire to reconcile traditional notions of gender roles with female participation in the public world combine to produce moral catalogs and introductory manifestos that stress moral purity as an argument for including women in public life. In Acosta's case the mission of the "mujer moralizadora" is defined largely in contrast to a Spanish American masculinity she identifies with politics: "While the masculine part of society worries about politics [ . . . ] [w]ouldn't it be wonderful if the feminine worried about creating a new literature?" (*La mujer* 388).[28] This reflection, which comes in the second half of the book, the half dedicated to "*mujeres literatas*" (literary women)—earlier chapters having dealt with the women associated with the French Revolution and charity and missionary work—goes on to give a gendered vision of just what this new literature might look like.

The notion of literary fame adds an important wrinkle, too. McFadden has noted the power of "female literary celebrities" such as George Sand and Harriet Beecher Stowe (4). These figures, she argues, served as key rallying points for the formation of female intellectual networks since their "works and personal examples served to call into existence 'virtual communities,' international in scope and significance" (4). McFadden asserts that even when, as in the cases of Sand and Stowe, the author herself assiduously avoided any identification with feminism, a ripple effect based on fame and influence "helped produce structures whose existence was an indispensable precondition to feminism's future" (3–4). In an era in which the influence of the naturalist novel as written and theorized by Émile Zola has come to hold almost the entire Western world in a thrall, participation in the debate over naturalism's meaning and effects connected women writers with a worldwide circuit of discussion and debate.

Going along with the chorus of Hispanic observers who find naturalism's depictions of immoral behavior an unacceptable use of literary expression, Acosta argues that the new literature would be known for championing public morality rather than scientific neutrality. Modulating this attack on naturalism somewhat, she argues that different literary styles correspond properly to different stages of development, and that if "the writer can pause along the way to gather poisonous flowers" in more advanced societies that already contain "readers of all types, many whose intelligence, ravaged by an excess of civilization, needs food seasoned with more and more violently exaggerated descriptions," the palate of a Spanish American readership demands "healthy and hygienic intellectual food" (*La mujer* 389).[29] The female writer, by this formulation, takes on a social role at least metaphorically connected with that of motherhood. If "adult" societies might need (or by Acosta's sarcastic reckoning at least think they need) spicier fare, the childlike stage of development in Spanish America demands not pabulum but at least a more moderately flavored dish, and one whose health consequences have been taken into account.

Aurora Cáceres, writing fifteen years later, would take the moral role of women in a more general direction in the introduction to her collection. With a nod toward preempting any charge of advancing feminism by attacking men, Cáceres introduces the caveat that her collection is not dedicated to overturning patriarchy or upsetting any perceived hierarchies between men and women. Assuring worried readers that "we see no antagonism between the two sexes," Cáceres seeks to deflect any charge of wishing to disrupt male privilege by defining her posture as one that accepts a male-directed vision with a secondary, spiritual role for women: "We consider the man as directing the progress of these grand evolutions and the woman as having influence in his spirit" (Cáceres 6–7).[30] Cáceres goes so far as to argue that the absence of a female-directed society might well serve as proof of an inherent inequality between the leadership abilities of men and women—"If the power of initiative and command existed in the woman, some society would have featured her as the directing element with the man seconding" (9).[31]

While this statement practically cries out to be read as a particular sort of feminism designed to produce incremental progress within assigned gendered roles, something along the lines of Teresa González de Fanning's emphasis on writing as an activity for self-development in women rather than part of a larger literary and media industry,[32] Cáceres is, on the other hand, equally quick to note the degree to which patriarchy has shaped not only the available professional and social roles for women but also the historical memory of those women who have managed to play an influential role despite those strictures.[33] Defining the female role as that of "a heroine of hunger in the proletariat and a heroine of self-denial in among the ruling classes," Cáceres also wonders just how many contributions of the sort her collection brings together have been lost (8).[34] Confessing that examples of influential women in "primitive times" are difficult to come by, she points out that the available pantheon of male figures must also be leaving many out, since historiography serves the purpose of present-tense pedagogy rather than historical memory per se: "History only keeps in its pages what can serve as lessons for posterity, making the grandeur of humanity known in its tragedies, its joys, its hatreds, its virtues, and its ambitions" (9).[35] This pedagogical vision of historiography—the historian as the provider of lessons from the past necessary to understand humanity now—links Cáceres's project to the entire family of biographical collections, feminist and otherwise, written with the aim of "saving" Spanish American youth from moral or political decline—a spirit in which a new sort of history is necessary not for accuracy or scholarship's sake, but in order to provide appropriate teaching materials for a perceived generation in need of new old models.

One of Cáceres's innovations is the use of a prepared questionnaire to which her subjects respond. She refers to the device as an interview and posits it as an effective technique for capturing "the mode of thinking" of a contemporary set of feminist thinkers (139).[36] Her collection, like Acosta's, includes both ancient and contemporaneous biographical subjects that, while generally divided by region and time period, produce a certain synchronic effect, as well as a flattening of national boundaries. Cáceres identifies feminism as its own intellectual passport, arguing that "a feminist is not a foreigner," given the probability of encountering like-minded thinkers "in whichever great capital she might visit" (341).[37]

Acosta and Cáceres's measured notion of female emancipation limits women's role to the media industry and the creative arts and shows great deference toward traditional gender roles in politics and business. The liberation they envision might be described as freedom to depict and report on the actions of powerful men. The public women exalted in both collections often combine literary expression and publishing acumen with experience in education, the other industry generally considered appropriate for women in nineteenth-century Spanish America. In this sense the collections serve to empower by celebrating progress already made. In a manner very much like that of the US industrial press cited admiringly by Sarmiento—those technical newspapers and quarterlies by which every agricultural and industrial innovation quickly became known and adopted by farmers and mechanics all over the country—Cáceres and Acosta are in a real sense creating the networks of female intellectuals they describe.[38]

## *The Collective Goes Meta: International Women's Networks*

Cáceres and Acosta also maintained a transatlantic platform that relied at least in part on the links between Spanish and Spanish American novelists nourished on a pan-Hispanic lecture circuit that sent Cáceres and Acosta to Madrid and that had brought Spanish luminaries such as Emilia Pardo Bazán to the New World.[39] Moreover, the art and publicity of the biography itself was a firmly international aspect of magazine publishing on both sides of the Atlantic in the second half of the nineteenth century. From Henry Barnard's *American Journal of Education* to Matto's *Búcaro Americano*, the popular and specialty magazines of the time tended to make biography a running section that used a theme such as education or feminism as an axis to transcend national and linguistic boundaries. Just as Barnard had run a hagiographic biography of Sarmiento to introduce the Spanish American educator to US readers as a fellow progressive, Serrano included Soledad Acosta among "Inmortales Americanas" in the pages of *Albúm Salón* in 1902. Referring to Acosta's native Bogotá as the "Athens of the New World" (a cliché that would be applied everywhere from Lima to Nashville in the early twentieth century), Serrano praises her as a writer capable of capturing "perfect physiological study" and "social thought" in the "torrents of inspiration" (torrentes de inspiracion) that flood the pages of her fiction ("Inmortales" 99).[40]

At the same time Serrano lauds Acosta the fiction writer, she also grants her the credentials of "eager and indefatigable educator" and remarks on how the two pursuits are especially related for a feminist:[41] "With her effective initiative she has stimulated the young female Pleiades to invade the field of reading and conquer fresh and beautiful laurels fully and without fear of their old obligations" ("Inmortales" 99). Serrano's link between literature and education hinges on both the need for some sort of initiative capable of upending those "old obligations" and the hope that literature will provide an especially fruitful professional field for that rising generation. (The word "Pleiades" appears so frequently in critical invocations of—especially but not exclusively—female Spanish American writers as to seem the result of an agreed-upon editorial conspiracy.) Serrano manages to praise not only Acosta's literary talent and educational acumen but also to note how rarely one could expect to encounter an intellectual with "a smoother, more feminine and more amiable manner" (99).[42] Serrano's attention to Acosta's "feminine manner" effectively preempts any critique that would define professional success as incompatible with traditional notions of femininity. An American writer, Acosta also manages to garner praise from Spanish observers who wish to see the members of the Spanish American Pleiades of writers counted as part of a larger, pan-Hispanic cultural heritage.[43]

A year after the publication of *Biografías de hombres ilustres*, the *Revista de España* would put on the full armor of metropolitan condescension to express the genuine and happy surprise at the cultural advancement of the American republics, an advancement credited to "the laudable use they have made of the sacred deposit their mother country entrusted in them in every genre of culture" ("Notas" 153).[44] The successful female writer provoked similar surprise, given the publication's definition of the female sex as "called by nature to other functions, not less honorable or transcendental" (153).[45] Acosta's ability to produce history as well as literature sends them into flights of gendered language as they praise the biographical collection as "an exemplar, not of fantasy and exquisite sensibility, but rather of austere penetration, severe judgment and grave and considered analysis" (153).[46] Mentioning Caesar and Livy as it praises

Acosta's ability to illustrate historical fact with narration, the *Revista de España* lamented that narrative history should have become a dying art in Hispanic letters and compared Acosta's living, breathing biographical figures with those of Plutarch. What really pleased the *Revista*, however, was Acosta's focus on the historical connection between Spain and Spanish America. Judging her focus on the Conquest as truly inspired, the journal expressed its wish that someday Acosta would become one of the watchwords of pan-Hispanic union "when the last remains of the clouds imposed between the children of a single country have vanished and all of the children of Spain form a single people" (156).[47]

What is perhaps most curious about the metatext on Acosta's biographical collection is the degree to which those who discuss it wish to make a biographical example of the text's author and editor. In the case of the *Revista de España*, Acosta's interest in the Conquest as a historical theme to be confronted head-on as a singular aspect of Creole identity—in opposition, say, to the Bolivarian tendency to look upon the writings of Las Casas and others as proof of the injustice of the Spanish Conquest and thus Spain's inadequacy as a metropole—marks her as possessed of a "moral tendency" that the publication credits as the real secret of her success as a fiction writer.

Cáceres's publication would inspire similar invocations of a pan-Hispanic literary community. The Spanish daily *Heraldo de Madrid* would go so far as to suggest that her book must be the precursor of another volume to come, given that it does not cover Spanish women and since, the reviewer is sure, "Aurora Cáceres, as a good American, loves the old Spanish mother" ("La mujer" 3).[48] The reviewer, whose piece is signed "Colombino," also praises Cáceres for having written a book that need not be included among "those undigested feminist tirades" (3).[49] Cáceres emerges as "one of our most elegant users of Castilian" but "Colombino" also manages to squeeze in a warning against American neglect of Spain and an oblique critique of feminist writing (3).[50] *Por Esos Mundos*, another Spanish publication, would strike a similar note, praising the book as "a feminine history" and the author's ability to dodge the fate of producing what its reviewer believed to be the curse of typical feminist fare—"that anti-esthetic gesture of the suffragists and academics" (*Por Esos* 894).[51] For these reviewers the narrative quality of Cáceres's collection, like that of Acosta, "saves" the book from falling into polemical and aesthetic traps.

Cáceres went to great lengths to maintain a transatlantic profile, including a number of European lecture tours, and one of the most interesting responses to her work itself and the figure that a popular female Peruvian writer represented in context was given by Ricardo Mazol, who described his experience of a 1910 Cáceres lecture at the Sorbonne for the Madrid newspaper *El Motín*. Mazol has nothing but praise to offer Cáceres; in fact, his only piece of advice is that she should feel less constrained by tradition, "consulting her own heart more than the stolid books of men" (6).[52] Where other observers praise moderation as an essential virtue against an assumed fear of too radical a feminist position, Mazol tries a different tack, calling for a freedom that insists on essential gender differences. Thus he calls for "a new literature, a new science, a new language, the form, tone and style that are best calibrated to the [female] sex" (6).[53] Literary "progress" for women is deemed necessary precisely because of a separation between male and female spheres.

But male-female relations is only a secondary hobbyhorse for Mazol. The real passion in his essay comes from his view of Cáceres's moment in the sun as an indication of Spain's cultural decadence. He is keen to point out the absolute lack of governmental or diplomatic representation from Spain—"Not even a miserable doorman from the Spanish Academy! Not even a *floor-polisher* from the Embassy!" (5).[54] Against this backdrop of absolute institutional neglect, in which Mazol counts himself and two colleagues as the only operative, if unofficial, representation from the Spanish-speaking world, the image of Cáceres emerges as indicator of what Mazol sees as the complete lack of Spanish presence in the world of letters:[55] "The sweet voice of Sra. Cáceres, sounded something like the praying of a daughter over a mother's tomb. Never did Spain seem so dead; it no longer hears . . . it no longer understands, not even those who speak its language . . . Dead!" (6). Mazol has trouble deciding whether to be happy about Cáceres's contribution and thus to paint her as a hopeful sign of pan-Hispanic regeneration or to imagine the shock and surprise of the Spaniards of previous generations, whose voices did resound "in the French colleges," if they should happen to realize that the halls of the Sorbonne would hear no Spanish at all "until it was presented on the lips of a woman" (6).[56]

But the problem of Hispanic decadence seems real and pressing to Mazol, and he declares Cáceres's collection of biographies worthy of a doctorate and suggests that it be presented as such to the Academia Española. He imagines that Cáceres's entrance would cause a long overdue scandal to erupt: "It seems to me that it is high time some of these bearded academics got up in shame and yielded their chairs to these women who, against winds and tide, have conquered acclaim that not all of the academics have won" (6).[57] Again, it's not clear if the emphasis lies more on those achievements made "against winds and tide" or on the extra shame the old academics are imagined to feel upon yielding their seats to a woman. But what most matters to Mazol is the question of awakening Spain first to and then from its decadence, and so Cáceres serves both as a symbol of what has gone wrong and the way to a possible solution.

Just as the *Revista de España* had found Acosta to be a laudable example of renewed transatlantic connection, given her interest in reviving history among Spanish American readers, so Mazol finds in Cáceres a starting point for the discussion of a possible renaissance in Hispanic letters.[58] It is Spain's future as a cultural power and not Cáceres's career itself that most depends on her acceptance by the Spanish academy, Mazol argues: "Otherwise, very quickly, before the Pleiades of Castilian writers streaming out of the American republics, that of our writers will have vanished" (6).[59] Cáceres's ability to provoke this sort of reaction from a Spanish observer demonstrates just how central a location she, her contemporaries, and immediate predecessors occupied in Hispanic letters.[60] Mazol's testimony also demonstrates the ability of biographical writing to effectively bridge gaps of literary genre. It functions as a work of education and moral inspiration as well as an academic project with sufficient reflected glory to bring Spain itself closer to a perceived cutting edge of cultural production. The book that rethinks history through narrated lives thus becomes a creative project capable of defining the literary present.

It's important to note that Cáceres and Acosta, along with Matto, wrote their biographical compilations from their own established, eclectic platforms. All three wrote travel books and extensive bodies of newspaper and magazine essays on a variety of topics. As Diana Arbaiza has argued in her discussion of Acosta, the movement between a *modernista* aesthetic of recovered and reimagined myths and symbols and the historical project of recovering lost bits of local and not-so-local historical knowledge was a logical one. In the context of future-centered Creole projects of national regeneration (Arbaiza refers to the movement headed by Caro and others, but the term could easily be applied to the tone of political debate in late nineteenth-century Peru), the past becomes something to be used for a symbolic future rather than a subject of investigation in its own right. Along with providing a fresh narrative of past lives geared to contemporary problems of pedagogy—Cáceres and Acosta, for example, both couch their volumes as influences that will lead Spanish American youth out of a perceived moral and political crisis—the biographical compilation also serves as a means of reshaping a present-tense "state of letters" and producing virtual communities that transcend national borders and, in some cases, chronology.

Acosta, who herself would certainly rank as part of the "Pleiades," at least when the term stretches beyond Lima itself, and Cáceres, who comes onto the scene two decades after the original *veladas*, but at a time when they remained a relevant cultural memory, would make their own contributions to furthering and shaping the vision of a coherent community of female Spanish American writers and intellectuals. Beatriz Urraca speaks of a "female inter-American intellectual network" fostered in Argentina's print journals, which published articles from writers throughout South America (153). In a sense Acosta and Cáceres's collective biographies also served the purpose of creating the textual simulacrum of a community. This effect becomes particularly pronounced when each concentrates on her own professional world, literature, and so weaves a narrative of writers and literary influence.

Both cite Staël as an exemplary woman of letters from another time.[61] Acosta finds that the scope and originality of Staël's oeuvre supersedes what she regards as the proper or normal limits of female agency. Defining her as "one of the few women of real, living genius," she explains that the scarcity of this kind of genius applies in her view particularly to women: "Women can have talent, intelligence, more perspicacity generally than men, but *creative genius* is a stranger to their nature."[62] Staël, she concludes, is best summed up as a kind of "very brilliant" exception that proves the rule (*La mujer* 245). Cáceres seconds Acosta's insistence on the notion of genius, crediting Staël with "creative genius" and, citing Paul Acker, "the revolution of Romanticism" (*Mujeres* 325–26). For Cáceres, who insists that "The woman who wishes to dedicate herself to letters, does not constitute a separate type," Staël can be said to have given the nineteenth century a kind of chronological harmony: "The nineteenth century is initiated as for the woman with the greatest, the colossal woman, as one critic calls her, Madame de Staël" (325–26).[63]

Staël serves as one example among many others of how the biographical genre allows Acosta and Cáceres to grant their subjects double agency. On the one hand, their announced belief in the biographical project as one that will influence the present generation of young women makes their books future-centered and puts the history of each woman included to use as a means of providing concrete inspiration in the present tense. On the other hand, the project also derives much of its rhetorical force from the tension between the individual and exceptional lives cited and the assumed noise and movement of the historical period they inhabit. For Acosta, Staël is an outlier not so much of her own time period but of human history itself. And while the praise of Staël's genius as an exceptional quality particularly unfitted for her gender places a clear limit on what Acosta is willing to call normal feminine behavior, her own beliefs about literature's social purpose make it clear that "genius" is, by her reckoning, far from the most important quality a writer can possess.

Defining the feminine by the presence of an overriding social mission—"Woman has in all times and places a great mission before her, and it is to be hoped that she will never forget it" (*La mujer* 247–48)—Acosta specifies the role she has in mind as that of moral sentinel, guarding the progress she associates with modernity: "Society finds itself returning to barbarism, and it is in the hands of the woman to impede it" (248).[64] Given a narrative based on progress and a female mission to maintain it, Acosta extols the United States as an example where material prosperity correlates with an increased presence and influence of women in public life, and lifts up Harriet Beecher Stowe, author of the antislavery novel *Uncle Tom's Cabin*, as an example of the moral result. Acosta has already praised Stowe and given a brief biographical summary in the chapter titled "Moralistas," so she does not repeat these accolades now that her attention has turned to the professional field of literature. What she does note, however, is a synergy between message and reception. Stowe can thus shine forth at once as an example of moral influence over a society suffering from the moral corruption of slavery even as, in the years after the US Civil War and emancipation, her popularity comes to represent the achievement of moral progress (356). At the same time, Stowe's books sell in sufficient quantities to make her a symbol of professional success, too, and thus proof that the role of moralist need not conflict with material reward and inclusion in public life.

The other point of convergence between Cáceres and Acosta is the vision of the present tense as a moment particularly appropriate for a rethinking of the past. Both demonstrate their faith in modernity's triumph as both a goal to which their books will contribute and an inevitable reality that makes their rethinking of history necessary and timely. Acosta, for example, describes the Spanish America of her present tense, ca. 1895, as one in which the individual republics are finally escaping from "the era of turbulence and political conspiracy that for more than eighty years darkened the social horizon" and confronting the pressing question "around the role that women will play in the new order of things that is being prepared" (383–84).[65] Cáceres, too, refers to the present tense with a combined sense of crisis to resolve and progress achieved, arguing that "the current condition of our societies demands from the woman greater energetic force, her passive condition of childish, unknowing companion has ceased" (345).[66] What Cáceres sees developing in place of the old order that believed it could afford to confine concrete social and political activism to the male gender is one in which the sphere of female influence makes the woman "the companion, not only in love, but also in sadness, in work, and in the ideals that make life happy" (345).[67] While she repeats the patriarchal gesture of imagining the female role as that of "companion," a redux, some one hundred and fifty years later, of Rousseau's narrative that brings a female presence in as the essential companion for his enlightened Émile, she is in effect using the old form to make a reimagined female role seem as unthreatening as possible. The expanded sphere of contribution, which in the context of a wide-ranging, collective biography means many greater subject headings for important female figures, effectively outflanks any attempt to limit the public agency of women on the grounds of gender roles. Femininity, she argues, already includes the public political roles assumed to be the purview of males.

## *Feminism and the Book to Come*

Along with the cumulative effect of dozens and dozens of biographies of influential professional women—from all over the world in the case of both books and from all over the world and a variety of time periods in Cáceres's study—both writers also turn their lenses to a regionally conceptualized Spanish America and find specific examples of working intellectual communities that unite the fields of literature and education. Acosta, who, when speaking of the shared colonial past, asserts the importance of a conceptual "American *patria*," argues that this patria "should constitute itself as a confederation in order to help each other, defend each other and mutually give each other glory" (*La mujer* 395).[68] Acosta's collection closes with an essay she has written for a Colombian periodical centered on the Lima novelist and essayist Mercedes Cabello de Carbonera. Lumping Cabello in with fellow Lima intellectual Lastenia Larriva de Llona, with whose work she seems less familiar, Acosta praises Cabello (and Llona) not so much for what they have accomplished in their writing lives, but for what their published works lead her to believe they are capable of writing—a synthesis of contemporary "American" reality: "to paint with graphic colors the natural beauty of *the Americas* our America, the historical customs occurring in these countries in past centuries and in the present" (405).[69] What these dreamed-of books—another kind of American novel in subjunctive—ought to accomplish, Acosta concludes, is precisely the opposite of what Cabello de Carbonera has produced so far, "the minute description of the disorderly customs of a class of Lima society, a leftover of European corruption, badly transplanted to the New World" (405).[70] Acosta is frustrated by the capability she sees untapped in Cabello de Carbonera's oeuvre, even as she acknowledges Cabello's success as a chronicler of Lima's political and financial players and notes that her novel *Blanca Sol* has been unusually popular, having sold through several editions—"an exceptional thing in Spanish America"—and made a serialized appearance in the United States (405).[71] What Cabello *could* be producing, Acosta argues, are "beautiful, *distinctly American* books," books therefore worthy of her "aptitudes as a writer, as a thinker, as a moralist" (405).[72]

Acosta's statement is at once a professional manifesto proclaiming the sort of literary products that women writers should be producing in Spanish America—a topic I will explore more deeply in subsequent chapters—and a general statement on the moral role of Spanish American women. If, as she argues a few pages later, "the mission of the Spanish American woman" can best be described as a positive moral influence on everyday conduct—"christianize, moralize, and smooth out the social norms"—then the Spanish American woman whose professional goal or destiny it is to be a writer takes on the task of creating moral examples of the sort Acosta's biographical collection has taken from real life (410).[73] The template of the life worth following remains an aesthetic and philosophical imperative as much for fiction as for nonfiction. And by focusing on a contemporary creator of texts, Acosta gives her own project a link into the future cemented by her own belief in the pedagogical utility of books. Just as her gallery of influential professional women on some level "proves" the intellectual and moral equality of women, so the specter of a contemporary who is already a bestselling author but whose potential as a moral influence has not been fully brought to bear on the reading public suggests a looming and on some level inevitable progress yet to be achieved. Part of what makes this magazine excerpt such an interesting coda for the entire volume is the way that it shifts from the general, international accumulation of professional biographies to a *distinctly American* directive. In Acosta's formulation, the cause of correctly capturing American customs and reforming them are one—the *distinctly American* novel is the novel that will at once depict and create a morally advanced American reality.

One aspect that even the picture of Cabello's subjunctive books to come shares with the popular genre of collective biography is what Gallego identifies as an emphasis on nurture over nature. Tracing the heroines chronicled in earlier chapters and featured for their moral uprightness and clear thinking in the midst of that crisis of crises, the French Revolution, Gallego notes that the moral qualities in question shine forth as "learned" (rather than "innate") (161). This elevation of what Gallego calls "the idea of transformation," means that Acosta's hope for a different sort of Cabello novel in the years to come might be something more than a mere rhetorical device, the reviewer's crutch of critiquing not the writer's oeuvre but a mythical oeuvre-not-written (161).[74] If, as in the stories of Smiles and Craik's working-class heroes, the life narrative flows more in defiance of circumstances and influences than under their control, then the further education of an already acclaimed novelist might be a plausible American project—another step in the escape from a Colonial mindset. The Cabello whose books Acosta hopes to see someday would fulfill the narrative arc of exemplary biography, becoming a life worth imitating as well as the producer of texts with a similar effect.

For Cáceres, too, the figure of the Peruvian female writer serves as a marker of possibility for the rest of Spanish America, and she sees Gorriti's Lima *veladas* as events that made the capital host to "the oldest and best represented female literary home" (189).[75] With the greater decade of distance between herself and those events, Cáceres has less trouble picking a heroine and basing her choice on past achievement rather than potential. From Cáceres's perspective, it is Cabello de Carbonera's friend and colleague Clorinda Matto who has already managed in *Aves sin nido* (*Birds Without a Nest*) to produce the *distinctly American* novel: "No writer has better adapted her life nor had her works receive more the influence of her patria" (190).[76] And Cáceres finds Matto's biography to be at least as interesting as her novel.

By 1895 Matto had been officially condemned when the journal she edited, *El Perú Ilustrado*, published a story deemed offensive to the Catholic Church, and in March of that year, her printing press was destroyed (S. Guardia 214).[77] Exiled to Buenos Aires, she continued her wide-ranging career as a woman of letters, editing the journal *Búcaro Americano* and continuing to publish articles and books of her own. What Cáceres finds praiseworthy in Matto's career, along with the American-ness of her fiction, is the perseverance she has shown in overcoming the considerable obstacles placed in her way by circumstance: "What most surprises us in her is her character, formed by energies, far from Peruvian, and her uncommon work ethic" (190).[78] With a heroism born of difficult circumstances—"Fate has turned her into a fighter, into a heroine of destiny"—Matto stands forth as a living, present-tense example of achievement under extreme difficulty (190).[79]

And if what Cáceres praises in Matto's fiction is just the sort of natural-world local color that would be impossible in novels set, like Cabello's, in a capital city—Matto's biography is distinct because it shows an *American* writer at home throughout the continent and therefore professionally immune (like Juana Manuela Gorriti before her) to the curse of political exile: "This bird accustomed to the high flight of the Andes, abandoned Perú with ease, making the move to the friendly republic, Argentina" (190).[80] There Matto's continued success as an editor and high-profile literary figure can be framed as the extension of her Peruvian career, and Cáceres provides a list of her editing accomplishments sprinkled with adjectives of praise so that *La Bolsa* is remembered as "an important Arequipa journal" and *Los Andes* becomes an "intrepid political journal" (191).[81] This mobile Matto manages to float as an editor and a writer above "fanatical persecution, political and even regional vengeance" (190).[82] Matto, as Cáceres points out, had been hounded not only by political opponents, but also, as a native of Cusco, by the same Lima society that features in Cabello's novel. An outsider in Lima *and* Buenos Aires who made a name for herself as a writer and also an editor, Matto's country was the country of publishing.

This Matto, the woman of letters distinguished by literary gifts, strength of character, and the necessary business acumen to navigate the precarious world of Spanish American publishing serves, like Franklin, Sarmiento, and Sor Juana, as both a symbolic and a functioning pedagogic presence. Her story teaches those women who read it to exercise those same gifts and to seek, in a republic of letters, the sort of freedom impossible in any single republic on the continent. The life that Cáceres recounts is also a life of teaching, in which Matto produces novels, articles, and even a literature textbook designed to put letters to work on the perceived crisis of public morality. Staël's treatise on the social purpose of literature had provided a blueprint for the convergence of pedagogy, aesthetics, and female emancipation by claiming the mantle of social reform as a necessary literary goal rather than a practical or utilitarian concern of secondary importance.

Writing on the heels of the French Revolution, Staël grounds her narrative in the question of literature's role in a political landscape she sees shifting from monarchy to republic. As skeptical as George Washington about political parties, Staël finds "urbanity of manners" itself to be a possible source of connection, since the forms of courtesy mimic realities that could develop through personal interaction: "It suffers us to see others long before we begin to esteem them, and to converse with them long before any acquaintance commences" (*Influence* 128). Likewise literature maintains a public function by personifying in its characters the new virtues that could never be assimilated to the entire public by abstract explanations alone (144–45). Therefore, from Madame de Staël's perspective, any attempt to cordon off literary creation as an artistic endeavor separate from didactic social improvement should be read as marginalization rather than protection:

> Certainly there is no career so limited, so confined, as that of literature, if we view it in the light in which it is frequently

considered,—as detached from all philosophy, having no aim but to amuse the leisure-hours of life and fill up the void of the mind: such an occupation renders us incapable of the least employment that can require positive knowledge, or that obliges us to render our ideas applicable. (139)

The binary between entertainment and philosophical improvement effectively makes "positive knowledge" the link between artistic creation and a larger notion of social progress. Staël is writing decades before Auguste Comte and his disciples would champion the narrative of phased social progress, but she shares with the positivists a narrative proof-test for artistic endeavors that asks whether they contribute to a general notion of political and moral advancement.

Staël also prefigures Latin American authors such as Cáceres and Acosta, by using the traditional association of femininity with moral piety as a tool for making an argument for women's involvement in public and especially literary life. In support of the education of women, Staël refers to a deep social need for moral arbiters and to women as natural moral judges who "cast an odium upon all base actions, contemn ingratitude, and honour misfortunes when noble sentiments have brought them on" (157–58). Unlike Cáceres, Acosta, and their contemporaries, Staël does not see a clear path toward mass participation of women in literary culture. She notes the particular difficulty that women writers would face from newspaper slander: "What authentic means can a woman have to prove the falsity of scandalous reports?" (164). She even imagines a sinister case of new idols replacing old ones. Just as pagans would blame "fate" for the failures, so she can imagine that in the present day "self-love, in like manner, wishes to attribute its failures to some secret cause, and not to itself," and she foresees a subjunctive future in which "the supposed influence of celebrated women might, in cases of necessity, be a substitute for fatality" (164).

While this concern overshadows any attempt to connect the dots, Staël's musings on the republican purpose of literature and women's education effectively unites the threads that will come together for the Lima Pleiades and its chroniclers. On the one hand, she articulates a moment of political crisis on the heels of revolution, presenting postrevolutionary France as a victim of political corruption and party bickering that have blighted the initial promise of the Revolution. Hewing to a revised but traditional notion of a female gender role tied to manners and morality, she makes a case for women's involvement in public affairs on the basis of that traditional role—a corrupt and immoral political culture needs especially the intervention of discerning voices of moral judgment. Finally, by making public morality the basis for literature's social purpose, Staël preempts any argument that would attempt to belittle didactic literature as somehow minor or lesser.

By this line of reasoning, literature that is separated from the regulation of public behavior is in fact "humbled and confined" to the realm of "words without ideas" and "ideas without consequences" (139). Staël does not write, as Cáceres and Acosta will, from within a real and or constructed network of female writers. In fact, she condemns the degree to which the Revolution has failed to advance either education or public agency for the women of France (155). But she does imagine that in republics (which in her late eighteenth-century moment are very much nation-states of the future, as hypothetical as any publishing project) male attention to politics might create an opening for female writers. As a proposal for female emancipation, this structure hedges everything on the social utility of literature itself, the notion that "confining" women to the world of letters will only serve to increase their influence in the public sphere. When she rhapsodizes about the link between aesthetic perfection and moral utility, Staël can conjure an almost mystical connection between words on the page and the behavior of a readership. Thus, in the republican life in which women become the authors, literature becomes "one of the principal powers of a free state" (242). Like Leibnitz, Staël dreams of a world in which clarity of language means improved political communication—"The science of politics must be created" (213). If writing as a political influence represents a stopgap measure in the long historical progression to political science, it is influence, by Staël's lights, that defines aesthetic perfection and so when "an impartial public are not moved and persuaded by a discourse, or a work, the fault *must* lie in the author; but it is almost always to what he is deficient in as a moralist, that his fault as a writer must be attributed" (240).

Acosta and Cáceres, writing a century later, uncover the same rhetorical synergy between moralism, aesthetics, and female emancipation.[83] So when Acosta imagines a literature to come, a subjunctive future republic expressed in terms that echo Staël's, she speaks in terms of literary moralism—the dream of a to-be-written literature that will unify pedagogy and aesthetics. This literature will be written by women, the argument goes, because of the unique collision of social progress and traditional notions of female gender roles. The traditional role of teacher and moral judge meets the open space of literary creation in a singular moment of political crisis and moral decadence. The twentieth-century Spanish American woman will be a literary teacher and a pedagogical artist.

# 4

# Novelistic Education, or, The Making of the Pan-American Reader

> For us, to defend and to spread culture is the same thing: to increase the human treasury of watchful conscience in the world.
> —Antonio Machado, *Juan de Mairena*, 2:62

## Introduction: Community of Women's Education

The previous chapters have focused on the power of narrative encapsulated in the life of a single, exemplary human being and multiplied in biographical catalogs and collections into virtual networks of human example. Threads naturally emerge, and much of the compositor's intentionality and skill serve to frame the collected lives around shared characteristics. Aurora Cáceres, Soledad Acosta, and Emilia Serrano (Baronesa de Wilson) all worked to create books that served as virtual embodiments of the network of pan-Hispanic women described by Leona S. Martin. This network took on global dimensions, too, as chapters focusing on the responsibilities and opportunities for women in the former Spanish empire appeared alongside descriptions of notable women from Scandinavia, Western Europe, and the United States. Literary women form a powerful presence in all of these narratives, as the compilers see the literary field through Staël's vision of it as an arena in which the private sphere could be rendered public, and in which the unconscious, electric influence of narrative might bring about changes in habit and public opinion that would be impossible through overt political demands.

Autobiographers, biographers, and compilers also join in framing their endeavor at least in part as a pedagogical one. Franklin and Sarmiento offered their own self-educations as examples for the youth of America, and Sor Juana Inés de la Cruz's ability to overcome social obstacles and find in books the sort of enlightenment that educational institutions were unwilling to offer a woman would likewise serve as a model to nineteenth-century feminists coming of age in societies where many of these restrictions, legal or social, overt or tacit, continued to function as barriers just as real as the lack of books and time that punctuate Franklin's and Sarmiento's narratives. Alongside the powerful educational analogy of the self-cultivated life—the heroic autodidact—these writers took on education as a direct topic of analysis and advocacy, too. Sarmiento's paean to US educational progress, *Las escuelas: base de la prosperidad i de la república en los Estados Unidos*, appeared in a number of editions published in New York City beginning in 1866 that were clearly geared toward a pan-Hispanic readership. Fourteen years later Emilia Serrano would publish her Sarmiento-inspired *La ley del progreso; páginas de instrucción pública para los pueblos sur-americanos* (Quito, 1880; Curação, 1891), another work intended to attract a region-wide following and to posit North American efforts toward a system of public education as an example for republics throughout the hemisphere.

The line that ran from New York to Buenos Aires to Quito and Curação would also connect Lima, Bogotá, and Valparaíso. Juan Manuela Gorriti's *veladas* took place, as has already been noted, in a house that was quite literally a school by daylight. When the exiled Argentine author mentioned as one of the pleasures of literature "this parenthesis that the pen puts around us in the midst of work," the "work" in question was most likely educational (*La tierra* 149).[1] Her salon featured essays on education as well as poetry and literary criticism, among them a series of impassioned lectures by Mercedes Cabello de Carbonera on the importance of educating women, lectures that illustrated the point with arguments designed to convince male listeners of the reasonableness of the cause and, as Graciela Batticuore has noted, with an advocate's voice that attempted to question certain aspects of male dominance without attacking traditional views of male and female roles (*El taller* 18). These events brought together an international collection of male and female intellectuals and made self-critique of the Spanish American republics an exercise in optimism for the possibilities of New World democracy rather than a simple lamentation of circumstances and missed opportunities. Batticuore speaks of an "ephemeral 'oasis' of American co-fraternity," and the discourse of educational possibility becomes another trope of Spanish American (and US) rhetoric, and a trope that easily binds itself to the cause of female emancipation and the anxiety about whether political revolutions have really brought about intellectual independence from Europe (20).[2] Educational anxiety, like book anxiety, manages to transcend material and political circumstances. Just as Horace Mann could sincerely despair at circulation figures for Massachusetts that Sarmiento would call the envy of the South American continent, so the McGuffey Reader, a wildly successful US textbook anthology, would include among its readings Henry Ward Beecher's *cri de coeur*: "We must educate! We must educate! or we must perish by our own prosperity" (McGuffey 77). It is easy to imagine Sarmiento repeating the refrain, changing only the last word.[3]

The terms of pedagogical discourse naturally lent themselves to cosmopolitanism, as reformers such as Mann, Sarmiento, and Charles Brooks embarked on official tours aimed at bringing innovative ideas home from Western Europe and Great Britain (and, in Sarmiento's case, the United States), and as writers such as Serrano and Acosta could cite their own travels to provide a kind of platform for their educational ideas—an assurance that they spoke from a perceived modern space that transcended their individual nationalities. In education as in no other field, foreign experience counted directly and crucially toward the authority of the national reformer. Specific proposals for reform—plans for school construction, teacher planning, governmental funding, and so on—appeared before a backdrop in which education came to be identified with a larger narrative of progress. Thomas Popkewitz's formulation that "the notion of progress is fundamental to pedagogical thought" (35) also works in reverse. Concrete plans for pedagogical reform become spurs to future American progress and by their very existence "proof" of an existing American sensibility. Reformist educators converged on the need for "a thoroughly American curriculum" to ground the independence of future citizens as a closely held value rather than a political circumstance (53).[4]

Education's status as a shared hemispheric enterprise was a feature of the times themselves, not an addition tagged on by ex post facto analysis. Along with efforts to apply directly the practical techniques and systems of other countries, the educational sensibility also included a biographical network of its own that posited the names and stories of great teachers and reformers as geographically and politically transferable sources of inspiration. In the United States, the *American Journal of Education* featured Sarmiento himself as a transnational exemplar in 1866, the same year in which his analysis of the US educational system was rolling off the presses in New York City. Praising Sarmiento's "cosmopolitan spirit," the *Journal* credited him with a particular perspective essential to the reformer, the ability to see his own nation through a global lens: "He can stand aside and look upon his own country as posterity alone can generally look upon what is passing at the present time" ("Educational Lessons" 533). Earlier that year the *Journal* had included Sarmiento's essay titled "The Dignity of the Schoolmaster's Work," which defined the office of the schoolteacher in quasi medical terms as "an adequate position to cure radically the evils of society" and the Spanish American schoolteacher in particular as an emissary of a still distant world of global communication—"like the guard of a telegraph, with his arms crossed in the midst of the desert" (n. pag.).

The global and hemispheric dimension of educational reform cannot easily be separated from the cause of female emancipation, either. As Francine Masiello has noted, the hemisphere's affinity for a broad narrative of progress became an especially important tool for feminists seeking legitimacy for their own efforts from a public that was heavily invested in traditional gender roles. In the decades after independence, she argues, women began to equate their own educational rights with "a commitment to national values" (Masiello 230). The "American feeling" these reformers were trying to communicate considered gender emancipation as part of a larger concept of modernity, *and* as an assertion of the continued spirit of the independence movement. Even Sarmiento's confrontational vision of "civilización vs. barbarie" could be sublimated into the argument for female emancipation. As Masiello puts it, reformers were rethinking "the binary opposites of civilization and barbarism as a polemic over gendered privilege," a move that made feminism as they understood it part and parcel to the humming circuits of modernity encapsulated in the telegraph (233).

Like the previous chapters, this one will continue to keep three threads of discussion in play: hemispheric Americanism, female emancipation, and the intersection of education and literary aesthetics. It will focus on the theoretical discussion of women as students and readers that held late nineteenth-century intellectuals in a thrall throughout the New World, but that reached special intensity among Gorriti's circle of writers and their contemporaries. At the same time, this chapter will survey the global publishing scene against which these discussions took place and a handful of notable and formally innovative publishing projects that emerged. I will be arguing that a certain kind of textbook writing appeared in response to a clearly defined notion of gendered reading—these textbooks made the site of reading itself an inspiration for narratives centered not on the heroic autodidact but on small communities of readers struggling together to come up with meanings and applications for what they read. Here I am applying William Acree's conclusion about textbooks in Argentina and Uruguay to Lima and its pan–Spanish American audience during the same time period: "Textbooks were the closest link between print, power, and collective identity" (159). The following and final chapters will discuss the novelistic theory that was created under the influence of educational discussions, that is, the educational novel, while this chapter analyzes the uses of narrative in explicitly educational texts, a phenomenon I call novelistic education. In both cases, we will need to hold at some critical distance the belief, inherited from twentieth-century literary criticism, of a firm opposition between the literary and the pedagogical.

Catherine Sheldrick Ross's recent essay on the connections between pleasure reading and public libraries sums up one consequence of this separation as the belief that "only bad art—for example, pornography or propaganda—roused readers to action in the real world," a belief she counters with the practical observation that "readers, on the other hand, often talk about books as a source of models for living, examples to follow, or rules to live by" (Ross 649). The life stories, self-told or otherwise, of the heroic autodidacts examined in previous chapters provide ample evidence of this "practical" use of books as a source of virtual living models. In this chapter I will argue that the same Spanish American compilers and biographers who forged virtual networks of influential women for a pan-Hispanic readership also made a vital contribution to the field of educational discourse and the production of textbooks and textbook anthologies. Here, as before, the concept of hemispheric Americanism on display is an ideological one. Fueled by a combination of ambition (American possibility, American futurity) and fear (European decadence and its bound, imported manifestations), Spanish American educators forged a definition of readership as a creative, emancipatory act, and a definition of America as a locus for progress.

This progress included gender emancipation as one of its primary manifestations, and it linked this goal back to readership with a vision of the female reader made up of equal parts mysticism and science. Like book anxiety, this mystical female reader cannot be attributed to any single author or literary tradition. It emerges in a broad array of eighteenth- and nineteenth-century sources and becomes the key for translating the political possibilities of the literary field as defined by Staël into concrete educational proposals and texts.

## *Defining the Female Reader*

For all of its rationality as a means by which information can be transmitted in tranquility and solitude, reading as defined by the nineteenth century was also a mystical endeavor, no less mystical than any other connection between human beings. Charles Brooks and Eugenio María de Hostos's use of the phrase "moral electricity" endowed the act of reading with a kind of magic, making it a pathway by which moral influence could pass from the writer to the reader without the latter necessarily being aware of the passage. The tension inherent in the very word *electricity*, as galvanic novelty experiments yielded to electric motors and electric lights, was the combination of invisible processes and visible results. Unlike religious mysticism, electricity produced tangible effects about which observers could agree.[5]

Hostos's formulation took Brooks's definition a step further by endowing the female reader with a particular moral sensibility. His argument begins with the concept of "moral electricity" and the assertion that "sentiment is the best conductor of this electricity" ("La educación" 37).[6] From there Hostos goes on to posit women as better conductors and receivers of moral electricity than men based on a difference in the relative quality of sentiment in both genders: "Sentiment is an unstable, transitory and inconstant faculty in our sex; it is a stable, permanent, and constant faculty in the woman" (37).[7] From the notion of woman as a superior reader and receiver of moral sentiment, it is a relatively easy leap back to the old cliché, dating at least to Pestalozzi, of woman as the natural teacher. So Hostos goes on to conclude that national resurgence, a topic of such concern to male politicos, might in fact rest largely in the hands of women: "Give yourselves mothers who teach their children scientifically, and they will give you a country that obeys reason with virility, that realizes liberty with extreme conscientiousness, and that slowly resolves the capital problem of the New World" (38).[8]

Appearing in the June 25, 1873, issue of *Sud-América: Revista Científica i Literaria*, a publication printed in Santiago, Chile, and intended for a wide regional leadership, Hostos's essay linked women's education to national regeneration—"a country that obeys reason with virility"—and made that formula for national regeneration part of a hemispheric discussion—"the capital problem of the New World." And where would the solution to this problem lie? Hostos was convinced that the New World needed to obey a particularly humane conception of reason, founded "not in corrupting force, not in indifferent morality, and not in the exclusive predominance of individual well-being," but rather "in science, in morality, and in work" (38).[9] As is customary among nineteenth-century arbiters of vice and virtue, Hostos describes the vices with much greater specificity. The juxtaposition of pure or at least grammatically unmodified science, morality, and work, with the contrasting influences of corruption, indifference, and excessive individualism displays a faith that vices are in fact corruptions of the virtues, that is, that part of sentiment's national and regional project is to restore a balanced and original version of scientific process as a driving historical force. Vice, on the other hand, emerges as the capture and subordination of this force to individual ends. Selfishness threatens the American republics, and increased empathy and identification with others will save them.

Hostos's argument is remarkable for the speed with which it manages to connect gender emancipation with a perceived New World moral crisis, but its overall sentiments follow a traditional notion of femininity that functioned, in the hands of different interlocutors, either to advance or deny the cause of female participation in public affairs. The idea of women as perfect or more perfect readers and teachers stretched back to eighteenth-century Europe and was alive and well in Spanish America in the decades leading up to Hostos's essay and Gorriti's *veladas*. The brothers Amunátegui, Miguel Luis and Gregorio Víctor, devoted significant space in their aforementioned 1856 survey of the state of Chilean education to the question of the moral influence of women. Working hard to cast literacy and increased access to education as issues capable of cutting across the divide between liberals and conservatives, the brothers praised reading as an intellectual version of steam power, a device that made distance disappear (14).[10] Increased literacy, they argued, with a nod to religious conservatives, would help make sermons available to everyone, everywhere—"Make it so that all know how to read, and the priest will be able to be present everywhere" (354)—and the widespread education of women would have a similarly sweeping effect: "The day in which all women know how to read, there will be no more ignorance in the world" (374).[11] This last assertion extends logically from the Amunáteguici's belief that "the woman is the best of teachers" (374).[12] If the need for educational reform logically appeals to everyone, from clergy who wish to make printed sermons omnipresent to free thinkers who would prefer other printed voices, then the education of women must be an equally universal need.

In Spain, the Galician-born author Concepción Arenal would argue from a more traditional Catholic perspective, in terms that echoed Hostos. Women, she asserted, were essential to any plan or hope for religious revival—"Religious regeneration can only come from them" (Arenal 102)—and she took the customary naturalistic step of cloaking this spiritual authority in medical vocabulary: "They can inoculate with their faith in a world corrupted by doubt, gangrened with indifference" (103).[13] Arenal's *La mujer del porvenir* appeared in Madrid in editions published in 1884, 1895, and 1913, suggesting that the perception of a need for regeneration was far from just an American concern and that it troubled the Spanish zeitgeist well before the crisis of 1898. If a Spanish writer such as Arenal could confidently position herself within a corrupted world, the American writer took on the added dimension of a perceived separation from the world and a notion of the American republics as places of asylum and regeneration.[14]

The notion of a particularly feminine duty, responsibility, or calling to produce moral regeneration plays a strong role in a number of the texts already discussed, such as Acosta's chapter on Spanish American writers, and it receives a full exposition in Matto's *Elementos de literatura* (Arequipa, 1884). Published in the same year as Arenal's *La mujer del porvenir*, Matto's volume was both a literary textbook for women and an argument for why such a textbook was necessary. Early on Matto takes the obligatory step of announcing the limitations of her vision. Her book is meant for the female reader, she insists, who by definition "is not called to the pulpit nor the turbulence of the [political] platform, but to the teaching of the family, the peacefulness of the home and the adornment of society, by her virtues in union with a painstaking education" (*Elementos* 3).[15] Matto goes on to cite the Reglamento de Instrucción Pública, the 1876 Peruvian law governing public education. One of its hundreds of separate "articles," article 109, deals with the education of women and specifies that it should include "elements of rhetoric and poetics, universal history, modern languages, calligraphy, drawing, and labors appropriate to the sex" (*Reglamento* 26).[16] While the wording and placement of the article clearly demonstrate the marginal position of women in both the law and Peruvian society, Matto also finds that it provides just enough language for greater political leverage.

Focusing on "rhetoric" as a basis for elegance and persuasiveness of expression, Matto argues that the largely subordinate position of women in Peruvian society makes rhetoric doubly important. Since women are largely excluded from public life, persuasion, she argues, is an even more important skill:[17]

> The bosom of the domestic home, and at the same time society in general, requires the study of rhetoric by women, who are marked to adorn the one and the other. As a teacher, as friend also, she is called to instruct, advise, and pour out consolation among those who suffer and weep. Mother, she exhorts, commands and dissuades; wife, she supplicates, persuades, and shares; in all of these cases eloquence will lend her support, giving her the triumph reserved for the virtuous and enlightened woman. (*Elementos* 7)

Matto, like Hostos, is uniting a number of argumentative threads into one compressed gesture. Having denied any intention of overturning the structure of gender roles in late nineteenth-century Peru, she takes the extra step of grounding her book in the language of the law itself. But once she begins to parse what "labors appropriate to the sex" means in practical terms, she finds numerous examples in which the private sphere demands the same skill set necessary for clergy, attorneys, and politicians, to wit, the ability to make persuasive arguments capable of changing the opinions and behaviors of others. Implied but of course not stated is the link that persuasion necessarily creates between the private and the public sphere, as influence exercised in the home affects the male family members officially sanctioned to practice influence outside the home.[18]

Matto finds it easy to move from rhetoric and persuasion to the literary, since cultivating the ability to persuade means studying, in print, the great persuaders of the past, and later on she argues that the female student is especially suited to literary study because "she is equipped with greater sensitivity, greater perspicacity and greater moral beauty than the man" (*Elementos* 68).[19] These theoretical reflections come only a few pages after Mercedes Cabello de Carbonera's satirical poem "Mujer escritora." Matto's textbook is an anthology, after all, in the style of McGuffey's Readers, and it takes pains to include not only women writers but also women writers writing about the phenomenon of women writers. Part of the poem is spoken in a conservative male voice that wonders what possible utility literary instruction could have for women:[20]

> What good are women
> who instead of taking care
> of our clothing and our table
> talk to us of Byron
> of Dante and Petrarch,
> as if these gentleman
> were giving them lessons
> on just how they should
> darn socks
> or make a stew? (*Elementos* 60–61)

Matto's inclusion of the poem serves to underscore the point she will make a few pages later—that women not only have the right to commune with Byron, Dante, and Petrarch, but that the very qualities commonly associated with femininity would in fact produce better readers.

Years earlier Cabello had spoken on women's education in Gorriti's *veladas*, and her essay on the topic had appeared in *El Correo del Perú* in 1874 under the title "Influencia de la mujer en la civilización." Meeting her readers halfway, Cabello had fallen back on the separation between reason and sentiment as an analogy for male and female spheres. The resulting metaphorical structure made the female reader spirit to masculinity's reason: "Draw the woman to the sanctuary of science so that she in turn may draw the man to the altar of God" ("Influencia" 40).[21] Both halves lacked something in Cabello's formulation, but the backdrop of a perceived moral crisis in Spanish American politics makes it clear which element she considers more lacking and more important. "Science" as she sees it, has already arrived, in the form of advanced communication (steam and telegraph) and advanced financial instruments (the speculation behind the guano and mineral booms), but widespread poverty, inequality, and persistent political instability remained part of the Peruvian social fabric in 1875 and would in the decades to follow. Cabello's yet unwritten novels *Blanca Sol* (1888) and *El conspirador* (1892) would address these issues head on. Speaking from an educational perspective, she finds that the goals of widespread public education and greater participation by women in the public sphere cannot be separated: "the moral regeneration of the people and the intellectual birth of the woman" are by her lights the twin challenges facing both Peru and Spanish America in general.

This link between the female reader/student and moral regeneration on a larger scale resembled book anxiety in its hemispheric manifestations. US writer and social reformer Bronson Alcott (1799–1888), whose experiments with classroom discussion as a basis for narrative had born fruit in *Conversations with Children on the Gospels* (1836), is a case in point. Alcott had voiced a similarly mystical notion of the moral female reader in his discussions with primary school students. Separating feminine emotion from masculine reason, Alcott had maintained that "the best teaching is done by women" (Alcott 163) and that sentiment was not the opposite of reason but rather a faster way of arriving at the same destination: "Woman divines. Her logic is swift; it darts to the conclusion; she sees it intuitively, while fumbling reason follows after" (159–60). This notion of femininity as a magical route to logical conclusions was also echoed by Alamos González's address to one of Gorriti's *veladas*, a speech that urged moving women's education forward at "full steam." What this would mean, he argued, was a larger social change in which nations that had previously ignored it would come to recognize and employ "this sublime, almost divine force called woman" (esta fuerza sublime, casi divina, que se llama mujer) (Gorriti, *Veladas* 348).

Alamos González's formulation of the feminine joins that of Alcott and Hostos in presenting it as an unseen force that will fill a visible gap in societies that the authors have declared themselves dedicated to reforming. If the mystical feminine is a pragmatic tactic for Matto and Cabello, a *treta del débil*, to borrow Josefina Ludmer's memorable phrase, that allows them to use existing prejudices as a form of leverage, then it takes on a structural role for the male writers, an unknown element capable of swelling or shrinking to fill whatever vacuum they see. Another effect of the stereotype of women as sentimental and of sentiment as a form of correction is the notion of the female reader as an antidote for selfishness. Hostos's specification of "the exclusive predominance of individual well-being" as a social threat to Spanish America thus met its antidote in the morality of the female reader, a morality that worked both as a filter for receiving written and spoken influence and as a real influence on others. As one commentator on the nineteenth-century United States has pointed out, the binary notion of gendered reading served to universalize the real influence of written texts to argue that "the literary text promoted activism in all its readers, male and female" (Vásquez xii).[22]

The analogical slippage between the student-teacher and writer-reader relationship was an important component of the mystique of the autodidact as well as an argument for the importance of the biographical collection. When the vocabulary of educational reform on a large scale becomes part of the conversation, the individual examples scale up to the level of nations and populations. In this case the language and circumstances of educational reform to some degree mirror the language and circumstances of the publishing industry, as the wide distribution of popular novels becomes possible on an increasing scale. Jonathan Gottschall's recent book *The Storytelling Animal* argues that "Stories serve the biological function of encouraging pro-social behavior" (Eagleman 17), that is, that the act of storytelling and story listening fosters imaginative and affective connections necessary for community behavior. This notion that narrative was social and communicative functioned as an article of faith among educational reformers in the late nineteenth century and especially among feminist novelists and textbook writers who found they could make traditional notions of femininity match this pedagogical goal. What Sarmiento said about the teacher and what P. Fuentes Castro said about the press, that they were in positions of unique leverage to mold public opinion and values, matched what Matto, Cabello, Acosta, and González de Fanning would say about novelists.[23] It also applied to their roles as textbook authors and compilers.

## *Rules for Reading and Writing*

Perhaps no single author more completely exemplifies the unifying importance of education as a motivator, as an organizing principle, for a career in letters, than Emilia Serrano, Baronesa de Wilson. Serrano's work as a biographer and compiler of biographies has already been analyzed. In *La ley del progreso (páginas de instrucción pública para los pueblos sud-americanos)* (Quito, 1880), she took a similarly cosmopolitan approach to define good readings in both senses of the term—that is, she produced a definition of how a reader should approach a text along with a set of criteria for deciding which texts would be most appropriate for young readers. We might call the indefatigably peripatetic Serrano the embodiment of the "female inter-American intellectual network" of writers whose pedagogical and literary ambitions tended to overlap (Urraca 153).[24] Her project, in keeping with the common frame of educational reform projects going back to Sarmiento, is at once regional and national in scope, as she addresses an Ecuadoran public, writing in fact under the auspices of the Ecuadoran government, and does so with a series of self-designed precepts intended to serve all of South America. The national model, to the degree her model is national, is a prototype for the rest of the region.

Serrano is especially comfortable with the synthesis of science and religion, and she also blends the educational mission into an Americanized concept of progress. Teachers are "priests of responsibility" who sacrifice themselves "for America and because of America," and their mantle, she argues, goes back to the roots of Christianity: "*Teach the one who does not know*, are the words of the Gospel, divine and eloquent phrases that enclose in themselves the greatest thought and the happiness of humanity" (*La ley* 7).[25] Serrano identifies herself as a close reader of Sarmiento as well as of US reformers such as Charles Brooks and Horace Mann, and her focus on linking the educational mission specifically with the Gospel recalls Olavide's novelistic epic of Christian enlightenment as well as Alcott's *Conversations with Children on the Gospels*.[26] In Serrano's discursive universe the presence of self-sacrifice leads almost naturally to a saintly pantheon. Seconding Sarmiento's notion of fame as the lasting and most important reward for the successful pedagogue, she suggests that those who sacrifice themselves to the secular/religious missionary order of the teacher will gain a kind of earthly eternal life in collective memory, as "much later humanity will look for the names of the propagandists, the innovators, of those who have contributed to the great work of civilization and will bestow on them eternal recognition" (14).[27]

Serrano also conforms to the kind of "golden rule" practiced by Sarmiento and the editors of educational journals throughout the hemisphere, the belief that in the present tense those who want to be remembered as "innovators and propagandists" would do well to begin creating that eternal pantheon of the great. She lifts up the examples of "el ilustrado Carlos Brookts" and praises the statue of Horace Mann erected in Boston, remembering the US reformer in messianic terms as a "true and sublime apostle of progress" (11).[28]

Along with this praise of US public schools as a model system inspired by exemplary reformers, Serrano also joins Sarmiento in praising the volume and extension of book circulation in the North American republic, and she cites print as "the omnipotent weapon against obscurantism," thus making Gutenberg the greatest hero of all (28).[29] What Serrano adds to the discussion is a very specific notion of what makes an effective pedagogical text. Basing her aesthetic of the book on a brand of synthesis not so distant from the combination of scientific and religious calling she hopes to see in teachers, Serrano argues that teaching books should balance entertainment on the one hand and "useful teaching" (enseñanza provechosa) on the other, ever adapting themselves to the necessarily short attention spans of young readers (33). Sustained attention is the perfect model for reading, as Serrano sees it, but since that faculty is only being developed in young readers, the authors of teaching books must take into account the limits of their readers while using the entertainment value of narrative to pull them closer and closer to the mature ideal. The textbook should probably be written in the same country in which it will be used so that the subject matter and modes of expression will approach the students where they are, and it should practice a stylistic moderation calculated to reign in the excesses of youthful imagination: "correct style to make the ear attuned to purity of language; good form, naturality of images, nothing of the exaggerated pictures that exalt the infantile imagination and above all, easily comprehended in the anecdotes, stories and episodes, plots and conclusions" (33).³⁰ Here Serrano is following Rousseau's insistence on a transparent relationship between sign and signifier, and his resistance to any pedagogical exercise that would call for language to be repeated or referred to without being perfectly and completely understood. Imagination could be a problem, too, since it would tend to blur the reader's understanding of the relationship between the book and the world, and so Serrano also suggests that the book not appeal too strongly or too directly to the child's presumably well-developed penchant for fantasy and make-believe.

If Serrano demands strict limits on reality and orthodoxy of style, she nonetheless insists that narrative's charms should be employed to the fullest as tools for manipulating the power of sentiment. Serrano uses "vibration" rather than "electricity" as her metaphor, and the overall effect is much the same: "To employ successively the charm of a narrative with the examples of vices and defects, the prizing or punishing of them, interesting the imagination of the child and appealing and making vibrate the fibers of its sentiments, its sensibility and its good heart" (33).³¹ Serrano also worries about what bad books can do, especially those "that sow perturbation" in young female readers, and she identifies the good sort of books by their results, too, as producing "noble sentiments" (35).³² And if bad readings in the sense of bad texts can cause problems, then "bad reading" is an even graver difficulty. Just as Rousseau raised concerns about the divide between language and meaning and the long-term consequences of asking students to repeat phrases and answers without understanding their meaning, so Serrano produces the image of readers poring over texts without a deep connection to the meaning of what they are ostensibly reading. These readers, who merely "go over the pages of a book, without looking for anything in it that orients, instructs or critiques" (35), serve as living proof of the need for involved instruction—for teachers who will demand a demonstration of what their students' readings are actually accomplishing. Here, as in the work of her US contemporaries, the question of active versus passive reading comes to the forefront. One of the dangers of the metaphorical invocations of electricity and vibrations for the transfer of knowledge and sentiment is the suggestion that such a transfer happens automatically and independently of the diligence or ability of the reader. Serrano wants to stress the need for deep connection in order for the vibrations to bring about the desired moral content. Her analysis remains vague, however, on precisely how this balance breaks down, that is, to what degree it depends on the writer and to what degree on the reader.[33]

## *The Cosmopolitan, Universal Classroom*

This question of where the reader's and writer's contributions to the communicative process begins and ends—a possible point of discussion for any literary text—takes on particular significance when the text in question is defined as an educational one. María Adelia Díaz Rönner's relatively recent (2001) theoretical treatise on children's literature identifies "didacticism" as a particular problem for the genre (21). She argues that the problem with notions of "messaging" in children's literature is the limiting effect that a preconceived moral or principle can exercise over the rest of the text: "Of a literary text it implies suffocating the variety it necessarily offers, and drives the receiver/multiplier to manipulate a single line of meaning" (22).[34] Literature, as Díaz Rönner is defining it, implies possibility, uncertainty, and even contradiction, qualities that are effectively engineered out of attempts to make a text communicate a particular moral message.

This concern becomes especially important when we consider the prevalence of the anthology format in the nineteenth century. Books such as Matto's *Elementos de literatura* or, in the United States, McGuffey's well-known Readers, compiled literary texts as lessons for their readers with the ensuing danger of reducing reading to the utilitarian exercise of ferreting out an aphoristic moral truth. González de Fanning's 1893 *Lecciones de economía doméstica* is in effect a normal school in book form, since it purports to teach its female readers how to become effective household managers, a task that includes the education of the household's children, and it makes an effort to fuse morality and aesthetics into something more organically linked than a gilded pill of moral instruction. Following Schiller's phrase, "aesthetic education," González de Fanning proposes the existence of moral aesthetics not as a separate arena where principles may be tested away from the pressures of everyday life, but as an allegorical construction in which actions might possess the same aesthetic qualities as works of art. Structured as a catechism, the text answers the question of the meaning of "beauty in the moral order" as charity, broadly defined and, especially, as "the sacrifice of one's own tranquility or one's own existence to the benefit of others or to country" (*Lecciones* 49).³⁵ González de Fanning insists that this sort of moral education demands a reading education, too, as children must be taught the arts of aesthetic perception in the moral field just as they are taught to understand literature or painting: "Children should be taught to appreciate it through appropriate readings, and, even more, through practical examples" (*Lecciones* 49).³⁶

When the question turns to just where these practical examples should be found, the answer for textbooks, like that of the biographical anthologies already discussed, emerges from a pragmatic cosmopolitanism—a vision of world literature and world history replete with examples that can be applied by analogy. Serrano, despairing at the task of outlining the perfect pedagogical text, can only manage a past-tense version of the book in subjunctive, remembering that somewhere in Germany she once encountered a book by an unknown schoolteacher that managed to capture the give and take of a classroom on its pages (*La ley* 31–32). She remembers that it addressed its subjects in turn—grammar, geometry, algebra—by way of student-teacher dialogues and that the result was a universalizing degree of clarity: "So clearly and well explained are the subjects, that the least intelligent or most childish could analyze and discuss them" (31–32).³⁷

Like Sarmiento confronting Ackermann's catechisms, Serrano is praising the reproduction of a largely oral classroom scene on the written page. But unlike Sarmiento, she does not enter the scene as a reader providing answers to the catechist's questions. Since the book contained both the questions and the answers in the classroom dialogue, Serrano remembers herself as a reader-witness who watched the magic happen: "The professor conversed extensively in his work, reflected and appreciated and set out examples that captivated his students and gave them the pleasure of learning" (31–32).³⁸ Not only does Serrano glory in the professor's presentation—however general her description of it—but also in the students' reception of it. She is witnessing a scene of comprehension to rival the scenes of reading remembered by heroic autodidacts, and the capture of this scene, an ideal of pedagogy, becomes the idealized task of the pedagogical text.

What's most curious about Serrano's description is her decision to present the fictional interaction between teacher and students as though it were a genuine experiment demonstrating the effectiveness of the professor's technique. In the book's fictional universe, the mystical connection between teacher and student succeeds, the moral electricity flows, and therefore the book itself has value not only as the enduring record of this fleetingly achieved ideal, but rather as a means of recreating it. This recreation, we can only presume, could take the form of imitation, of teachers setting out to make their own classrooms resemble those of the unknown German author, but Serrano's framing of the book as an ideal educational text suggests that she expects a similar electrical circuit to be completed between the reader and the teacher-author.

It is also ironic that even Serrano, who includes shared national origin between text and student among her list of virtues for pedagogical literature, finds herself forced to fixate on a foreign model. One of the striking features of nineteenth-century discussions of textbooks is the interplay between nationalistic and cosmopolitan or transnational visions of the act of reading. At the same moment that reformers such as Serrano and González de Fanning make their proposals within clearly defined national frames—Serrano's book is in fact being financed by the government of Ecuador—the ideological commitment to republicanism as a form of government means that they adapt a set of principles designed to be applicable to republican governments everywhere. These reformers translate and adapt, finding the rhetorical and structural tools for the American republican textbook in a variety of texts from a variety of national circumstances. The classroom itself became the universal space in which the allegories of learning and national construction could be carried out across national, regional, and linguistic boundaries.

The Spanish and Spanish American vogue of an Italian text, *Cuore: libro per i ragazzi*, a novel by Edmondo De Amicis (1846–1908), underscores the portability even of very particular local circumstances when attached to an educational frame. First published in Italian in 1886, it appeared in a Madrid edition translated by Hermenegildo Giner de los Ríos in 1887. It was composed during the literal period of construction for Italian nationalism, and it appealed to Spaniards seeking unity in the wake of the Carlist Wars and Spanish American observers, such as González de Fanning herself, looking for narrative forms to develop a curriculum of national sensibility. By the time González de Fanning praises the book in an essay focusing on the "mother's library" in her 1905 collection *Educación femenina*, she can cite its appearance in "44 successive editions" as proof of its enduring popularity and thus its ability to transcend the specific moment in which it was written (*Educación* 78). This transcendence is also geographical, and González de Fanning finds that the story of a young student who comes to understand the breadth and diversity of his young national identity easily transcends the specific circumstances of the Italian peninsula: "It's one of those that could be called human, since it comprehends the feelings of the human heart as it beats in the snowy Siberian steppe or in the burning regions of the tropics" (78).[39] These geographical details, the Siberian steppe and the tropics, encompass an enormous range of climate extremes and clearly exceed the territory of De Amicis's Italy.

González de Fanning is also prepared to make a broad statement about how any reader, regardless of his or her home country, should react to the experience of De Amicis's text:[40]

> Very poorly gifted would be the child or very unwholesome the domestic education it had received, if on reading *Corazón* he did not feel inclined to imitate the beautiful examples that this moral cinematographer is bringing into view, especially if he has a careful and discreet mother who, avoiding unconscious and slipshod readings, fixes the child's attention in every salient characteristic, and reminds him whenever the moment requires it. (80)

Along with a belief in the universal intelligibility of De Amicis's message—not only should it resonate in contexts beyond the borders of the newly formed Italian state, it should also appeal to every sort of sensibility that comes into contact with it—González de Fanning's words offer a definition of good reading as attentive reading. The ill-educated reader who might miss the message could only be the sort of reader who never learned to slow down and pay attention to details.

Her use of the word "cinematógrafo" to emphasize the power of accumulated anecdotes is nearly a neologism in 1905. The word would not appear in the Real Academia Española's dictionary until 1925, and the Oxford English Dictionary's thread of citations for the English equivalent—"cinematograph"—begins in the mid-1890s, a bare decade before González de Fanning's book was published in Paris. The word signified not the moviemaking person or "cinematographer," but rather the moving picture camera, the recently invented machine that made movies possible. Her analogy between moving pictures and De Amicis's series of vignettes about life in a school that brings together students from different regions of Italy highlights the cumulative effects of anecdote, or as she puts it, the use of fragmentation to keep the narrative from becoming monotonous: "Every chapter has its own action and message; they are like pearls on a string that come together without touching or getting mixed up, as each one completes the clear beauty of its neighbors" (79).[41] Just as Serrano uses the specific example of the remembered but unnamed German book that encapsulates a professor's successful relationship with his students, González de Fanning finds in De Amicis the embodiment of her own vision of the pedagogical aesthetic—a hybrid narrative structure in which the larger frame lends itself to division into detachable and memorable units. The narrative effect therefore unfolds not as a slowly evolving impression of a larger whole but rather as a series of lessons that accrete to a moral sensibility—a curriculum divided into teachable components.

When she focuses on a specific episode from *Corazón*, such as the moment when the Piedmontese instructor commands his students to welcome the newcomer from Calabria, she describes the scene in visual terms as a "means of engraving in the hearts of the children the feeling of national brotherhood" (79).[42] The notion that a value can be "engraved" in a student harkens back to forms of visual art much older than the cinematograph, and its use here also suggests that context can be transferable by analogy—that patriotism in one place and time can inspire similar feelings in another. Finally, by choosing the episode in which a group of students from the Piedmont learn to sympathize with a new arrival from a peripheral region, González de Fanning asserts a relationship between sentimentality and national unity. The young Peruvian reader of De Amicis can learn to place herself in the perspective of another just as the characters in the book do. As in Serrano's vision of the German professor with his students, the narrative recreation of an educational circuit on the page leads readers to recreate the circuit again in their own interactions with others.

De Amicis would become a singularly important example for Spanish American and Spanish observers who wished to argue for the possibility of human community against the array of political, economic, and ideological forces that seemed to be working against coherent national identity in Spain and the New World. Elvira Bermúdez's prologue to a 1973 Mexican edition of *Corazón* identified the book with "the era of national integration" while finding that a distant reading, the only sort of reading possible for Mexican students a century and an ocean away, gives rise to something else: "It is not a crude nationalism, but rather a clear, clean, and cordial patriotism" (xxvii).[43] Bermúdez even imagines the Mexican reader making a series of analogical substitutions for the place-names featured in De Amicis's narrative, and she imagines that this substitution might not even need to be a conscious one: "A young Mexican reader—perhaps unconsciously—might read Durango where it says Turin, Distrito Federal where it says Roma" (xvii).[44] She goes on to provide a list of analogical cities, pairing Veracruz with Venice, Acapulco with Naples, Monterrey with Milan, Guanajuato with Florence, and the marginalized Yucatán with Calabria or Sicily. She brings historical figures together by analogy, too, finding echoes between Hidalgo and Garibaldi, Morelos and Mazzani.

Time and space add irony to the pairings, especially given the penchant for New World names as more recent copies of the old (Mexico's colonial designation, after all, was New Spain). In this case, while the Italian cities might be older than their Mexican counterparts and thus the originals of the pair, the Mexican heroes come first chronologically, as Morelos and Hidalgo were about to make their entrances on the stage of Mexican Independence when Garibaldi and Mazzani were born, respectively, in 1805 and 1807. This is another way of saying that Mexican Independence predates the formation of the modern Italian state, and so when Bermúdez suggests the appeal of De Amicis to Mexican readers, she is suggesting not a model for national imitation but rather a literary manifestation of something that had already happened in Mexico, a retelling of Mexican history from another perspective. Nationalism and the obsession with the local combined with the difficulty of reconciling different forms of local identity thus become a transferable and universal dilemma, a universalism Bermúdez imagines in geographical terms: "In every country, some of them less and some of them more, they have their heroes and their battles, their laborious north, their happy south, its beautiful beaches, its bustling ports and its lordly capital" (xxvii).[45] What Mexican students will therefore learn, as they unconsciously read "Guanajuato" where the text says "Florence," is to read themselves into a universal version of history in which marginality and difference punctuate any effort toward national unity.

As specifically as Bermúdez's terms match the specifics of nineteenth-century Mexico to those of nascent Italy, the kind of analogical reading she proposes swept through the Spanish-speaking world in the decades after *Corazón* first appeared in Spanish. Edward H. Worthen's analysis of the book's popularity in Spanish emphasizes the prestige of its translator, Hermenegildo Giner de los Ríos (1847–1923), the younger brother of Francisco Giner de los Ríos, the famed educational reformer responsible for bringing Krausism to Spain and founding the Instituto Libre de Enseñanza in 1876. Worthen notes that the book also garnered official government sanction as an educational text in Mexico and Argentina (137), and he also points out that De Amicis was something of a Hispanist himself, having authored travel books about Spain and a novel *Sull'Oceano* (1889) that chronicles Italian immigrants in Argentina and Uruguay (140). These ties to the Hispanic world were compounded by De Amicis's popularity. His work made such a deep impression on Argentine society that he received job offers from two Buenos Aires newspapers, *La nación* and *La prensa* (Worthen 140–41). Worthen concludes that *Corazón* "has probably been more widely read in the Hispanic nations than any other literary work, with the possible exception of *Don Quijote*" (142n1), a distinction that makes it that rarest of literary phenomena, the contemporary classic in translation.

In Spain José Ortega Munilla praised the work's "moving sincerity" while also describing it as a successful literary microcosm of society and turning to the metaphorical language of medicine, so familiar to writers and critics on both sides of the Atlantic as a way of discussing writing in moralistic terms: "It is a reduction of society to something like a microscopic preparation, in which the observer can analyze at his leisure the resiliencies of the soul" (Munilla 3).[46] Here the Spanish press echoes what naturalist writers such as Zola and Spanish American observers like Matto will claim about the social and scientific utility of the novel, but in this case the novel in question is anything but the product of a naturalist aesthetic—focusing as it does on the mystical bonds of patriotism among schoolchildren. Like the social novel being theorized in Lima in the 1890s, *Corazón* brings realistic technique and naturalistic precision to the very unnaturalistic task of inculcating a sense of public morality in its readers.

Whatever the scientific merits of De Amicis's writing, the Spanish press would continually stress his ability to connect emotionally with readers. So thoroughly does De Amicis penetrate the Spanish psyche that one Madrid newspaper, *El Día*, would praise a discourse by Tolosa Latour, famed pioneer of children's medicine, as possessed of "the sweet vagueness and the indefinable charm" of the Italian writer ("Un discurso" 1). This sentimentality would take on political importance as well, when a correspondent for *Vida Socialista* narrated a visit to a Rome workers' hall that housed a bust of De Amicis, "the sweet and tender writer of the children, of the workers, of the candid souls; he who had a heart for an inkwell and an olive branch for a pen" (*Vida* 8).[47] In all of these examples, sentiment serves as a glue capable of repairing social fissures, and De Amicis's success as a writer and public figure serves as proof of the efficacy and viability of this approach.[48]

If De Amicis emerges as a soothing voice for national anxiety in the Spanish-speaking world, the particular causes and characteristics of that anxiety differ from place to place. González de Fanning is worried above all about political corruption rather than separatist national movements, and she turns to reading as a source of moral lessons that will make children less susceptible to corruption and as a habit of mind that will make them accustomed to associating effort with reward rather than expecting rewards based on social or family connections (it is the absence of this circuit of effort that becomes the moral back story of Cabello's *Blanca Sol*). González de Fanning's belief in *Corazón* as an almost foolproof text has been noted. But guidance still matters, however much the joy of narrative and the intrinsic desire to read might fuel the child's progress. What most troubles González is the prospect of disorderly reading. She asks what will happen if reading proceeds without plan or analysis and if the reader never learns techniques for determining which ideas are most worth remembering:[49]

> Those parents will never achieve their goal who buy books and give them to their children who, beginning those readings with the vehemence that corresponds to their age later abandon them with the inconstancy that also goes with their age. It is necessary to teach them to understand, to judge and compare accurately; only that way can you make them assimilate and pick out the useful, the good and the beautiful; the rest is casting the seed to the mercy of the wind that grabs it, stirs it up, and sterilizes it. (*Lecciones* 80)

In much the same way that her essay on "Las literatas" proposes writing as a form of education useful to all and not only as a means of expression practiced by an elite group to be read by everyone else, this passage makes literary criticism an essential skill for anyone who would learn by reading. Where Horace Mann's well-known aphorism "light reading makes light minds" referred to the problem of students reading the wrong sort of books, light novels instead of more substantial nonfiction, González's approach focuses on reading as a verb. She expresses concern over habits of mind and approaches to the written word. Youthful enthusiasm is not enough, she argues, because it is by its very nature fleeting, and the skills she wishes to emphasize take longer to develop.

González de Fanning's approach is curiously paradoxical in that it calls on parents and teachers to provide greater guidance—she's not comfortable, say, with the prospect of an enthusiastic youth given free rein over the library—but also looks to develop qualities of judgment in the young reader that will make the reader capable of discerning moral content and, quite literally, of filtering out the useful content from everything else. This approach assumes, among other things, that it would be impossible for a tutor or parent to act as a permanent filter. Finally, the sustained reference to the Biblical parable of the sower, a story that would undoubtedly have been familiar to her readers, provides a metaphysical connection between the acts of teaching and reading. In the parable Jesus likens the dissemination of his own message to the act of casting seeds randomly over the earth. Some seeds fall on rocky ground, others among weeds and competing plants, and others on fertile soil with few obstacles to growth. In the last example the seeds produce fruit-bearing plants, and in the first two they do not. This parable, which appears in three of the Gospels, indicates a certain randomness to the power of the pedagogue—the message is sent far and wide and always succeeds in taking root somewhere, but largely for circumstantial reasons beyond the sower's control. In González de Fanning's reworking of the story, books become the seeds and neglect on the part of parents and teachers risks producing students whose disorderly reading habits make them inhospitable ground for the messages being translated on the page. This retelling demonstrates the emphasis she wishes to place on pedagogy: no book can be teacher-proof, and no message can survive disorderly reading. González de Fanning's picture of readings turning into lost seeds also emphasizes the importance of discernment on the part of the reader. Anything can be lost to a certain kind of bad reading. The heroic autodidact, á la Sarmiento, would be, by González de Fanning's lights, at best a lucky exception, since the books by themselves can teach many things but not how to read.

Finally, it is worth pointing out that despite González de Fanning's vagueness about what exactly "the good, the beautiful, and the useful" should entail, she endorses a specific morality of work and reward in which reading plays a part. Her conception of national virtues relies on the sort of expansion that makes the individual student or family the microcosm of a larger group. Early on in *Lecciones de economía doméstica* González de Fanning describes the woman's role in family life as that of "Minister of Finance of the family" (*Lecciones* 6). The entire notion of "domestic economy" or "home economics" is a moral one, she argues, because of, rather than despite, the financial nature of the discipline. Home economics "encourages love of work and of an ordered life; honorability and exactitude" and thus works against "the idleness that is the most frequent cause of vices" (*Lecciones* 7).[50] These virtues come to be national as well as personal when fomented in many families at once, she concludes, and thus work against political and municipal corruption in its large and small forms (*Lecciones* 7).

Her recommendation of De Amicis's *Corazón* as the single most important book that a mother can offer her children speaks not only to the specific virtues of sympathy and self-sacrifice she sees expressed in the work's content, but also to a particular kind of reading she wishes to encourage. The use of a foreign text, indeed a translation, is of little consequence because her philosophy emphasizes the reader's need to seek virtue wherever it can be found. Having linked aesthetics and morality, González de Fanning proposes a notion of taste and critique that organizes written material in search of moral lessons. The child's relationship with the text thus becomes a feedback loop in which the presence of those lessons reinforces the child's propensity to find them. De Amicis's Italy differs from her Peru in a number of geographic, political, and linguistic aspects, but his book and González de Fanning's philosophy agree on the mystical link between the small community of the classroom and the larger society—nation or nation-state—that it shapes and reflects. Even the Peruvian student being taught at home by a parent or other family member will connect, in González de Fanning's conception, with De Amicis's narrative of classroom scenes, a space capable of transcending differences of language, geography, and culture within the shared ideology of the independent republic.[51]

## *Shaping the Global Classroom*

If *Corazón* provided the singularly inspiring space of a republican classroom to Spanish American feminist educators, it was only one of a handful of global texts that made up a universal western library of narratives that demonstrated and performed education. With its recurring characters and progressive temporal structure, *Corazón* fit the description of a novel, like its predecessors *Émile* and *Eusebio*. Alongside the educational novel, another kind of text, the educational anthology, dominated the canon of accepted textbooks and became the prevalent choice of American authors who wished to create a New World educational canon of their own. In the United States Noah Webster's famed 1776 textbook commonly called the *Blue-Backed Speller* had helped make American rather than British place-names the touchstones for US education in geography and politics. William Holmes McGuffey's renowned series of Readers anthologized moralistic stories, political speeches, and other documents in the interest of fomenting a New World sensibility that, like that of Benjamin Franklin and Teresa González de Fanning, would prize industry above all other virtues and condemn as false any ease or pleasure enjoyed without it (Sullivan 161).[52]

In Spanish America a lineage of educational periodicals also played a significant role in the development of a pedagogical aesthetic. Projects geared toward adult readers and with political themes that billed themselves as instruments of public education went back at least to colonial times and the original *Mercurio peruano* (1790–1795). The emergence of independence as a military and political cause gave birth to other "educational" efforts such as Miguel José Sanz and José Domingo Díaz's *El Semanario de Caracas* (1810–1811), while another editor with ties to the Caracas rebellion, Andrés Bello, would plot unfinished projects from his exile in London designed to educate a pan-Hispanic public about its own literary and historical heritage—*La Biblioteca Americana* (1823) and *El repertorio americano* (1826–1827) (see Jaksić, *Andrés Bello* 67–69 for more on these projects). And the Lima group's Cuban contemporary, José Martí, created *La Edad de Oro*, an educational magazine for children that appeared in four editions in 1889 and promised its readers an effective presentation of useful knowledge: "We will tell you everything you want to know, and in a way that you will understand, with clear words and excellent pictures" (Martí, *La Edad* 4).⁵³ Aiming at a conversation "with the gentlemen of tomorrow, and with the mothers of tomorrow" (4), Martí's publication sought to cement a clear sense of American identity in which any "child of America" might be a reader (5).⁵⁴ Finally, along with a concentrated set of readings designed to teach civic virtue, *La Edad de Oro* offered the promise of community and continuity. Martí's introduction invited young readers to send their questions directly to the editor and promised to print the best of those letters in its pages, while also proposing a semiannual contest in expository writing with books and free copies of the journal as a prize (4).⁵⁵ Here we see another echo of the warmth of human contact Sarmiento found in Ackermann's catechisms that reminded him of his old teacher—the printed page serving not only as a route to one-way communication but also as the conduit for a virtual community.

Just as the catechism engineers reader response into its structure, so the plan for *La Edad de Oro* imagines the long life of the periodical as a relationship between its editor and readers. Its short print run—less than a year—underlines the gap between the logistical difficulties of publication and the chimerical promise of human connection. Another narrative tack common to the nineteenth century struck a balance between the thematic prescriptions of the catechism and the continuous evolution of the periodical. Following the lead of French-language classics widely available in translation such as Fleury's *Catéchisme historique* (1679) and Marie Leprince de Beaumont's *Magasin des enfants* (1758), Serrano would publish *Almacén de las señoritas* (Paris, 1865) and Soledad Acosta would produce *Conversaciones y lecturas familiares* (Paris, 1896). Serrano follows Leprince de Beaumont's organizational structure by framing her narrative as a series of readings interpreted by a group of young women under the guidance of a teacher, a kind of narrative classroom not so different from that imagined by De Amicis.

Acosta's book goes further into novelistic territory, as it weaves readings and lessons into a conventional plot structure and gives its characters identities outside of the classroom setting. Her book represents a significant aesthetic touchstone for uncovering the intersection of narrative and pedagogy in the Lima group. Seldom analyzed by critics, it performs at once as a novel about pedagogy in a community and as a guide to pedagogues and students. This new social twist on the pedagogical novel makes the master narrative a community's struggle to understand texts and one another rather than a single heroic learner's encounter with books in a void. While the composition of educational narratives invites all manner of analogy between the student and the nation or the larger community, these communal narratives bring in difficulties of communication and thus point to language and sentiment as tools of understanding necessary to keep the republic from fragmenting. In this section I will be arguing that Serrano and especially Acosta, use an available idiom—the catechism as narrative—to project a vision of educational community that reproduces and attempts to address the difficulties both see as inherent to the new American republics—an inability to identify with fellow citizens and a cognitive dissonance in which elements that should be paired, work/reward, language/meaning, have somehow come unglued. The interpretive work their classroom communities attempt to perform is therefore political work, too.

In the cases of both Serrano and Acosta, theory and practice meet in an inherently global context. Serrano's title is a literal translation of Leprince de Beaumont's (1758) work. *Almacén y biblioteca completa* continually saw print in Madrid, Paris, and Burgundy between 1778 and 1903, with Mexican editions coming off the presses in 1865 and 1927. One Mexican edition called itself *Nuevo almacén de los niños, dispuesto bajo el mismo plan en que se escribió en francés madama Leprince de Beaumont, y enriquecido con nociones de historia y geografía de Méjico* (Mexico City: Buxó y Aguilar, 1864), thus promising to use Leprince de Beaumont's text as a narrative or methodological frame for Mexican content, performing the work of converting Florence to Guanajuato and Venice to Veracruz rather than asking students to do so in their heads while reading. Two books published in 1890 in Bogotá, capital of Acosta's native Colombia, used the title *Almacén de los niños* without making any overt nod to Leprince de Beaumont, listing the authors, respectively, as Elías Montalvo y C. and D. Ignacio Borda.[56] Serrano's title, which used Leprince's basic frame but with different content, enjoyed a transatlantic popularity all its own, with numerous editions published in Paris and Mexico City.

In a global educational community that increasingly saw the value of a text that combined discreet narratives to emphasize predetermined notions of civic virtue while building linguistic and rhetorical skills—

McGuffey's Readers typically included the word *eclectic* in their title—Leprince de Beaumont's appeal is easy to grasp. French by birth, she was working as a governess in London when she began to put together a French-language book, *Magasin des enfans* (*The Young Misses Magazine*), to give her British students age-appropriate materials with which to learn the new language (Clancy 285).[57] Where Fleury's *Catechisme historique* and McGuffey's Readers structure themselves as textbooks, anthologies of texts the students are expected to read with questions and discussion topics designed to shape what will actually happen in the classroom, Leprince's approach prefigures De Amicis's vision of the classroom as the spatial and temporal frame for an original narrative. By taking the extra step of producing both the assigned readings and the classroom scenes in which students and instructor work together to decipher them, Leprince produces a text that in many ways resembles a novel, as the class becomes a cast of characters (with names that underline their symbolic roles, "Lady Witty," "Lady Sensible," etc.) and the reading and interpretation of each text takes on the structure of a chapter. De Amicis, perhaps himself inspired by Leprince de Beaumont, managed to give his episodic saga a semblance of order by taking on the recurring theme of national unity in a context in which that unity remained very much in doubt. Such a tension is largely absent from the eighteenth-century British context in which Leprince writes, but her student-characters do struggle with the task of learning how to locate, politically, figuratively, and geographically, their island empire with reference to Europe and the Americas.

Leprince de Beaumont, whom María del Carmen Marrero Marrero would identify as "a great fighter for women's rights" (Marrero 177),[58] would also write a book about the education of boys—*Le Mentor moderne*—while always adhering to a child-centered philosophy that favored student initiative over the instructor's mandate (Marrero 179–80). Two points of focus stand out in Leprince's work—morality and geography—and these themes constantly intertwine with the author's emphasis on the act of reading as a practical and symbolic educational exercise. One early British edition of *The Young Misses Magazine* included praise from "the Authors of the CRITICAL REVIEW" who celebrated Leprince's ability to make aesthetic appeal serve pedagogical ends: "Here we find the useful and agreeable happily blended, a short and clear abridgement of sacred and profane history, and some lessons in geography" (v). This seemingly unlikely triangle of the Bible with secular history and secular geography allows Leprince's instructor to establish a set of hermeneutical rules for her students. She notes the difference between "story" and "tale"—"A story is an account of what is true, and a tale is a narration invented only to amuse young persons" (9) and presents the Biblical portion of the curriculum as a kind of super-story in which the skepticism employed in the interpretation of normal stories should be cast aside. In fact, the teacher argues, in the case of sacred history, the story should be seen as trumping empirical evidence: "Remember, my dear children, that this history is the only one which you may not doubt the truth of, it is more certain than that it is now daylight" (32).

By making the book about more than sacred history, Leprince also manages to keep a practical and empirical frame on moral topics. On the heels of a reading in which a prince loses and then recovers the moral voice of his own conscience, her narrator offers the advice that "If you really intend to be good you must write down all the naughty things you say and do, every evening," thus combining the Christian imperative of confession with the use of daily writing as a pedagogical plan—just the sort of synthesis that González de Fanning would employ to argue that writing could work to the moral benefit of women. Fables relating to the act of reading also abound. One anecdote features a villainous captain who "although he did not love reading, he had a large library, to make people believe he was a man of sense and learning" (Leprince de Beaumont 1.85). This unused room later becomes a godsend for a more virtuous character, a soldier who "became capable of commanding an army" by reading the heroic biographies of successful commanders (1.86). Another tale has a frivolous group of older sisters ridiculing the younger "because she spent the greatest part of her time in reading good books" (1.46), while a third introduces a woman brought up in the city who wishes to improve her own inner life and agrees to follow the educational program of a shepherdess in which "The whole day was divided betwixt prayer, reading, work, and walking" with a surprising result that "she found herself a thousand times happier amidst her rural affairs, than in town" (1.211–12). In this last anecdote the notion of reading as a cure for superficiality meets the cliché of rural wholesomeness versus urban corruption—the city student is saved by going into the forest to read.

Along with these specific anecdotes, Leprince de Beaumont also includes direct commentary on the importance of the act of reading and the kinds of reading to be emphasized and avoided. One student reflects to another on the insufficiency of wit in the absence of books—"you do not want wit, my dear sister, but you must adorn it by reading, and making proper reflections on what you read" (2.193)—a formulation that stresses commentary and critique as necessary steps for the reader. Reading can be done badly or well, by Leprince's reasoning, and she uses the metaphor of digestion to underscore the importance of method: "And as the glutton is not properly nourished, and, on the contrary, is often troubled with indigestion, in the same manner your hasty reading is not well digested, and does not give you any greater knowledge" (3.120). So important is the moral quality of restraint and moderation, that even reading could become a dangerous appetite, so the governess asserts that reading too fast or too greedily will negate any positive cognitive effects. Summing up the importance of regular encounters with books, the governess also reinforces the notion of every student as an autodidact—"Reading instructs, points out our faults, and gives us motives and means of correcting ourselves" (2.269). Reading serves not only to provide methods and suggestions for self-correction, but also to inspire the desire to perform self-correction in the first place. Leprince de Beaumont's governess is arguing, in effect, that reading functions as a kind of mirror capable of shifting the student's perspective on her own life. In a move that prefigures contemporary, twenty-first-century arguments for fiction reading as an activity that expands a reader's ability to imagine herself or others from a different point of view, Leprince de Beaumont—unwilling to privilege novel-reading over scripture and history—finds a similar benefit in nonfiction.

The constant presence of the governess who not only guides her students but also stops to explain to them (and the reader) the justification for her pedagogical techniques gives Leprince de Beaumont's book a theoretical perspective on teaching that is impossible for a catechism or anthology such as those of Fleury, McGuffy, or Martí. Serrano and Acosta seize upon this dimension for their texts, too, creating classroom spaces conspicuously located in the New World, and weaving metacommentary about books and language into the pattern of included texts, invented or cited, and the discussion of what they mean. Early on in *Almacén de las señoritas*, the reader is introduced to a distinction between "cuento" and "historia" that precisely matches Leprince de Beaumont's discussion of "tales" and "stories" (19). Soon the family patriarch suggests a broad rule for reading, that the first question should be, "Of what use is this book I am holding?"; his question at once affirms the importance of reading with method and dismisses the notion of reading as a pleasurable act (*Almacén* 19).[59] Having fixed on moral educational objectives that include self-denial and moderation, these authors find it difficult to frame reading as a wholly pleasurable activity, even when they use pleasure as an argument for its efficiency as a means of transmitting information. Serrano's text consistently stresses the importance of education for women as a plan B against financial disaster rather than a career-oriented plan A, and she also includes admonitions designed to keep intellectual and social independence in check. A girl, she argues, "should repress her caprices, and conform to the will of their parents and teachers" (134) and remember the importance of modesty and moderation: "The best dress for a young girl is moderation and simplicity" (289).[60]

This inherently conservative approach to social mores is even more pronounced in Acosta's *Conversaciones*. Critics have long noted the uneasy synthesis between Acosta's Catholicism and her dedication to feminism as well as the contradictions between the concern for social justice her writings display and her belief in the racial and economic superiority of Colombia's Creole elites. Some have focused attention on the deep economic and cultural reach of her desire for female participation in cultural production and the economy writ large (see Dónoan and Gómez Ocampo). Others have focused on the oppositional nature of the educational project—the elitism in her characters' frequent desire to "educate" the often sympathetically drawn but othered masses (Marín Colorado), or to note the conflicts that can erupt between a belief in the dignity of work on the one hand and an esteem for established aristocrats over working-class strivers on the other (Aguirrea). The book's dual role as an agent of social control and social emancipation is a structural condition for Acosta's *Conversaciones* and a topic of debate within her text.

*Conversaciones* takes place on a plantation removed from the hustle and bustle of Bogotá. The large and wealthy landowning family entertains visits from a botanist and a priest who spend their Sunday afternoons—thirty of them, making the novel's span a literal "month of Sundays"—giving lessons to the family's children about church history, local flora, and an almost innumerable array of topics that arise in the

*El Perú Ilustrado* offers a profile shot of Soledad Acosta de Samper, the Colombian woman of letters who made a deep impression on literary Lima. Courtesy of the Library of the University of California, Berkeley.

heat of discussion. The two teachers do not always agree, as the priest maintains a predictably conservative skepticism about the social consequences of independence and rising literacy rates while the botanist extolls the progress made by female scientists in Great Britain and the United States as sources of inspiration for young Colombian women. On the other hand, the priest's conservatism allows him to make observations that might be more difficult for liberals invested in the historical narrative of the republic, such as when he complains that the end of colonialism has in fact made life worse for the country's indigenous population because of the republic's half-hearted commitment to educating all of its citizens and inability to dismantle the racial hierarchy inherited from the colony. When he exclaims "Independence was done in this country by the whites and for the whites!" (*Conversaciones* 112–13), he is both erasing the important contributions to the independence movement made by nonwhite Colombians while at the same time noting with cold realism the fact that a change in government has not made racial hierarchies or injustice disappear.[61]

The priest also turns what could have been a nostalgic commentary about colonialism—"the common people were much happier in the time of the Spanish" (112–13)—into an indictment of republican neglect when he condemns the available school system as mere "simulacra of schools" and suggests that the teaching of reading as a basic skill accomplishes little in a social arrangement in which access to the printed word is still the property of moneyed classes and urban settings: "Since in the countryside they will never see a book or even a paper, what good are we doing by obligating them to learn something they will never practice?" (112–13).[62] The botanist is of course more sanguine about the future of Colombian readers. One of the reasons that access to the printed word and formal instruction should be widened, he argues, is the possibility of awakening the hidden genius of the population. Not only does he imagine the possibility that scientific superstars could arise among the "gentes del pueblo," he also suggests that "everyone, even the most stupid beings, has a seed within" (168).[63] That "seed within" (and once again we are returning to the imagery of the parable of the sower) can of course bear fruit only if the right conditions are provided, and those conditions include access to books and the guidance of instructors.

These digressions by the priest and botanist into the nature of reading and the educability of the Colombian public bring a strong current of metacognition to the classroom discussion, and while this metacognitive dimension takes up a fraction of the text, it frames the narrative within a larger discussion of educational reform. If narratives such as *Eusebio* or *Émile* suggest but never articulate practical questions such as "Is this educational model scalable?" Acosta's text goes to great lengths to make them part of the structure of the text. Here the narration of an idealized educational experience for a few students becomes at least the site of a discussion of what could be done for the many.

In Acosta's case, as in that of Leprince and Serrano, the educational narrative clearly takes precedence over the educational discussion. Most of the book's pages are devoted to paraphrased or verbatim readings—the instructors will quite literally mention an interesting title and begin a "reading" from it that appears in the text as a multipage direct quotation—and to the ensuing discussion. Leprince's text punctuates each day's lesson with instruction in British geography and even goes so far as to recommend a specific text—"Mr. Palait's *Introduction to Modern Geography*"—which the governess urges her charges to convince their parents to buy. Both of Acosta's instructors extol female heroes—scientists and early Christian martyrs—as examples for Colombian women, but the belief in the universal power of the text falters when the discussion shifts to the larger population. The botanist's insistence on the "seed within," comes tempered with the negative impetus for educational reform, the backwardness he perceives in most of the nation's population (and here, as in Serrano, "nation" slides rather easily into "region"). He calls for more education for mothers by invoking not the natural seed of genius hidden within but rather the natural tendency to pass along "the bad customs, the bad habits, the vices and errors of the common people" (272–73).[64] When he searches for a metaphor, the one he seizes on is a dam—symbol par excellence of modernity's struggle against nature. All of these vices have proliferated, he argues from the lack of a *dique* capable of stopping or redirecting their natural flow.

What the common people—so present as a topic in the discussion and so absent as voices—really need, the doctor argues, is "mental nourishment appropriate for their limited and immature faculties" (275) and an educational program calculated to make them see themselves as something less than fully modern subjects, "an education that gives resignation and comfort" (276).[65] This educational problem is a political problem, too, he concludes, since not all citizens in the republic can be regarded as moral and educational equals. Recognizing a gap between "the entirely white part of the population, which has inherited civilization from its ancestors," and the "common people," the botanist concludes that "complete democracy is very difficult in Colombia," and that it will effectively have to wait until the rest of the population catches up with ruling elites (275).[66] The botanist's particular choice of words makes civilization an inheritance rather than the result of an educational process, and the emphasis on those inheritors as the *entirely* white citizens of Colombia underscores the degree to which he sees that inheritance confined by strict racial categories.

This racialized notion of civilization coexists uneasily with the idea of books as a pathway to self-improvement. Following the botanist's arguments to their logical conclusion, we might say that he identifies reading as a laborious substitute for inheritance, and the only alternative for those he would categorize as "uncivilized" by virtue of racial inheritance. This is of course the same botanist who referred to the "seed within" that can be awakened in "even the most stupid," and nowhere does he acknowledge or attempt to resolve this contradiction. Critical treatments of Acosta, which have tended to focus on her novels, have noted that her own combination of elitism and dedication to educational reform reflect the botanist's contradictions. I want to argue that these two notions of human perfectibility as achieved by study and reading on the one hand, or membership in a ruling racial and social class on the other, also reflect a tension at the heart of the educational reform project and the notion of the ideal citizen as the ideal reader. The contradiction becomes all the more pronounced when we consider it in terms of the female reader-citizen, who is often confined to the domestic sphere even as this sphere is defined as the "real" locus of education for future male and female citizens alike.

One way to read the botanist's comments would be as a negation of reading as a force for social change. He seems to be arguing that categories of racial hierarchy in fact define who is and who is not civilized, and it is difficult to see how a trait or set of traits could be inherited *and* learned from books. On the other hand, the unresolved nature of the contradiction opens up another possibility—that the botanist sincerely believes in racial hierarchy, in the power of racial inheritance so important to nineteenth-century race theory, but that he sees reading as a method, however slow or inefficient, of counteracting it. Luisa Ballesteros Rosas has noted the absence of "El pasado indianista" in Acosta's vision of late nineteenth-century Colombia (Ballesteros Rosas 297–98), but the botanist's racism functions at the very least as a tacit acknowledgement that any imagined Colombian nation would have to include many, many citizens not among the "entirely white" ruling elite.[67] Books, by this second reading, would be the only possible means of widening the circle to include the country's sizeable Afro-Columbian and indigenous populations. And if the botanist is content to use a theory of racial inferiority to slow the process down—thus the argument for incomplete democracy in the present tense and for providing working-class students with intellectual food appropriate for their "immature palates"—these measures serve only to postpone an eventual reality of greater equality. If he really believes in the power of books and book distribution, he must feel more than a little uneasy with the notion that greater access to texts will forever produce "resignation and comfort" within the existing hierarchy rather than threatening to overturn it.

## *Store and Repertoire*

The trilingual confluence of *magasin*, *almacén*, and *magazine* for compilations intended for students adds an etymological wrinkle on the edges of the words' dictionary definitions. The *Oxford English Dictionary* traces *magazine* in English from the middle French *magasin* and traces that term to the Arabic *maksan/maksin* whose meaning it gives as "storehouse." Both the OED and the Dictionary of the Real Academia Española (DRAE) agree that this Arabic word is also the root for the Spanish term *almacén*. In all cases the word's original meaning has nothing specifically to do with words or texts but rather refers to a storehouse or warehouse where many different sorts of goods are kept and or sold. Sixteenth- and seventeenth-century definitions provided by the OED include "a place where goods are kept in store"; "a country or district rich in natural products, a centre of commerce"; and "a ship which supplies provisions." One early definition (traced to 1600) bridges the gap between goods and words by a figure of speech, "a store or repertoire (of resources, ideas, rhetorical weapons, etc.)," and the definition employed by Leprince de Beaumont's *Young Misses Magazine* appears in 1639, a century or so before its original publication: "a book providing information on a specified subject or for a specified group of people." The OED's examples for this final definition generally refer to professions, "The Mariners Magazine" or specific activities, "Negotiator's Magazine." In Leprince de Beaumont's case the "young misses" take on a quasi-professional group identity. The more familiar definition, to contemporary ears, of *magazine* as "a periodical publication containing articles by various writers" only appears in 1731, roughly the moment in which Leprince de Beaumont's book was coming off the presses.

In Spanish the etymological narrative leans even more strongly in favor of physical objects rather than words. None of the definitions accepted by the DRAE refers to a book or periodical publication, and the one definition that makes any reference at all to letters does so in the most physical and concrete way: "Each of the boxes which contain a set of matrices of the same type which are used in a linotype machine" (Serrano, *Almacén*).[68] By this definition (which also appears in English-language discussions of the linotype), the magazine is the raw material waiting to be transformed into the letters of a typeset page—a basic and literal example of the literary repertoire of a writer or speaker.

What unites all of these definitions is the notion of the *magazine* or *almacén* as a storehouse for future activity, a place where the goods, weapons, or words of the future stay safe and ready for a skilled user to take them up. The early North American clergyman and intellectual Cotton Mather, whose *Essays to Do Good* (1710) Benjamin Franklin listed among his foundational reading experiences, explained that rhetoric would be the primary weapon in the battle he saw between religious truth and its opponents—"Your *Pen* will stab *Atheism* and *Wickedness*, with an Efficacy beyond other means" (Mather 149). Remembering, as Acosta's botanist would, the intellectual potential that could be awakened by reading, Mather would ask a rhetorical question: "Who can tell what Good may be done to the Young Scholar, by a *Sentence* in a *Copy-book?*" (110), and he would demand that his America counter the "*Devil's Library*" (158; all italics in original) by publishing "BOOKS that have in them the Salt of Heaven" (170). Publications such as Leprince de Beaumont's *Magazine* and Serrano's *Almacén* attempted to update the models provided by the traditional compilations assembled by Fleury, McGuffey, and many others by providing templates for literary discussion and narrative "proof" of the positive effects of reading. They used the rudiments of plot to show character development as a response at least in part to reading, an idea that had long been a staple of the biographies and autobiographies of American heroes.

The other essential ingredient to textbook culture as constructed by the feminist writers of the Lima circle was the interpretive community that took the place of the isolated individual reader so prevalent in heroic biography and autobiography. Vásquez's study of US educational thinking during the nineteenth century stresses the degree to which individual study was seen not as a wholly independent endeavor but rather as a means of making the individual eventually fit for society— "Self-culture is not meant, then, ultimately to isolate the individual and his authority, but to connect" (41). Vásquez also argued that notions of the individual's place in a community varied according to gender expectations. In a society that tended to equate education with progress and that blurred the Enlightenment's secular and religious meaning in the narrative of religious/intellectual conversion, female self-culture, he argues, became even more community-oriented than male self-culture as, "For men, conversion ended with the individual; for women, conversion was interactive" (93–94).

In the reading community as imagined by Serrano and Acosta and the principles of readership laid out by González de Fanning and Matto, the reader's curiosity and skill serve both to mark her membership in a community and to demonstrate her commitment to that community's narrative of progress. By setting their scenes in physical classroom spaces they are, in effect, creating a new vision of a normative educational experience with female students and readers.[69] Bronson Alcott's mystical formulation of the gendered reader made femininity contiguous with progress in a traditional head/heart binary—"The Reason is always conservative. Conscience is the reformer" (*Notes of Conversations* 136)—and the narrative of corruption and crisis in late nineteenth-century Lima demanded reading reformers bent not only on "revising domesticity,"[70] but also on bringing about the sort of moral revival they believed to be the bailiwick of women. Their vision of the social force of female readers demonstrates Caulfield's conclusion "that gender played a primary role in defining and representing modernity and civilization, and that women were primary targets for reformers" (Caulfield 475).

The hemispheric and transatlantic nature of American perspective allowed these writers to equate the New World with intellectual progress and thus to subsume even nation-specific works like those of De Amicis and Leprince de Beaumont into a broadly conceived American identity that served as a base for particular approaches to Columbia and Peru. Goldgel has described the nineteenth-century nation-building period in Spanish America as one in which the construction of separate states served as much to reinforce as to fracture regional identity given the obvious fact that these states were being constructed "on the basis of a nationality largely common to all of them" (*Cuando* 28).[71] These shared notions of Spanish American nationality intersect the inchoate US nationality also under construction via educational projects, albeit with several decades' head start. What brings them together is a notion of pedagogical reading capable of shifting and appropriating Old World texts while simultaneously taking on the task of becoming producers of new ones capable of fulfilling the void at home. Book scarcity and moral crisis emerge as symbiotically related problems. In a climate of belief in the power of narrative and the act of reading to generate unseen, electrical forces, these twin problems would be impossible to solve separately. The production of readers and writers was therefore a simultaneous project rather than a sequence. New World readers would make the demand for New World books and vice versa.

# 5

# Educational Aesthetics and the Social Novel

## *Lima and the Global Novel*

Anne Garland Mahler introduces the concept of "an ideological stance of anti-imperialism" (112) in her 2015 article on the Civil Rights movement in the United States and Latin America and its link to the Tricontinental anti-imperialist alliance of the 1960s, which united Asian, African, and Latin American intellectuals. One of the advantages of ideology as an organizing principle, she argues, is the agency it conveys on individual subjects and the group as a whole, since membership is based on the advancement of an ideology and not confined by language or geography. In the case of late 1960s imperialism, this means that resistance can happen anywhere and that anyone might participate. What emerges then is "a resistant, global subjectivity" that defies "trait-based and circumstantial conditions" (113) and that thus functions quite differently from "postcolonialism."

While the nineteenth-century writers and texts dealt with in this study are oceans and decades away from the Tricontinental alliance, Mahler's approach is similar to the one I have taken to define the hemispheric consciousness of the period. This approach rejects mechanical parallels between an American North and South of the sort made popular in the early twentieth century by the Bolton thesis and instead focuses on shared concerns about books and readers in the newly independent republics, concerns that in certain key moments transcend regional differences and other particularities of place. This ideological Americanism explains the shared book anxiety of Sarmiento and Horace Mann, an anxiety that transcended the vast differences between the state of publishing in the nineteenth-century North and South. Another key element of this approach is a focus on intentionality. Roberto González

Echevarría has pointed out the difficulty of separating literature and metaliterary discourse in the nineteenth century. Citing Madame de Staël and other nineteenth-century authors of well-known literary histories, González Echevarría notes that "it is possible to argue that literary histories are not really metadiscursive, but rather that they belong to the textual economy of the period in which they are written" (8). This seemingly obvious observation becomes more important if we accept González Echevarría's distinction between literary tradition and literary history. If the first is the timeless result of writers reading and being influenced by other writers, the second, he argues, is a Romantic idea, a product of the same historical period that produced Spanish American Independence. This means, as González Echevarría puts it, speaking of Spanish American literature, that "it is not a recent literature, as some would suggest, but rather a literature whose foundational peculiarities are more concrete and intense than those of European literatures, but not necessarily different" (8–9).

The cited phrase works both as a rejection of and a possible basis for a circumstantial literary Americanism. Certain European literary traditions and nation-states long predate the Romantic period—Great Britain, France, and Spain among them—while the United States and the Spanish American republics came into being as independent political entities just as the literary history was coming into its own as a genre. This historical convergence is only magnified by the preeminence of the novel as a literary genre in the period. González Echevarría's work on the origins of the Spanish American novel emphasizes the slipperiness of prose as a literary medium that can be made to resemble all manner of nonliterary communication, and Claire de Obaldía's work on the essay makes the same point from the opposite direction when she points out a special affinity between the novel and the essay, also harkening back to the Romantic period: "A writer must reflect or philosophize about his art, and so the novel must include a philosophy of the novel" (Obaldía 244). What emerges is a circumstantial trifecta for the novel in the Western hemisphere as the political reality of independence coincides with the emergence of the (often, but not always, national) literary history, and, within the novel itself, the necessary presence of a theory of the novel.

These circumstances alone would be enough to support the hemispheric American novel as an academic topic of interest. The axis takes on an ideological dimension when we begin to consider the presence of an educational impulse not confined to the New World but heightened by the particular New World perspective on industrializing Europe as an advancing specter that threatens to outpace American progress in publishing and school reform. Governed largely by monarchs and empires, this Europe looms, paradoxically, as a retrograde political influence on the vanguard of technology, a source of moral and political decadence freakishly endowed with the tools to expand its influence across the globe. In the preceding chapters, I have explored American conceptions of the links between education and book publishing, and I have argued that progressive idealism paired with anxiety about retrogression and European influence created a hemispheric American ideology that transcended temporal and geographical circumstances. Couched in ideological rather than circumstantial terms, my analysis has focused on the self-conscious consideration of Americanism by nineteenth-century authors, north and south, rather than on "hidden" alliances or parallels revealed by ex post facto analysis.

To put it in simple terms, the authors I have worked with "go meta" on the importance of writings that include their own, and often in the midst of literary and educational texts. Whereas the last chapter explored the period's tendency to bring literary texts and literary aesthetics to bear on the world of textbook production, this chapter focuses on the novel, and in particular on the same circle of Lima-based writers who were producing biographical collections, educational textbooks, and essays about biography and education, even as they were composing what they called "social" novels and writing manifestoes and descriptions of just what that novel entailed. Cabello de Carbonera, Matto, González de Fanning, and Acosta all participated in the literary life of Lima during and after Gorriti's *veladas*. All four of these writers worked as professional educators and/or published educationally focused texts, and all of them participated in the burgeoning world of newspaper and book publishing, spheres that were essentially impossible to separate when the very printing presses used by the book publishers were often owned by newspapers and when the likeliest location for a novel's debut appearance was by installment on the pages of one of those newspapers.[1]

All four of these writers also exemplify Obaldía's notion of the implanted theory of the novel—their novels contain arguments not just for novel-writing in general but also for the writing of a particular sort of novel calculated to sway public attention on issues of national or regional concern. While some of these writers' works enjoyed tremendous popularity during their lifetimes—Cabello's *Blanca Sol* went through multiple editions and Matto's *Aves sin nido* would be compared to Harriet Beecher Stowe's *Uncle Tom's Cabin*—they were largely left out of the canon of Spanish American literature formulated during the twentieth century. Their own attempts at literary historiography, works of theory, and biographical collections became even more forgotten and difficult to find than their novels. A resurgence of attention to the nineteenth-century Spanish American novel and in particular to the vibrant community of female novelists has returned these authors, especially Cabello and Matto, to the forefront of Spanish American letters. Studies by Doris Sommer, Nancy LaGreca, Ana Peluffo, Francesca Denegri, Thomas Ward, Lee Skinner, Mary Berg, and others have broken new ground by providing close readings and critical frames for examining the contribution of Spanish American women to the development of the nineteenth-century novel. Among their suggested critical directions are a focus on the inclusion of Spanish America's indigenous populations, a use of sentiment to sway public attention, and overt treatment to the economic barriers to social mobility for women and men in an aristocratic society under the thrall of speculative capital.

This chapter will focus on the theoretical contribution this group of writers made to the question of the novel and the novelist's role in society. First, I will frame their vision globally, tracing the development of the idea of the social novel as a reaction to a particular vision of French naturalism and particular readings of foreign authors such as Leo Tolstoy and Harriet Beecher Stowe. Conducted against the constant backdrop of debates on just how "moral" or "social" the novel should seek to be—Juan Valera versus Emilia Pardo Bazán in Spain, Walter Besant versus Henry James in Great Britain and the United States—this question and Lima's relationship to it moves at the speed of reading and translation rather than the chronology of composition and publication dates. Lima's combination of provincialism and connection to the global world of literature makes it possible for Stowe, whose major works had been published decades before, to share the stage with Flaubert, Pardo Bazán, and Tolstoy, who were themselves in the process of writing novels and articulating the aesthetic and social goals to which they believed the genre should aspire. Finally, all four writers combine an intensely localized American anxiety about corruption as a corrosive political force with a self-conscious vision of themselves as practitioners of a global literary form. In plots that often mimicked the educational narratives I have already explored, they proposed individual struggles as allegories or even specific remedies for inequality and injustice, always imagining their own hemisphere as the last, best hope for such remedies to take hold.

Gender, I will argue, plays a role in the theory of the social novel similar to that already seen in biographical collections and educational writings, in which a reified traditional notion of female identity serves as a lever for vastly expanded public influence. Just as the proponents of women's education anticipated their readers' bias by basing their argument at least in part on women's role in raising *sons*, so the social novel would elevate the female novelist as a moral redeemer of a society in which male-dominated politics has become hopelessly corrupt. Assiduous readers of Germaine de Staël, the novelists of the Lima group saw literature as a route around traditional barriers to women as participants in politics. This elevation of the novelist as a kind of public moral educator also depended on a synthesis of literary aesthetics and pedagogical technique. The new social novel was an aesthetic project aimed at eliciting precisely prescribed reactions from its readers. Thus the three theoretical arcs explored so far—ideological Americanism, gender emancipation, and the fusion of education and literary aesthetics—all play an essential role in this particular conception of the social novel. Written from a locus of Spanish American crisis with the full consciousness of a growing world literary market, these novels and their theories seek to create the role of novelist-teacher and to suggest or overtly argue that women are particularly well suited to exercise it. Having chosen literature as the field most open for female participation in the public sphere and having practiced and theorized a formulation of the social novel that turned many of the conventional stereotypes about that feminine sphere into sources of authority, the women authors of the Lima circle found their own standing bound up in the debate over what the novel should do. The stakes in the debate over the social novel therefore encompassed not only a way of writing they sought to popularize, but also their own status as writers and public figures.[2] Cabello, Matto, and their contemporaries put all of their chips on the table when they argued that their novels and the novel in general should be viewed first and foremost as a source of social redemption.

Lima's literary debate about the role of the novel in society clearly takes place in a capital that feels itself connected to a larger global conversation; the evidence stares up in black and white from the pages of a February 1890 issue of *El Perú Ilustrado*, printed by Peter Bacigalupi and edited by Matto. Commerce meets literature between ads for cod liver oil, baby carriages, and even Bacigalupi's old printing press, as Matto offers her readers a portion of one side of the literary conversation between Juan Valera and Emilia Pardo Bazán, two of the best-known and best-selling Spanish authors of the period.[3] In the context of Lima's daily and weekly newspaper industry, *El Perú Ilustrado* took its place alongside *El Correo del Perú* as the voice of a liberal elite celebrating what Ana Peluffo refers to as "cosmopolitan modernity" that tended to create space for female intellectuals (*Lágrimas* 263).

In this case the featured writer is Juan Valera and the words an extract from his 1887 book *Apuntes sobre el nuevo arte de escribir novelas* (Notes on the new art of novel writing). Valera framed his book as a response to Pardo Bazán's, *La cuestión palpitante* (The pressing question) (1884), which itself was written in the wake of Émile Zola's *Le roman expérimentale* (1880) and *Les romanciers naturalistes* (1881). Pardo Bazán had, without wholeheartedly endorsing the movement, found naturalism a useful point of departure for discussing the possibilities of the realistic novel. Her book had made a big splash in literary Lima, where it inspired Mercedes Cabello de Carbonera to take up the topic of the novel's role in society and impressed Matto as an articulation of "a feminized version of canonical naturalism" (Peluffo, *Lágrimas* 206).[4] Along with its critical engagement with contemporary French fiction, Pardo Bazán's study offered a left-handed compliment to Valera, identifying his style as too elegant and classical to be realistic, "taken, more than from the spontaneous Cervantes, from the mystics, pure writers par excellence" (Pardo Bazán, *La cuestión* 170).[5] In this particular issue of *El Perú Ilustrado*, Matto chooses a passage of Valera's book that directly responds to this compliment.

He begins with a citation from *Les romanciers naturalistes* in which Zola condemns the literary vocabulary of his own era as "one of the most monstrous jargons of the French language" and pleads that what is needed is "less artfulness and more solidity" (*Les romanciers* 374, 376).[6] Valera uses this critique of naturalism by a naturalist to underline his own belief that there would be something particularly absurd about

A page from Matto's *El Perú Ilustrado* selling Worcestershire sauce and the publisher's old printing press. Courtesy of the Library of the University of California, Berkeley.

the invention of Spanish naturalism, since it would necessarily emerge as a double example of "artfulness" or, as he puts it, "the imitation of an affectation" (Valera, "Folletín" 1226).[7] As far as Pardo Bazán's less-than-enthusiastic praise for his own virtues is concerned, Valera happily pleads guilty to the charge of being more "mystical" than "spontaneous," and he does so in terms calculated to call the term "naturalism" into question. The chronicling of genuine religious experience, Valera argues, is "the real naturalism," and he goes on to define *his* notion of the term as "the simplicity, the candor, and the complete lack of any artifice of those who speak or write in good faith, because they have something to say" (1226).[8]

Having demonstrated his willingness to shrug off the mantle of Cervantes, undoubtedly the most famous Spanish author to nineteenth-century readers in the Western world, Valera goes a step further, staging an opposition between the entire legacy of the Spanish picaresque and that of the religious mystics, and again declaring that it was the latter who wrote most "naturally": "The Fathers wrote, in general, with the goal of being understood by the little ones, uneducated women and common folk, and to the end of teaching them something they judged to be of maximum benefit for the health of their souls. Therefore they thought more about the content than the form of what they were saying and were, and could not be otherwise, very natural" (1226).[9]

Valera's assertion of content over form tacitly asserts a principle that was already becoming the foundation for the notion of the social novel (and the social novelist) in Lima. Rather than attacking Cervantes or the other authors of the picaresque tradition, authors who had become Spain's claim to fame in a nineteenth-century literary landscape where the novel was beginning to hold preeminence over poetry and drama, Valera uses a literal definition of naturalism to allow the mystics to leapfrog these authors as more authentic examples of a "natural" style. He derives their authority from their intentions rather than from their influence on other writers. And while influence over ordinary readers is the ostensible goal of mystical writing, Valera offers nothing in the way of evidence that the mystics were necessarily read or received as they wished to be. Since they sought moral influence rather than literary fame, he argues, the texts they wrote were necessarily aimed at the sensibilities of uneducated readers. Their writings therefore subordinated aesthetic concerns to the task of communicating with an unsophisticated audience. Valera, of course, posits the mystical concern as the individualized salvation of souls and their technique as putting readers in closer touch with the divine. So a certain "social" element is missing. But when Matto, Cabello de Carbonera, Acosta, and González de Fanning offered their own theoretical defenses of the novel and the novelist, they too would stress the active virtue of changing readers' behavior as the sine qua non for any aesthetic imperative. Just as the logic of the textbook anthology perceived literary aesthetics as a means to a communicative end, so the Lima vision for the social novel would put the moral imperative of the religious mystic to work on human society, transferring its passion from humanity's communication with the divine to humanity's communication with itself.

Appearing as it did in a magazine edited by Matto, this Valera excerpt, the first of many that Matto would print, reveals just how strongly the Lima writers felt connected to literary conversations across the Atlantic, a connection that (as revealed, for example, by the disproportionate billing afforded Pardo Bazán's lukewarm praise of González de Fanning in Spanish America) was not precisely reciprocal.[10] A few months later, for example, Matto would print a column by a correspondent in Spain reporting on a dinner party at Pardo Bazán's house attended by one of the foundational historians of Spanish literature, Marcelino Menéndez y Pelayo (1856–1912). The article mentions that the discussion—"a rain of intelligent sparks"—included Pardo Bazán's mention of a desire to write a Spanish cookbook and Menéndez y Pelayo's suggestion that he would put together a new edition of the works of Pablo de Olavide ("En casa" 1523). Neither project seems to have ever appeared in print, but by putting them in the gaze of her Peruvian readers, Matto manages not only to produce gossip-column-style entrée into the lives of the distant and influential but also to suggest that one of those influential figures dines with his mind on Peru or at least on Peru's most famous ex-pat Enlightenment writer. Part of the thrill, then, of being a reader of *El Perú Ilustrado* was membership in a virtual global republic of letters.

## *Toward an American Theory of the Novel*

Pardo Bazán's *La cuestión palpitante* had demonstrated the asymmetrical nature of this virtual community when it spoke of Spanish America not as a literary vanguard in its own right, but as a large and mostly untapped market waiting for enterprising Spanish publishers (175–76).[11] These publishers would need to develop an enhanced ability to possess and defend copyright given what Pardo Bazán sees as the New World tendency toward literary piracy. She also finds fault in a Spanish psyche unwilling to conceive of literature as a marketplace in which readers should be willing to pay for their entertainment and writers are artisanal merchants deserving of a fair price for their wares: "We save our communism and our stinginess for novels" (*La cuestión* 174).[12]

Pardo Bazán's foil for the Spanish sensibility is Great Britain—"There the novel is considered neither a pastime nor a mere aesthetic pleasure, but rather an institution, the fifth power of the state"—and while she praises British attention to the moral power of the genre, quoting Trollope's observation that "novels are the sermons of the current time," she believes British moralism carries an artistic price (158).[13] Endowed with a sense of moral purpose not so different from what Valera finds in the Spanish mystics, namely "moral and docent purpose, impulse to correct and convert, and eagerness to save the reader," the British novelist might have a fatal flaw, she argues (159).[14] Pardo Bazán worries above all that the very concern for humanity that sparks the philanthropic impulse to reform the lives of readers threatens to soften the novelist's approach to her own material. The pious reformer who is too devoted to her own characters "detains the scalpel" somewhere short of "the ultimate pleats of the soul" (159).[15]

The conflation of the pen with the scalpel, of the writer's tools with those of the physician, was something of a nineteenth-century commonplace in the wake of naturalism. In *Le roman expérimental*, Émile Zola had argued that the genre represented a perfect platform on which to apply scientific methods to materials that had generally been considered outside the bailiwick of science, namely "the life of the passions and the intellect" (*Le roman* 2).[16] Defining the novelist as "observer" and "experimenter," Zola proposes a slogan, "Observation shows, experiment instructs" (11), to demonstrate the vast influence that novelists could exercise by adopting the experimental method, and he offers a brief job description for the novelist willing to take that step: "In a word, we should operate on personalities, on passions, on human and social acts, as the chemist and the physician operate on base and living bodies" (16).[17] A few pages later he boils the novelist's role down to another concise definition, "We are, in a word, the moral experimenters, showing by experiment how a passion behaves itself in a social environment" (24).[18]

One does not need to read deeply into the Lima of ca. 1890 to find similar application of scientific terminology to the role of the novelist. Matto herself would pen a trilogy of novels—*Aves sin nido* (1889), *Índole* (1891), and *Herencia* (1893)—that she expressly defined as experimental projects with a diagnostic edge. But where Zola's "teaching" restricts itself to knowledge about how passions and personalities work in a social environment, Matto lobbies for the inherent connection (if we continue with a medical metaphor) between diagnosis and treatment. *Aves sin nido*, for example, begins with a prologue explaining the novel as a representation of its own time and place and a tool for changing it: "It has to be the photograph that stereotypes the vices and virtues of its people, with the necessary corrective moral for the former and admiring homage for the latter" (*Aves* 1).[19] By this reckoning the novelist becomes a surgeon who reveals and explores contemporary society—her patient—and applies remedies that range from reform to full-fledged extraction by virtue of her influence on readers: "In its pages it contains many times the secret of the reform of certain types, if not their extinction" (1).[20]

In *Índole*, which lacks the declarative prologues of the other two novels, Matto breaks off the action in mid-stream to remind readers of the clarifying role of the "observing novelist who, carrying the corrective in the points of his pen, penetrates the mysteries of life, and at the same time before the multitudes passes through that dense veil that covers the eyes of the blind and fanaticized inhabitants" (*Índole* 250).[21] *Herencia*, on the other hand, begins with a dedication to Nicanor Bolet Peraza that gives Matto occasion to complain about readers' tastes. In a world in which "sweet breaths of breeze and white beams of moonlight" no longer command readers' attention, she argues, it has become almost necessary to clothe moral remedies in realistic depictions of decadence and vice: "If they find the corrective spiced up with morphine, with wormwood, with all of those bitters that are repugnant to perfect natures, they don't only read us, they devour us" (*Herencia* 24).[22]

Here Matto is alluding to the old problem of the relationship between the genre and readers' tastes, the question of to what degree the novel responds to predilections already present in the reading public and to what degree it shapes those predilections. José M. Gómez Hermosilla, a Spanish critic, who, like José Luis Munárriz, channeled Hugh Blair's manual of rhetoric into a different linguistic and literary milieu, cited Blair citing Francis Bacon to make the case that fiction gives taste a chance to align with morality with greater precision than in the real world. What the novel offers that life cannot is precisely "a more general distribution of just rewards and punishments" (316).[23] Finally, by presenting agreeable examples of virtuous behavior, the novel, by Gómez Hermosilla's reckoning, can train the reader's palate: "They direct themselves straight to the heart, to make it love the perfect and detest the defective" (321).[24] Matto clearly believes that a novel centered on civic morality and empathy can triumph against the vicissitudes of public taste, and she posits the novelist's job as that of spotlighting (diagnostically) the social customs that fall short of that ideal and proposing (in terms of treatment) alternative ways of being. She and her fellow social novelists would have agreed with Richard Rorty's comment on the relationship between literature and moral progress: "Only the imagination can break through the crust of convention" (923). "Breaking through" convention as opposed to highlighting or revealing it gives the novelist a public role in areas not confined to the literary.

In Matto's view, as in Cabello's, a not-so-subtle transformation has shifted the role of the writer from the experimental surgeon envisioned by Zola, who investigates to find out how social bodies work rather than with an eye toward changing or saving them. Matto's writer is a moral surgeon, physician, and pharmacist diagnosing the illness, describing necessary measures, and thinking in terms of what sort of instructions the pill bottle should carry. Her dismissal of Pardo Bazán's fear that too much moralism might make the novelist unduly timid relies on what she sees as a difference between America and Europe. What Matto herself has to say on these points takes the discussion to a local and also hemispheric level. Matto explains that writing novels is a different business: "In those countries in which, like ours, LITERATURE is still in its cradle" (*Aves* 1).[25] *Aves sin nido* treats among other themes the plight of Peru's indigenous population in the Andes, and Matto goes on to specify her purpose as that of communicating the notion "of bettering the condition of Peru's smaller populations" to her Lima readership, "and even when it's nothing more than simple commiseration, the author of these pages will have achieved her purpose" (2).[26]

One of the desired effects, then, of Matto's photography of Peru's social environment, will be a unity based on sentiment among citizens separated by geography, ethnicity and sometimes language, but united by nationality. She also posits the corrections her novel will offer as spurs to modernization, betraying the American anxiety about falling behind the rest of the industrialized world (although from Matto's perspective the "industrialized world" would almost certainly have included the United States). She argues in effect that she will be "signaling points of no small importance for national progress; and *doing*, at the same time, Peruvian literature" (2).[27] In this sense Matto's is a classic project of national literature. She is telling stories that anywhere else "would have their troubadour, their novelist or their historian to immortalize them with the pen or the lyre, but that in the isolation of my country, barely manage the discolored pencil of a sister" (*Aves* 2).[28]

The condition that Matto refers to as "the isolation of my country" becomes an essential one to her project, dictating not only the very fact that her novel needs to be written but also that she and not a singer or a historian or (at least implied) a male novelist should be the person to write it. The anxiety she expresses—that an American world exists outside of memory and the book—is corollary to the book anxiety discussed in Chapter 1. Del Valle, the would-be American encyclopedist, had wished in the wake of independence for the material conditions to chronicle *everything* going on in the American continent, and Matto finds herself before a similar dilemma on a smaller scale but with the means and the will to solve it. Her book need not be hypothetical.

Matto's colleague Mercedes Cabello de Carbonera had sounded a similar diagnostic note in the middle of her 1886 novel *Sacrificio y recompensa*, when she asked "Why shouldn't the novelist imitate the physician who searches for and studies the means of avoiding certain diseases?" (*Sacrificio* 81).[29] The discussion carries over into the debate about just what and how the realistic novel should depict when Cabello's narrator argues that a certain kind of realism (which bears more than a little resemblance to Zola's naturalism) paints an incomplete picture of humanity because it focuses on "the parts that are most disgusting, base, and ruinous to hold them up as the only thing real and true" (81).[30] Against this trend she posits her own hope in another portion of humanity: "And we leave out that there is in the human soul a noble, elevated, and beautiful side, which the novelist should study, should stimulate and hold up as the only means of reforming customs?" (81).[31]

Cabello's sentence bears some parsing. Her insistence on the "reform of customs" as a proper goal for the novel references a large body of Spanish American fiction and nonfiction known as *costumbrista* writing, which sought to depict the social mores of the capitals and more frequently the provinces of the region with varying practical and artistic aims. She also prefigures Matto, whose prologue to *Aves sin nido* previously cited soon fades into a prose novel and the voice of a character who makes his own metadiscursive declaration: "Frankly, miss, you should know that custom is law, and no one can take us out of our customs" (*Aves* 16).[32] The separation between descriptive and proscriptive science becomes, in the words of Cabello's narrator, a question of ultimate purpose, of what the novel is for. If the realistic school she cites errs by focusing too much on the base rather than the elevated human qualities, it also does so with the specific end of showing them to be the alpha and omega of the "real" and "true." Cabello's proposal differs therefore not only by endeavoring to depict other, more elevated aspects of human character (and in both cases she is vague about just what those characteristics are), but by doing so with the goal of "reforming customs." She does not necessarily question the veracity of what the naturalists are after, but rather suggests that her approach is the one that will be effective in changing how her readers behave.

The difference is subtle but categorical. Cabello defines the novel as a tool for enacting social reform and chooses the human characteristics she will emphasize accordingly. A few years later her prologue to a second edition of her *Blanca Sol* (1889) would attribute the ascendance of the novel in the nineteenth century to its role as "the link uniting literature and the new experimental science" (el lazo de unión entre la literatura y la nueva ciencia experimental) (*Blanca* iv), and she would throw down a gauntlet to her professional colleagues based on this historic role:[33]

> It will therefore be necessary going forward to divide novelists in two categories, putting to one side those who, as Cervantes said, write pages to entertain young ladies, and [to the other] those who can make the novel an instrument of research and study, in which the art lends its powerful assistance to the sciences and looks at mankind, freeing it from ancient traditions and absurd worries. (vii)

Cabello's choice of words for the frivolous sort of novel in this binary takes direct aim at the entrenched misogynistic cliché of the popular novel as feminized and therefore less serious than other forms of literary expression.[34] In her case she is presenting herself as a female novelist aspiring to the male-gendered seriousness of science. Cabello also links grammatically and conceptually the tasks of studying and depicting humankind with that of changing its values and behavior. The serious novel as she defines it calls out prejudices and superstition not merely for the amusement of the reader but as a way of hastening scientific progress, of ushering in modernity as a mindset or a custom.

In 1892 Cabello would take another step, moving from the declarative prologue and/or aside in the midst of the novel, to a book-length work, *La novela moderna: estudio filosófica* (1892). Beginning with the assumption that her own present tense is best defined as "Period of transition and radical reform" (Epoca de transición y de reforma radical) as far as the novelist's art is concerned, Cabello charts a middle course between what she views as the excess of romanticism and naturalism, explaining the latter as a natural reaction to the former: "Just as romanticism had damaged hearts with its excess of fiction and idealism, so the naturalist school has damaged them with its lack of ideals, its atrophy of sentiment and complete suppression of the moral being" (*La novela* 21).[35] Her course will employ something resembling a naturalist toolbox but with a sensibility and a sense of social purpose more reminiscent of the Romantics.

Cabello's text exhibits an easy familiarity with a hemispheric and transatlantic circle of writers. She cites Pardo Bazán's description of Spanish literature as "a reflection of the French" and suggests that her Spanish American colleagues should not despair at the Spanish American republics' lack of distinctly defined national literatures operating independently of Spanish influence: "if not even in the country of Monroe, Miss Stowe and Longfellow has this benefit been achieved" (31).[36] Cabello praises Pardo Bazán as part of a wave of Spanish writers she sees at the vanguard of literary progress: "The Spanish school" as she calls it, "will be the one to innovate naturalism, converting it to psychological and philosophical realism" (31).[37] Cabello's choice to name Spain rather than France as the locus of the novel's future shows a level of comfort with the metropolis that we might read as the absence of a threat. She fears that Spanish American novelists will be unduly influenced by their French counterparts while noticing that the Spanish authors she cites admiringly write books that "lack the certain indefinable, inexplicable something, that makes the pages of a book palpitate, as though animated by the soul" (32).[38] It is this *je ne sais qua*, she insists, that gives French authors such as Daudet, Guy de Maupassant, and Mirabeau their powerful international influence.[39]

But the production of attractive texts that vibrate with life can never be an end in itself in Cabello's vision of the novel. She takes the time to condemn the notion of art for its own sake as an absurd truncation— "It is like pursuing the idea of a faculty without an object, of a principle without a consequence, of a cause without an effect" (35).[40] To say something like "l'art pour l'art," she concludes "would be like saying science for science, negating its influence in all of the knowledge that has to do with studying and curing the sufferings of humanity" (35).[41] Here Cabello is rejecting the notion of art as somehow separate from the utilitarian principles she sees governing science. In her view it can be neither an autonomous zone for reflection (Schiller's version of aesthetic morality) nor a purely recreational space with pleasure as its own final purpose. Even if art were to be imagined as giving pleasure and nothing else, she argues, the experience would necessarily lead to *something* else: "Pleasure is not an end; and even if it were, from there would be born an action benign or malignant for our spirit" (35).[42] The novelist must serve something, and the choice she is debating is not whether the novel should be seen as a moral agent but how the novel's social agency could best be applied.

### *Art, Morality, Context: Reading Stowe from Peru*

Cabello in essence makes a straightforward call for the novel as a work written toward a moral end and perfectly suited to exercise an influence on social custom. With the notion of law as an expression of social custom going back at least as far as Montaigne, her discourse carries special resonance in a region in which the distance between written constitutions and the actual practice of government had long been a commonplace for historical and political analysis. The phrase uttered by Matto's "voice of the people," that custom was what actually determined law, was one that had been repeated, asserted, or alluded to one way or another by a line of Spanish American thinkers going back at least to Simón Bolívar and Francisco de Miranda, often accompanied by a lament for the relative ineffectiveness of written codes and constitutions. If this article of faith held sway in Spanish America, another publishing event in the United States had, in its national and international reverberations, proven that the agency Cabello saw in the novel was not exercised on the consciences of individual readers alone, that it in fact produced far-reaching geopolitical consequences.

Harriet Beecher Stowe's novel *Uncle Tom's Cabin, or, Life Among the Lowly* was first published in 1852. Within a year of its publication, Spanish-language versions appeared in Spanish America (Mexico City, Buenos Aires, Bogotá) as well as in Barcelona and Paris. A decade later the US Civil War and the legal abolition of slavery would give the book credible claim to have played a major role in the reshaping of the US political landscape.[43] Lisa Surwillo has traced the novel's influence on mid-nineteenth-century Spain, noting that newspaper excerpts and theatrical adaptations gave the work an entrée into the Spanish zeitgeist that far exceeded even what the translation's impressive circulation would imply (769–70).[44] Spain and Spanish America were, like Russia, locations where the book's descriptions of the chattel slavery practiced in the United States, could easily be applied.[45] Surwillo notes a curious irony in the reluctance of Spanish censors to target Stowe's novel, even when a rigorous censorship of texts depicting *Cuban* slavery, such as Gertrudis Gómez de Avellaneda's *Sab*, had been recently practiced in Cuba as well as Spain (772).[46] Progressive Spanish newspaper editors even managed to print excerpts of *Uncle Tom's Cabin* in the space left blank by censors who had removed articles deemed dangerous or subversive. Stowe's text had become so well known that it was "no longer a literary novelty but a way to hint at what had been suppressed" (Surwillo 771).

Stowe's legacy would leave deep tracks in Spanish-language critical discourse on novelists and the novel on both sides of the Atlantic and for decades after the initial publication and translation of *Uncle Tom's Cabin*. In Spain Antonio Neira de Mosquera called Stowe a founding writer of "the humanitarian novel" in 1853 (188), and eighteen years later Leopoldo Augusto de Cueto's omnibus review of the oeuvre of Gómez de Avellaneda would focus on Stowe in its attempt to contextualize the social role of the female writer. Her novel, he declared, "was a more powerful weapon for the cause of freedom for blacks than all of the doctrinal discourses pronounced to that end in Congress in Washington and in the abolitionist meetings" (630).[47]

In 1890, as Matto and Cabello were at the peak of their own careers and as Matto's journal put the Spanish debate over naturalism on full display for Lima's reading public, the same Juan Valera who extolled the legacy of the mystics brought up the memory of Harriet Beecher Stowe when he took on the task of reviewing US utopian writer and social reformer Edward Bellamy. Bellamy's novel, *Looking Backward 2000–1887* (1887) is told from the perspective of an industrialist who falls into a deep sleep in the cellar of his Boston town house and wakes up over a century later to find that a socialist revolution has created a classless society. Like More's *Utopia*, the book takes on the form of a travel guide to a new and exotic landscape but with the added touch of familiar Boston place-names. Valera's essay, which appeared in *La España Moderna (Revista Ibero-Americana)* under the title "Novela-Programa," strikes a tone somewhere between mild sarcasm and outright condescension. Valera is troubled by a naive American optimism that he couches in hemispheric terms as "a certain brave confidence in the future of humanity" ("Novela-Programa" 38).[48]

While Valera sees this belief as lacking historical and philosophical foundation, he recognizes a certain raw power in Bellamy's optimism, a power perhaps capable of converting belief in the book as an effective agent of social change into a kind of self-fulfilling prophecy: "There is in that place a certain emulation, a certain juvenile petulance, that is useful, because it will persuade many that America will achieve what Europe has not; it will resolve problems that here we take for irresolvable, and it will realize ideals that we, tired out, done in, and old, have abandoned for unrealizable and chimerical" (38).[49] There can be little doubt that Valera, who will also write, "The lyrical poetry over there inculcates in its best works that to desire is to be able," remains convinced that the "tired out" Europeans have a more realistic take on human history (39).[50] Valera even makes a point of praising Bellamy's sexism—the radical reformer has at least not had the temerity to suggest that male and female social roles be equalized or made interchangeable (42)—and he addresses his American readers directly, mock-praising their well-developed faculties for "sensibility and fantasy" (45).

Stowe comes onto the scene when Valera attempts to give context for that American optimism in the power of novels to incite social and political change. Bellamy might appear to be an eccentric or a crank to readers without his naive faith in socialism and progress, but in the context of US literature, he is attempting to fulfill a literary and historical niche whose force cannot be denied. Valera sees "the anti-slavery triumph" of Stowe's novel as an obvious precursor to Bellamy, and he surmises that Americans expect "other, more complete triumphs" (44). He is also prepared to see Stowe's legacy as emblematic not only of a certain sensibility toward social reform in US circles but also of an American sensibility, full stop. He addresses his Spanish-language readers, presumably scattered throughout the continent, as "ustedes," and he speaks of historical optimism as a New World characteristic in general, invoking not only the supposed location of the island that inspired More's *Utopia* but also the old trope, still dear to reformers and publishers north and south, of the hemisphere as a last best hope for escaping Europe's political and moral decadence. Valera recognizes Stowe's influence as linchpin of this argument, a piece of hard evidence in its favor, even if he is not prepared to drop his sarcasm.

A few weeks before running the Valera–Pardo Bazán debate, Matto's *El Perú Ilustrado* had included a more wholeheartedly positive allusion to Harriet Beecher Stowe in a reprinted book review praising Matto's own *Aves sin nido* as "the first novel, really national, with the flavor of the land itself, that has been published in these times" (Ariel 1255).[51] Along with its capture of a Peruvian reality, the reviewer, identified only as "Ariel," praises Matto's concern for Peru's indigenous population, a group the reviewer describes as having been left out both by Christianity and by the benefits of industrial progress (1255). In this sense Ariel sees Matto's path as following "that goal, consummately humanitarian and philosophical that the author of *Uncle Tom's Cabin* pursued, over in the country of Francklin [sic]" (1255).[52] Part of being a national novel, by this definition, is taking on the task of including territory and people beyond the confines of capital cities, something that Matto's upbringing in Cuzco and knowledge of Quechua makes her unusually qualified to do.[53]

Ariel also suggests another narrative of emancipation beyond that of Peru's indigenous Andean population. Matto's status as a female author whose very success flies in the face of prejudice and stereotype is reminiscent of that of Pardo Bazán, and Ariel declares that it also signifies an even greater breadth of inclusion, that Peru, too, will be part of a narrative of female emancipation: "This is undoubtedly the era of the woman really truly liberated, in the dominions of thought, and Peru cannot evade the century's imposition" (Ariel 1255).[54] While focusing more on Pardo Bazán than on Stowe as a symbol of female authorship, the reviewer's leap from indigenous emancipation to the obvious feminist implications of authorship traces a logical move that would be repeated throughout the second half of the nineteenth century. (We might well ask if it was Stowe's status as a pioneering female author that prompted Valera to find the time for a few words in praise of Bellamy's endorsement of traditional gender roles in his socialist utopia.) Acosta's treatment of Stowe as an exemplary female role model was discussed in a previous chapter. Here it bears remembering that Acosta includes Stowe in two biographical chapters, one focused on women of moral influence and the other on women writers, and that her praise includes sales figures from the first print run—"300,000 copies, that were sold out in a few days" (*La mujer* 172–73)—as a means of expressing Stowe's influence in concrete terms.[55] Other feminist writers would take a similar approach, finding Harriet Beecher Stowe to be an important example of the social benefits of women's participation in the public sphere (Silva, "Justicia" 280), or as proof that formal education could serve to multiply rather than corrupt the moral influence of women in society (Muñoz, "De la mujer" 41).[56]

Friedhelm Schmidt-Welle makes this sentimental bond with an oppressed population the basis for his comparison of Matto and Stowe. Noting that critical evaluations of US nineteenth-century literature have tended to stress latent Puritanism as the salient force behind the didactic tone that characterized the era, Schmidt-Welle argues that a look at Spanish American literature from the same time period calls this explanation into question ("Harriet" 133). Catholic Spanish America produced a largely didactic literature, too, and Schmidt-Welle suggests that the common thread was a postcolonial necessity to connect with a subaltern population (133). This impulse differs from the missionary desire to spread Christianity among the subaltern population because both novels express their Christian zeal (be it Protestant or Catholic) as simultaneously moving in two vectors: "to Christianize not only in the 'Other,' but also among the Christians, with the desire of causing them to feel mercy themselves" (135).[57] One of the effects of this double-vectored pedagogy is what Schmidt-Welle refers to as pedagogy "at the discursive level" in which the novel at once depicts the education of certain characters and expects to have a similar pedagogical effect on its readers (142). Schmidt-Welle acknowledges that the sentimental bond creates a categorical difference between those who feel the sympathy and those who are its objects, especially given "the contradiction between the acceptance of the 'Others' and the supposed necessity for modernization at the expense of their culture" (144).[58] He settles on the phrase "sentimental liberalism," attributed to Leslie Fiedler, to sum up the intentionality, promise, and limitation of Stowe and Matto's approach.

The role of sentiment along with the question of what the novel should want to do in its own society is an undertone for discussions of Harriet Beecher Stowe as the book becomes, in Spanish American circles, a shorthand for a larger conversation about the novel's role in social reform and the role of emotion as a communicative tool for helping to bring that reform about. This debate became inseparable from the implications of Stowe's status as a female author, which became a kind of riddle for skeptical male critics, causing varied degrees of discomfort.[59] Neira de Mosquera's positive note on *Uncle Tom's Cabin* uses the occasion to genderize the virtues of female novelists. Women are better than men, he argues, in matters relating to "feeling" and "imagination," "because the mission of the woman is to feel and be fertile, while the man's destiny is to think and examine" (188).[60] On the same page, Mosquera proposes a universal literary criterion—"Intelligence does not choose sexes. The literary republic focuses not on the author but on the work"—but he finds in his particular view of femininity an explanation for what he sees as the recent success of so many female novelists (188).[61]

We might say that Mosquera's rhetoric hews to the argument that women have a particular literary gift, a thread he could presumably have followed back to Staël or seen taken up by contemporaries such as Amalia Puga, who in 1892 argued for the importance in the surge of female novelists that included Matto and Cabello by asserting, "Just as there is in the man an aptitude for scientific investigation, so there is in the woman an extraordinary ability in the aesthetic reflections of art" (201).[62] In Neira's case, of course, the characterization functions as a limitation—he presents an affective vision of femininity that necessarily excludes rationality. Feminist rhetoric of the time was recasting that trope as a virtue. Concepción Gimeno de Flaquer's 1905 conference at the Madrid Ateneo would define feminine virtue in part as the ability "to find the poem of existence in the affective life linked to the intellectual life" (242).[63] In this formulation the task of literature is articulated as a production that combines rational and affective spheres, and the woman's supposed confinement to the affective sphere becomes a virtue once she is freed to connect with a rational one. The narrative of female emancipation thus presents a female figure prepared to move between both spheres and implies a male counterpart who remains stuck in the rational.

If movement between the affective and rational spheres meant authority, then one way to complicate or frustrate that formulation was to imagine that women's grasp of the rational sphere would necessarily be incomplete or, worse, that the entrance of affect into rationality would create a grotesque hybrid rather than a more harmonious vision of humanity. Thus Augusto de Cueto's positive rendering of Gómez de Avellaneda as part of a tradition that includes Stowe also manages to strike a suspicious note, praising the Cuban writer for managing to resist what he sees as the disturbing trend "of desperation, of dogmatism, of reformist presumption" that he sees rendering many novels by women writers less entertaining than they might be (630). What Augusto de Cueto does find time to praise, however, is a moderate counter-trend in which he sees Gómez de Avellaneda taking part, that of "those women who, without pedantry or fanfare, cultivate their understanding and contribute, in letters or in the arts, to civilization in general and the brilliance of their country" (637).[64]

Cueto's fear that women would become pretentious and dogmatic if permitted to study and gain public influence was a misogynistic cliché that Cabello, Matto, and their contemporaries saw as a real obstacle to the widespread acceptance of female intellectuals in general and female authors in particular. González de Fanning's essay "Las literatas," which appeared in the 1893 collection *Lucecitas* with Pardo Bazán's ambivalent prologue, posits writing as a valuable recreational activity if not a profession for Spanish American women. Even this carefully positioned argument comes couched in protective phrasing that foresees the objections readers taken in by the cliché will likely make. She argues that "when writing becomes the custom of many and not the privilege of a few, then pedantry and presumption will also become less common," and further bolsters this position by quoting Socrates: "'I only know that I don't know anything,' the sage has said, and the truth is that vanity and petulance seem to be the exclusive attributes of ignorance" (*Lucecitas* 246).[65]

It was perhaps this sentiment that persuaded Pardo Bazán to remark that González de Fanning's writings possessed "a certain submission and sweetness that betray the female spirit's adaptation to the mold to which so many centuries of moral and material subjection have cast it" ("Prólogo" vii).[66] Pardo Bazán's skepticism extends to the literary merit of González de Fanning's work, too. This is best revealed by the sort of praise she offers by calling her "a useful woman in the broadest sense of the term" and characterizing her literary endeavors as a break from her professional life as an educator: "Letters represent her recreation, an amenable solace—a very noble solace, of never before pondered effectiveness and virtue for curing the pains of the soul" (vii).[67] Peluffo's in-depth reading of the prologue notes that for González de Fanning and her publisher, this kind of measured praise may in fact have represented the best sort of publicity, since it "served to confirm the 'moral' character of Fanning's work" ("Emilia" 69).[68] Peluffo also sees in Pardo Bazán's evaluation a desire to separate content and aesthetics, or, as she puts it, "to establish a polarization between the aesthetic projection and the ideological substratum of the work" (67).[69] By this reckoning González de Fanning works with progressive intentions but without the necessary formal toolbox or without the audacity to use all of the tools at her disposal.

Pardo Bazán's separation of González de Fanning's professional identities as an educator (she had founded and directed a school in Lima) and her literary vocation prefigures a division between the aesthetic and the didactic that would damage the legacy of the Lima circle in the historiography of Spanish American literature at least until the end of the twentieth century, and in this respect their critical fate mirrored that of Harriet Beecher Stowe. A case in point is Augusto Tamayo Vargas's 1940 volume *Perú en trance de la novela: Ensayo-crítico biográfico sobre Mercedes Cabello de Carbonera*, which attempted to revive Cabello as an important figure in Peru's literary landscape but nonetheless found itself balancing her intentions with their literary execution. Tamayo Vargas, who is convinced that Cabello's theoretical and literary work is indeed important, takes an approach similar to Pardo Bazán's, but reaches the opposite conclusion: Cabello, who "never managed to escape from the pamphlet" somehow created characters whose conduct defied her intentions. Comparing her position to that of Pirandello in *Six Actors in Search of an Author*, Tamayo Vargas couches Cabello's success as a novelist as a case of the novel's characters becoming more interesting and more powerful than the cause the author has created them to serve—"But the characters defeated her. As in a work by Pirandello: they defeated her" (70).[70] There can be little doubt that Tamayo Vargas has no intention to praise Cabello's writings when he describes her novel *El conspirador* (1892) as "full of teachings" (148) or when he rates "the half romantic half pedagogical tone" as characteristic of nineteenth-century Lima, and tapping "deep roots even in our own day" (95).[71]

As far as Harriet Beecher Stowe's own writing is concerned, the debate about how to deal critically with her work emerges soon after its publication. DeForest's selection of *Uncle Tom's Cabin* as the closest available approximation of the "Great American Novel" carries with it the explicit desire that better examples should be produced. Alongside the novel's praiseworthy depth of vision, DeForest finds glaring faults, too, counting among them "a very faulty plot"; "a black man painted whiter than the angels"; "a girl such as girls are to be, perhaps, but are not yet" (28). These critiques—all of which center on a supposed lack of realism, a distance between the world painted in the novel and one experienced by readers—depend not only on a particular reading of American reality but on a supposed straightforward realism as the novel's aesthetic object.[72] It is perhaps these emergent tinges of an idealistic or romantic sensibility that Martí refers to when he calls Helen Hunt Jackson's novel an improvement on Stowe (Martí, it's worth pointing out, was Jackson's translator when he made that claim) ("Ramona" 1).

In the United States David Reynolds charts the novel's twentieth-century neglect as a measure of the sway of the New Critics, who, as "conservative Southern agrarians" were ill-disposed to appreciate "socially relevant, message-oriented fiction, especially when written by women or from a Northern perspective" (258), and who "found the novel lacking in the qualities they valued—paradox, ambiguity, organic unity" (272). But writers who approached the novel from a left-leaning sensibility and one that favored the cause of racial justice would find it problematic, too. This narrative of the ebb in Stowe's critical fortunes mirrors Ana Peluffo's summation of the oblivion into which Matto's *Aves sin nido* was soon cast despite the fanfare and positive reception accompanying its publication in 1889. If the book was initially attacked by religious conservatives because of its anticlerical politics, it was later disregarded for the use of sentiment, a tactic that met with equal disapproval from conservative and avant-garde critics in the early twentieth century. Much depends on the context of reading. If mid-nineteenth-century critics read Stowe as abolitionists or defenders of slavery, and so drew separate conclusions about the book's merit, the twentieth-century debate was not purely an aesthetic one, either, as US critics such as James Baldwin and Kenneth Lynn argued from a post-slavery United States in which racial injustice remained a pressing and unaddressed problem (see Parfait 188). In Peru ca. 1890 this context functioned both locally and globally. Locally the novel spoke to a society that was defining itself, at least in progressive circles, around its ability to include the indigenous population within the idea of the Peruvian.[73] Globally, but also personally, for novelists such as Cabello, Matto, and González de Fanning, the links between sentiment and gender and between Stowe's biography and the professional role of the female novelist meant that the debate was an existential one. It would not be possible to win on gender and lose on aesthetics or vice versa. The critical viability of the protest novel signified nothing less than the relevance of female novelists. And the discussion of the world's most famous protest novel could therefore not help but hit close to home.

## *Tolstoy and the Profession of the Novelist*

This link I am making between female emancipation and the aesthetic triumph of the social novel tapped deep roots into the literary debates that rocked the Western world at the end of the nineteenth century. Just as Cabello and her contemporaries kept themselves apprised of the details of Valera and Pardo Bazán's discussion of realism, so they could not avoid the entrance of Leo Tolstoy onto the global literary scene. Decades after the publication of *War and Peace* (1869) had first made him famous worldwide, Tolstoy emerged in the last decades of the nineteenth century as a symbol of the moral agency that the position of novelist could afford. Tolstoy's shift to religious and philosophical writings in the 1880s carried symbolic importance for critics who were debating the moral and philosophical importance of the novel. This shift would finally culminate in the 1898 publication *What Is Art?* where he ventured to define the purpose of art as "making understandable and accessible that which might be incomprehensible and inaccessible in the form of reasoning" and included Stowe's *Uncle Tom's Cabin* on his very short list of works of the "highest religious art" (132). But even before his controversial artistic manifesto, Tolstoy had become a lightning rod of critical attention not just as a novelist but also as an example of the sort of public figure the novelist might aspire to become.

In France Eugène-Melchior de Vogüé published *The Russian Novel* in 1886, a positive, indeed almost hagiographic paean to Russian novelists, Tolstoy among them, as morally serious alternatives to the naturalists. But Vogüé is careful to praise Tolstoy's moral influence via fiction as one that needs no meta commentary. It is a style that works, he argues, precisely because it does not indulge the temptation to preach in fictional prose: "The moral lesson springs only from facts and results, both bitter and wholesome" (249–50). As far as Tolstoy's shift in focus away from fiction and toward an emphasis on the practice of moral and social reform is concerned, Vogüé is quick to disapprove—"Should not the creator of masterpieces feel that the pen is the only tool he should wield?" (266)—a reply that justifies the artist's separation from life by virtue of a belief in the essential moral influence of art.

William Edgerton has noted that Vogüé's book coincided with the popularity of Dostoevsky in Paris and with Emilia Pardo Bazán's visit to the French capital. Her book, *La revolución y la novela en Rusia*, was published in Madrid in 1887, a year after Vogüé's, and it so faithfully followed the French author's line of argument that "she has frequently been accused of plagiarism" (Edgerton, "Tolstoy" 56). Both writers shared a sense that Russian fiction provided "a way out of the blind alley of materialism" (61), and Pardo Bazán praised Tolstoy specifically as a writer who aspires to do more than entertain—"quiere iluminar y enseñar a las generaciones" (he wants to illuminate and teach the generations) (*La revolución* 262)—while extolling Russian writers generally as participants in a creator-reader circuit more ambitious than that of Western Europe. "The Russians ask more of the novel than we do," Pardo Bazán argues, and this difference in public expectation creates a different kind of writer: "They seek a novelist who will be the prophet, let us say, of a better future" (*La revolución* 265–66).[74] Pardo Bazán's praise for the Russian novel-reading public comes with a slight toward her native Spain—"The serious and deep novel dies here without an echo" (276–77).[75] While Pardo Bazán might stop short of the assessment offered by Paulino Fuentes Castro in an 1874 issue of *El Correo del Perú*—"It is the public who makes the writer, not the writer who makes the public"—she clearly sees in Russia a dynamic impossible to create in her home country, a shared social and artistic vision that goes far beyond entertainment or aesthetic perfection ("Literatura" xxxii).[76]

Pardo Bazán and Vogüé's influence shines through clearly in Cabello's other important work of literary criticism, *El conde Leon Tolstoy* (1896), which employs the Russian author as a cudgel against Émile Zola—"Zola next to Tolstoy is a novelist who suffers from intellectual near-sightedness" (*El conde* 16).[77] She also seconds Vogüé's discomfort with the formal shift from fiction with a moral message to expository prose and public advocacy in a pithy formulation of her own, "Tolstoy the philosopher is less a philosopher than Tolstoy the novelist" (8).[78] And she resorts to the metaphor of electricity to describe what, she agrees with her predecessors, is the pernicious effect of nihilistic tendencies in the Russian zeitgeist. Speaking to the effect that ideas can have over time, she sees them building silently and then erupting, "as electrical fluids condense in the atmosphere, in order to come loose later in a terrible storm" (25–26).[79]

But Cabello's context is different, too, and not only because of geography. In the decade between Vogüé's publication and hers, Tolstoy's novella *The Kruetzer Sonata* (1889) had appeared. One of its characters, an old man on a train spinning tales of lost love, unleashes a retrograde critique of modern educational reforms that Cabello interprets as a deeply insightful call to arms. The old man, who holds forth to a crowd of younger passengers, lays the blame for much pain and suffering on the educational reforms that have purported to grant equality to women. But the old man's message is not as nostalgic as it might appear at first glance, since he suggests that the problem with modern reforms is that they imagine that only women must change in order for the balance of power between the sexes to be significantly altered. He declares, "The education of women will always correspond to men's opinion about them," and that legal and educational movements toward equality fail because men refuse to see women as equals: "They emancipate women in universities and in law courts, but continue to regard her as an object of enjoyment" ("The Kreutzer" 384, 385). A real shift, he concludes, will require changes in the way women and men think about their relationships to one another, and such a change, like "customs" in the formulation of Matto's rural philosopher, does not necessarily come about because of political or legislative action: "High schools and universities cannot alter that. It can only be changed by a change in men's outlook on women and women's way of regarding themselves" (386).

The words of Tolstoy's character invite a number of possible interpretations. We might read them as a sly and curmudgeonly attempt to prove that equality is too difficult a goal even to attempt and, as a corollary, that the reformers themselves must necessarily be either cynical or quixotic. It also betrays more than a hint of moralism, the suggestion that sexuality and men's (and women's) approach to it can become more powerful than any economic or educational leveling. Cabello shifts this negative interpretation slightly but substantially to read "The Kreutzer Sonata" as an argument that a greater feminist revolution is necessary, that, as far as the nineteenth-century woman is concerned, "The cause of her slavery does not reside in herself but in the concupiscent passions of man" (*El conde* 11–12).[80] Cabello cites Schopenhauer in her praise, and she employs the philosopher's notion of the "eternal feminine" (eterno femenino) as a model for progress rather than a static marker (11–12). If the cause of feminism needs to reform the behavior of men and women, then such reform can work only if it makes customs and habits change at the most personal level. We have therefore arrived, by her line of reasoning, at a task that laws cannot perform and thus have entered the bailiwick of the social novel.

It is this question of the change and reform of habits of mind that is the salient quality of Cabello's Tolstoy and the central insight she sees in his legacy. Tolstoy, she argues, provides an optimistic counterpoint to Naturalism. A positivist herself, Cabello has little difficulty with historical and scientific determinism per se, but since her belief structure espouses a narrative of progress, she needs a determinism that produces movement rather than stasis and, as a novelist, something that will put fiction close to the levers of power. Cabello sees all of these threads come together around the notion that "the man of today is the work of the man of yesterday, and the man of tomorrow will be the work of the man of today" (47–48).[81] Her professional creed as novelist is one she sees embodied in Tolstoy, too, that "this world in which our spirit is fed, we can form and build it to our will" (60).[82] Fiction is her tool of choice for this world-building.

## *From the Local to the Global*

Cabello's view of fiction specifically and art in general as a direct route toward social change rather than a detour around the normal path of politics resonates deeply among Cabello's European and North American contemporaries and indeed throughout the nineteenth-century discussion of the novel. The 1898 appearance of *What Is Art?* and its definition of artistic expression as irreducible to reason or exposition would follow the course of *El Perú Ilustrado*'s 1887 review of Cabello's novel *Sacrificio y recompensa* as "elevating with admirable skill the sentiment of the good to the level in which it can be understood by anyone and can easily exercise its healthful influence in all the social classes" (Rev. 10).[83] The reverberating echoes extend to Great Britain and Harriet Martineau's praise of Walter Scott's novels as more direct means of preaching and philosophy. Martineau had asked the philosophers of the world a rhetorical question, "whether they would look for thumbed copies of their writings in workshops and counting houses, in the saloons of palaces, and under many a pillow in boarding schools" (29). In her view the fiction writer's product physically traversed all of these spaces with an intimacy that was merely a metaphor for its powerful mental and emotional engagement.

The transatlantic debate between Henry James and British novelist Walter Besant had covered similar ground in the 1880s. Besant, the moralist, claimed that "the modern novel converts abstract ideas into living molds" and provides "a higher morality than is seen in the actual world" (10), while acknowledging the convergence of morality and narrative: "The world has always been taught whatever little morality it possesses by way of fable, apologue, parable and allegory" (9).[84] James, in contrast believed that "morality" would need to be more strictly defined to function as an aesthetic criterion and that the limits Besant wished to impose on the genre and the intentions of its writers were unrealistic and unnecessary. Where both come together is in their belief that narrative is something more than a simple diversion from everyday existence, that something has imbued it with a transcendental force. James's formulation is perhaps uncharacteristically concise: "The only reason for the existence of a novel is that it *does* compete with life" (54).

Nancy LaGreca has numbered Cabello among a group of female novelists for whom the creative freedom of fiction allowed a form of progress impossible in the real worlds they inhabited. She argues that "they *dreamed new women* for a modern age," creating living examples of female role models that would have been impossible without the imaginative space afforded by the novel (2). Much had remained the same in Lima between the inauguration of Gorriti's *veladas literarias* with Cabello's call for women's education and Abel de la E. Delgado's diagnosis of the Peruvian political sphere as one in need of a feminine influence and Cabello's 1894 book on Tolstoy (Gorriti, *Veladas* 37). When Cabello and E. Delgado spoke, Peru was adjusting to a post-Guano-boom economic world in which a gulf between expectations and the reality of commodity prices provoked a region-wide economic crisis.[85] In Peru this narrative of crisis and internal conflict became even more pronounced with the War of the Pacific (1879–1883), which ended in spectacular defeat and invasion by Chile. While the recovery from the war gave space to something of a golden age for Lima's literary and newspaper publishing scene (Gargurevich 169), the political climate remained unstable, with political disputes that frequently escalated into armed conflict between warring factions. The result, as Antonio Checa Godoy has summed it up, was a literary climate in which serial publications tended to be short-lived and literary and political expression was subject to continual (and continually shifting) restrictions (Checa Godoy 131).

With this in mind it should not be surprising that Cabello, Matto, and González de Fanning frequently engaged in the sort of exasperated self-critique of their nation that would become commonplace in, say, post-1898 Spain, and that found its US voice in the satirical writings of Julia Ward Howe or in the melancholy autobiography of Henry Adams. All three writers allude to a national crisis of values in which wealth and the appearance of wealth mattered more than any other personal characteristic. Matto and González de Fanning would focus on Lima itself, "the arrogant sultan of South America" (la engreída sultana de Sud-América) (*Herencia* 30), in Matto's words, as a capital city that has lost its soul in the pursuit of commerce and the appearance of modernity. Manuel Burga and Alberto Flores Galindo have characterized republican Peru of the late nineteenth century as an oligarchy that had still not adjusted itself to the Industrial Revolution, and one in which Lima symbolized displacement, ruled by an aristocracy that felt itself (and given the vagaries of land transport, often was) closer to the capitals of Europe and North America than to its own provinces (16). This perceived displacement also manifested itself in references to educational failures at the personal level. Matto, González, and Cabello's novels feature characters whose upbringing has left them ill-suited for the practical task of making a living by honest means (see Cabello, *Blanca Sol* 4 and *El conspirador* 94; Matto, *Herencia* 96; González de Fanning, *Ambición y abnegación* 6 and *Indómita* 20–21), and they all decry the city's political corruption. Matto and González de Fanning's works take this critique to deterministic lengths. Matto's narrators muse about the negative effects of diet (*Aves* 81) and climate (*Herencia* 94, 243), and González resorts to racist stereotypes, introducing, in Roque Moreno, a tragic figure whose faults she defines by his mixed ethnicity (*Roque* 8). Cabello's conspirator, who narrates his own autobiography from prison as a tale of political mis-education also resorts to racial stereotypes when he describes what he sees as the venial and corrupt nature of the Peruvian electorate and which he blames at least in part for creating the political climate that has nourished his own existence (*El conspirador* 137–38).

It could be argued that in every case the negative portrayals serve to cast in relief the difficult task facing those who wish to bring about reform through education in whatever manifestation of the term. Speaking of the nineteenth-century novelists of the region, Marín Colorado has pinpointed a significant structural problem with reformist programs of the period, a desire for generalized progress and inclusion juxtaposed with notions of the ideal citizen that rely on race and class rather than any clearly articulated qualitative definition: "Between the 'civilizing desire' and the reality of its execution we can understand the paradox of our modernity" (273).[86] The unbridgeable gap between educational intention and reality and between the subject positions of the educator and the student remain recurrent themes. Acosta, the Colombian novelist whose time working in Lima with *El comercio* made her at least an honorary member of the group, made this trope of the frustrated educator the central figure of her novel *Una holandesa en América* (1889) in which the protagonist, who has been brought up in Holland by her mother's relatives, returns to her Irish father and the family plantation in rural Colombia upon her mother's death. After chronicling the difficulty of reigning in her rebellious siblings and her morphine-addicted father as well as the supreme differences of climate separating the world of the plantation not only from Northern Europe but also from the cultured spheres of Bogotá, the novel leaves its protagonist happily resigned to her role as a beacon of civilization in the midst of a beautiful but menacing wilderness, consoled by what she sees as the central human joy, "the sincere conviction of having strictly fulfilled our duty" (*Una holandesa* 270).[87]

The frustrated educator manages to serve at once as a national and regional symbol.[88] It was in 1875, the same year in which Gorriti's *veladas* began, that *El Correo del Perú* published Manuel María Seguín's "El americanismo en literatura," which called for an aesthetics of calmness to counteract a climate of political intrigue and which couched the region as a youthful person stuck in a tumultuous phase of development: "Political events have worn us out, and we will be worn out even more by the deep and melancholy meditations inappropriate for a country that finds itself in action and with all of the movements of childhood" (389).[89] Seguín's bleak assessment of the political landscape ca. 1875, before the War of the Pacific shattered Peruvian society, demonstrates the degree to which anxiety over perceived instability functioned as something of a constant. This perception of youthful lack of development also serves as a regional marker of identity—defining Spanish America in terms of its educational need—and current events and the failings of individual characters thus feed into the larger narrative. The appearance of a Cuban exile in the Lima of Cabello's *Sacrificio y recompensa* inspires a character to proclaim that "in Peru we are all Cubans at heart" (94).[90]

As Peru, Cuba, and the region itself take turns as metaphorical students or patients, the characters and narrators use a mixture of metaphor and literal detail to further an educational motif. Cabello characterizes the disaffected protagonists of *Blanca Sol* and *El conspirador* as victims of particular forms of bad education offered in Peruvian society. In the first case what stands out is a concern for reputation and appearance over substance—a result of the neglect of women's education—and in the second case, in which the protagonist/narrator is male, his own education mirrors the political chaos that so troubled Seguín. Remembering himself as a student who worked "without method, or discernment," the conspirator describes his resulting mental state as "a chaos of badly founded principles."[91] Matto, too, for all of her interest in determinism, would describe the task of the new generation of Peruvian reformers as that of being "in struggle against vices that enjoy the privilege of being rooted" (*Aves* 97).[92] The social novel thus unfolds as a project within a project, a story about the story of attempted education and reform.

What the larger frame of the novel as a reforming device adds to the specific examples is an optimism of scale, a belief that over time the power of narrative can fight ingrained and unexamined custom with new customs that—because narrative functions nimbly and more subconsciously than straight persuasion—might escape examination and become ingrained even before the readers know exactly what is happening. In 1898 Tolstoy would liken "the evolution of feelings" to the "evolution of knowledge" and identify art as the engine of this sentimental revolution, "replacing lower feelings, less kind and less needed for the good of humanity, by kinder feeling, more needed for that good," and his formulation neatly summarizes the power of the social novel's appeal from the perspective of the Lima novelists (*What* 123). It is a means of enacting even deeper change when laws and reasons fail, and ironically, a form in which even or especially the story of failed educational endeavors becomes the vehicle of enduring reform.

## *"Fiction Does It Better"*

The critical fate of Tolstoy's *What Is Art?* mirrors the separation between education and aesthetics that became an article of faith with the advent of modernism. One US critic, writing late in the twentieth century and identifying himself as an admirer of Tolstoy's moralism, would call it "the most outlandish book ever written on one of the century's favorite subjects: art" (J. Allen n. pag.), while Edgerton explained it as a symptom of Tolstoy's own philosophical intransigence, calling it "a hedgehoggish idea," carried "to the very end of its logical consequences" ("The Critical" 159). Even attempts to revive Tolstoy's argument in the name of artistic education would acknowledge a critical consensus that deemed it "a view without much merit" (Trivedi 38). What Allen and others found most troubling about the sentiments expressed in *What Is Art?* was the narrowness of its criteria. If successful works of art must prove a positive moral contribution combined with widespread popular success, then many, many works will necessarily be left out.

Temporal perspective is part of the difficulty here, as twentieth-century critics survey the nineteenth with an eye toward formulating a literary narrative, a history rather than a tradition, to return to González Echevarría's formula, while Tolstoy's criteria remain firmly rooted in the present tense. While he might look backward half a century to Harriet

Beecher Stowe and interpret her book's reception and influence as having proven itself, given its obvious historical impact, the question he poses for the artist remains that of what art can do now. Cabello, Matto, González de Fanning, Acosta, and their contemporaries are likewise writing from a present tense in which they see art, and specifically the novel, as a possible field for women's intervention in the public sphere at a moment when the stakes could not be higher, when a region-wide anxiety about influences from Europe and corruption at home leaves the value and future of the hemisphere republican experiment in question.

I have argued that the threads of education, female emancipation, and the theory of the social novel became distinctly intertwined even among a group of writers with significant political, philosophical, and religious differences. González de Fanning and Acosta remained devout Catholics throughout their careers and promoted a politics of respectability that Cabello de Carbonera would call into question, while Matto's attempt, however flawed, to provide space for an indigenous voice in the discourse of Peruvian-ness stood in contrast to the more conservative identifications of race and class that held sway in the works of González de Fanning and Acosta. All managed to agree, however, that the novel played a social role in shaping the new republics and that a combination of local and global circumstances made that influence especially necessary in late nineteenth-century Spanish America.

In 1875, just as Gorriti's *veladas* were getting under way, *El Correo del Perú* published Rómulo Mendiola's attempt to domesticate realism for American needs. Arguing that "l'art pour l'art" tends toward destruction and decomposition—goals that should be anathema in countries and regions that are building themselves (52)—he posited that "the essential condition of art is morality" (61) and that "the mission of art is to educate" (60–61), a sensibility that would find its Old World echo in the Tolstoy of 1898.[93] For Cabello, Matto, and the rest of the writers in their circle, defending and writing the social novel was at once an act of patriotism and self-liberation. The moral novelist takes on the mantle of shaping public opinion, a role whose scope and possibilities exceed those of presidents and representatives.

Finally, lest we confine the intertwining of art and education to the nineteenth century, along with the habit of using the word *literature* to apply to all manner of printed material, the field of education and educational writing maintains much of the sensibility of nineteenth-century

Lima. The line of reasoning between art, perception, and experience that traces back to US educational reformer John Dewey, syncs up with Schiller's notion of aesthetic education as limned by Doris Sommer: "Reason is quite helpless here because arguments attract counter arguments but not the will to change" (Sommer 92). Recent cognitive experiments have purported to measure increased emotional empathy (Djikic et al., "On Being Moved") and increased open-mindedness and flexibility (Djikic, Oatley, and Moldoveanu, "Opening the Closed") as a short- and long-term result of the experience of reading fiction. In her 2013 essay "Why Fiction Does It Better," Lisa Zunshine uses pedagogical vocabulary to provide a utilitarian justification for reading fiction. Noting the emphasis on metacognition as a bedrock of the Common Core standards proposed for US public schools, she points out that in terms of producing metacognition, fiction is the ultimate gilded pill in comparison with nonfiction, because the need to relate to the explicit or implicit perspectives of characters and a narrator means that "it always functions at a higher metacognitive level than nonfiction, and it can achieve that higher level without explicit use of metacognitive vocabulary" (n. pag.). Here we might say that Zunshine is echoing the tone of the authors of the social novel in Lima in a landscape in which educational goals follow a cognitive rather than a moral line of thinking.

Of course, empathy is a form of cognition, too, and part of the process of integrating a new perspective seamlessly into one's own imagination is identification, emotional or otherwise. Whether posited in terms of content or of method, the notion that fiction could be or should be beneficial to the reader has proven itself capable of shifting its ground, lowering its profile, and above all surviving critical efforts to the contrary. Henry James's formulation—"The only reason for the existence of the novel is that it *does* compete with life" (Besant and James 54)—also suggests one of the key justifications for the social novel as an aesthetic project. If fiction can compete with life, it can offer alternative lives; and if it can teach readers to understand and even inhabit those alternative lives, it provides a forum for experience and growth impossible in the "real world" those readers inhabit. Per LaGreca's assessment, the novelist of the nineteenth century can dream up social roles that her society does not offer. She is also creating herself as the authority behind those dreams.

## CONCLUSION
# Publication as Mission and Identity

> It seems to me that the best art is political and you
> ought to be able to make it unquestionably political
> and irrevocably beautiful at the same time.
> —Toni Morrison

### *Did It Work?*

Toni Morrison's synthesis of the aesthetic and the political appears in "Rootedness: The Ancestor as Foundation," an essay that takes on the topic of what writing accomplishes and should accomplish within a community of readers. The North American novelist takes care to acknowledge that her position will not necessarily be widely shared in a critical climate in which "if a work of art has any political influence in it, somehow it's tainted." Morrison takes a contrary perspective: "My feeling is just the opposite: if it has none, it is tainted" (64). Focusing on the development of the novel in English, Morrison finds that from its inception, it has "provided social rules and explained behavior, identified outlaws, identified the people, habits and customs that one should approve of" (57–58). A certain moral dimension is thus inscribed in the DNA of the form, especially since the realistic depiction of recognizable lives and relationships necessarily comes to serve as an example for readers. However idiosyncratic its characters and the situations they face, the form develops social norms or develops exceptions that acknowledged norms throw into relief.

A lot of time and distance separates Morrison (1931–) from the generation of writers this study has explored, a generation that passed away in the early years of the twentieth century and, tainted with the stigma of didactic intent, indeed fell into a sort of critical oblivion. Morrison, writing from late twentieth-century America, demonstrates just how global and just how current the debate over what the novel should do remains a century after the *veladas* and the transnational and transatlantic debates over the meaning of the new popularity of the genre. One of the advantages of our own temporal perspective is the opportunity to look at the decades after the development of the social novel in Lima and ask the perfectly natural question of whether or not the experiment worked. Did the success of *Blanca Sol* or *Aves sin nido* and the broader discussion of the need for greater emphasis on moral education blunt the crisis of political corruption the Lima writers saw in their own city? Did it bring about a greater sense of national and regional independence? These questions cannot be easily sidestepped when the discussion centers on a group of writers who made the expressed intention of causing social change an essential component of their aesthetic. To varying degrees these writers promised to change the world.

When William DeForest praised Harriet Beecher Stowe's *Uncle Tom's Cabin* as the nearest example to the "Great American Novel" he hoped would soon appear in greater numbers, he based his claim for the book's influence not only on the belief that it had helped bring about the US Civil War but also on the claim that it had changed the common denominator of public morality. If the relative ethical merits of obeying or disobeying the fugitive slave law were a possible topic of conversation in the United States ca. 1858, DeForest argued, they had become a settled moral point by 1868 when he took up his pen. DeForest credited Stowe's novel with helping to bring about this change of public opinion. The Lima circle would have agreed with both the conclusion and the method of DeForest's thinking, since it credited a change in social custom as the real driver of a new legal regime and not the reverse. Custom legislates, DeForest and Cabello and colleagues maintained, and Stowe's novel had changed law by first changing custom.

Of course the very fact that Stowe's work would remain the quintessential example of the moral novel—cited in favor of and against the concept—for decades after its publication and indeed into the twentieth and twenty-first centuries says something about its singularity both as a work of art and as a historical event. A sea change did occur in US law and custom in the wake of its publication, but DeForest cannot really prove to what extent those changes were brought about by the novel.

Here it becomes easy to play the role of the skeptical Juan Valera and state that no sweeping change in Peruvian society came along to support the idea that the Lima group's novels were significantly altering human behavior.[1] The country did manage to enshrine indigenous recognition in its 1920 constitution, an act that could be interpreted as part of the legacy of Matto's work, but by the time this occurred, Cabello had died in an insane asylum, likely suffering from a case of syphilis contracted from her late husband, while Matto herself had been forced into an exile in Argentina that would continue until her death in 1909, a cruel mirror image to the exile journey that first brought Juana Manuela Gorriti to Lima and made possible those literary *veladas*.

In 1933 the Peruvian feminist and APRA founder Magda Portal would identify Matto as an important *precursora* (along with Flora Tristan), while arguing that the sporadic successes of female writers in Peru had failed to translate into real political leverage. What the country had managed to produce, she argued, were "writers, poets, great patriots" rather than transformational political leadership (5–6). Portal argued that the failure of Peruvian feminism up to her day could in part be attributed to the lack of a pathway between literary and political influence. Where Germaine de Staël and the Lima circle saw letters as a backdoor into politics, Portal saw parallel passageways whose interlocking doors remained closed to women. Did it work? To Portal it seemed clear that whatever progress literature had inspired had been woefully insufficient. The writing and reading of moral novels had not significantly changed the narrative of female exclusion from Peruvian political life.

## *Networks and Canons*

Any social novelist would likely object to the did-you-change-the-world criterion, however much the genre's pronouncements invite it. After all, even important change might not become apparent for decades, and if some sort of broad moral evolution were to take place in a nation or region, it would likely be impossible to tie that evolution to a single source. An unbiased questioner intent on proving the importance rather than the irrelevance of the social novel might begin by asking where Spanish America would be in the twenty-first century without *precursoras* such as those of the Lima circle. Some of the most important work on nineteenth-century women writers in recent decades has focused on introducing or reintroducing forgotten voices into the canon of Spanish American literature. In a sense this work has sought to rescue the canon itself by giving it a deeper relevance with regard to what was actually being written, read, and written about in the nineteenth century. The literary influence of these authors and any possible spillover between literature and politics or social customs effectively vanishes when their names and words are left out of anthologies and histories of Spanish American literature. Recovering the authors of the Lima circle as individual authors of transcendent literary works is thus an essential step in the construction and maintenance of the history of Spanish American literature.

By focusing on the Lima circle as a network that performed feats of publishing and circulation in a variety of print genres, I have sought to deepen and extend the arguments these scholars have made for an alternative intellectual history of the Americas. This alternative history hews closer to the evidence as presented in primary source documents than the official histories it seeks to correct. Cabello, Matto, Serrano, Acosta, and their contemporaries participated in a well-documented global discussion that linked literary aesthetics with the discourse of educational reform, and to the degree that twentieth-century literary histories wrote them out of the master narrative of Spanish American letters, they obscured a number of the topics that nineteenth-century Americans were actually talking, thinking, and writing about.

In this study I have expanded the canon revision already underway in contemporary scholarship in two directions. On a geographical vector—across the space of their own time—I have considered the Lima group as an intellectual network and traced its constant and vital contact with other networks in the Americas and Europe. This includes not only direct interventions such as Matto's decision to publish portions of the Valera–Pardo Bazán debate or the inclusion of a dispatch from the United States in Gorriti's *veladas* but also the shared readings by which members of the network claimed predecessors such as Germaine de Staël and Harriet Beecher Stowe and treated them as quasi contemporaries. The depth and prevalence of the Lima circle's engagement with these writers demonstrates not a subservience to European or US authority but rather a willingness to map out a new discourse on progress and modernity from the materials at hand. When better-remembered writers from the twentieth century like Teresa de la Parra (Venezuela) and Rosario Castellanos (Mexico) made the alternative intellectual history a rhetorical technique for the feminist essay, they were channeling a move already developed and refined in Lima decades before.

It is also worth pointing out the importance of the editorial work of the Lima circle and their contemporaries in preserving and publicizing the lives and works of exemplary women in the journals they edited and the biographical compilations they authored and/or assembled. This editorial work would serve as the foundation for the alternative intellectual histories of recent scholars. Indeed it would not be an exaggeration to say that the writers of the Lima circle provided examples of how the assembly of an alternative canon might be undertaken while being themselves the sort of writers who would need to be recovered a century later. Their essays and scholarship provided, in effect, a blueprint for their own recovery. Publishing history is part of this story, too, because the availability or lack of availability of printed materials so often served as a source of inspiration. The perceived marginality of these writers is one of the most perverse effects of the oblivion into which they were placed or allowed to fall. Celebrated at home as writers, teachers, and public intellectuals and welcomed (and published, and published about) throughout the Americas and Western Europe, they were anything but marginal in their own time.

The other vector along which I have attempted to expand the new alternative intellectual histories of Spanish America is the hemispheric obsession with writing, reading, and publication, as sources of intellectual and political legitimacy for the republics of the New World. This vector, centered as it is on a specific (if extremely large) location, cuts across time. I argue that the belief in the power of the book necessary to sustain the project of the social novel calls forth a long line of arguments that stretches back at least to the independence movements. Here again the transcendent aura of the work of art meets the more prosaic notion of systematic communication—the hemispheric popularity of educational texts aimed at autodidacts brushes up against the hopes and fears embodied in the nascent systems of public education. In republics where public education was one of the great progressive causes of the late nineteenth century, the do-it-yourself educational text became a proxy for public education prior to its establishment and a prototype for the sort of educational text the founders of those systems would want their schools to use. Sarmiento's memory of Ackermann's catechisms as his own school-away-from-school and his desire to make a textbook edition of Franklin's autobiography nicely encapsulates this process.

The Lima circle did its editorial and textbook work in a hemispheric context in which the perception of book scarcity became a relative measure of attitude rather than a statistic. A sense of the New World market as a blank slate that needed to be populated with its own books to avoid a flood of European imports managed to tie a knot of anxiety between the desire for intellectual independence and the need for educational systems that generally followed European models. This anxiety would join itself to the paradoxical view of the New World as a disordered space in need of a stronger moral frame on the one hand, and as a last, best hope for the moral redemption of a decadent Europe on the other. Morality mingled the personal and the political, and referred both to corruption as well as the persistence of monarchies and empires, a sensibility that Gretchen Murphy has described as "identification with the Western Hemisphere as a source of democratic difference from European monarchy" ("The Hemispheric" 553). The nineteenth-century publishing industry in the New World was nourished by a mixture of pride and insecurity.

## *Authorship and Pedagogy*

For the members of the Lima circle, this sense of hemispheric responsibility coupled with opportunity inspired a will to publish and a will to teach, sometimes in the classroom and sometimes by publishing. Since teaching implied professional participation in the world of letters, their national and regional patriotism was necessarily linked to their professional advancement—in theory, the more books and magazines they sold proclaiming gender emancipation, the more they themselves came to embody the concept in practice. In this sense the Lima circle could not be called marginal in a historical sense any more than a geographical one. They were not isolated among intellectuals in their own time, and their discourse formed part of a longstanding narrative of republican progress.

Almost a century after the disappointing aftermath of the French Revolution had prompted Staël to propose literature as a form of politics by other means, the Lima circle took on the identity of professional writers and editors as a way of becoming public intellectuals. As editors and biographers, they provided textual examples and rules of reading for a generation of Spanish American readers that explicitly included women. Their readers, like those who would have first read Staël, were coming of age to face the stark gap between the social mores that governed their personal lives and the republican rhetoric that ostensibly held sway in the political lives of their region. With so many avenues to formal intervention closed, they resorted to what Christopher Conway has called "the social utility of writing" (*Nineteenth-Century* 57). Just as the book served as a platform for a social message, so the mantle of author served as a new social position that permitted mediation between the public and private spheres.

At the beginning of the twentieth century, the Peruvian feminist Elvira García y García would argue that "moral education should be received throughout all of one's life" (69–70).[2] For Cabello, Matto, Serrano, Acosta, and González de Fanning, this belief—which they accepted implicitly—could not be separated from the art and business of writing. They were sure that their readers needed moral education, they were confident their writings could provide it, and they translated this confidence into a powerful argument for writing as a form of progress. The writer would create the future public and the act of writing allowed women to occupy a powerful position that politics alone could not deny.

# NOTES

## INTRODUCTION

1. "De aquí una contradicción, aunque sólo aparente. La poesía enseña y no enseña. Para resolver bien esta contradicción, explicarla y conciliarla todo en síntesis, sería menester un libro. Y un libro sabio y profundo, de que yo no me siento capaz." All translations from Spanish and French are my own except in cases that cite published English editions; in those cases the original Spanish or French text has not been included.
2. "Una salita contigua al salon de clases, donde no hay sino bancos y pizarras, mapas y pupitres" (Gorriti, *Lo íntimo* 149).
3. María Nelly Goswitz credits the *veladas* with "the creation of an intellectual platform in favor of the Latin American woman writer on a continental scale" (la creación de una plataforma intelectual en favor de la escritora latinoamericana a un nivel continental) (133). Peluffo emphasizes the importance of the concept of "sisterhood" (sororidad) in international women's networks in the nineteenth century, along with the importance of transatlantic connections among feminists ("Rizomas" especially 209, 212–14).
4. The female networks discussed here long predate what Manuel Castells calls "network society. By seeking to use literary networking and influence as an alternate route to political power, however, they do invoke what Castells calls "the fundamental dilemma in the network society," namely, the fact "that political institutions are not the site of power any longer." What replaces political institutions, Castells argues, "is the power of instrumental flows, and cultural codes, embedded in networks" (23).
5. Schlau cites Matto's relationship with Gorriti and Cabello as a particularly important example of this form of networking, and she argues that critics have tended to de-emphasize the importance of that female network while exaggerating the influence of Manuel González Prada in Matto's technique and worldview (60–61).
6. See Rosanvallon (44) for more on the revolutionary roots of the term. Gannett (24), "An Efficient" (208), and "Luis Blanc" (2) are examples of its use in US and Spanish publications.

7. See Goldgel for more on nineteenth-century newspapers' emphasis on "enthusiasm" as the quality to be communicated on the page, a communication sometimes compared to "electrical fire" (fuego eléctrico) (59).
8. Mary Louise Kete has argued that it is precisely this emotional binding force that made sentiment so distasteful to US writers in the century after the Civil War, when the notion of a transcendent national community was used to support the repression of racial and political minorities (161).
9. Jaron Lanier's recent treatise on the social and political implications of web 2.0 draws a parallel between the extra-technological powers ascribed to the Internet in the twenty-first century and those once ascribed to the printing press. Lanier stresses the importance of keeping in mind the fact that humans, not machines, set the political agendas that new media will reinforce or introduce. As he puts it, "Printing presses in themselves provide no guarantee of an enlightened outcome," and he uses the often impressive technological savvy of totalitarian regimes as a case in point (46).
10. William Acree Jr. has argued convincingly that education was inherently connected to gender emancipation in nineteenth-century Spanish America in both the domestic and the public sphere (*Everyday* 162) and that even educational philosophies that emphasized the domestic had the effect of transforming it into "a matter of national importance, which in turn led to greater numbers of girls attending schools" (163).
11. Beatriz Ferrús Antón argues that the division between the "gender essay" and the "criollo identity essay" spills over into fiction writing, too, and she employs Pratt's distinction to "the great national novels" (las grandes novelas nacionales) and "the serials written by women" (el folletín escrito por mujeres) (258).
12. "Todo el mundo puede decir, sin exageración, que ha leído este libro" (Rodríguez 138).
13. "Victor Hugo dijo que toda lágrima borra alguna cosa" (Rodríguez 143).
14. "Toute larme, enfant, / Lave quelque chose" (Hugo n. pag.).
15. Parfait details a similarly tear-centered discussion of Stowe in the wake of James Baldwin's critique of her novel's sentimentality, a discussion in which Kenneth Lynn took an opposing tack: "In what seemed like a reply to Baldwin's 1949 charge that in Stowe's novel tears actually hid an absence of emotion, Lynn argued that tears encouraged the moral regeneration of the nation" (188).
16. Baldwin condemns the book as "a very bad novel, having, in its self-righteous, virtuous sentimentality, much in common with *Little Women*" (14). See David Reynolds (*Mightier* 258–59) and Parfait (182–88) for more on twentieth-century critiques of the novel.
17. "Cuando tiende a robustecer ese poder tranquilo, benéfico y real, que ejercemos en primer término, sobre nosotros mismos, y en segundo, a través de nosotros, sobre el medio que nos rodea" (García y García 64).

18. Nancy LaGreca has credited Cabello, along with her contemporaries Rufugio Barragán de Toscano (Mexico) and Ana Roqué (Puerto Rico) with the creation of new female role models for their readers: "What makes these three women novelists' stories unique, urgent, and necessary is that they *dreamed new women* for a modern age" (2).

## CHAPTER 1

1. Gooding cites the specific example of Faraday's cage, a "conducting container large enough to allow an observer to get inside with the electrometer." When placed on stage before the public, the observer inside the cage became the observed and therefore "this container would have to allow an audience to see the electrometer, too" (127).
2. "Si vous savez donner cette commotion électrique don't l'être moral contient aussi le principe" (Staël, *De la littérature* 381).
3. Staël's theory of a universal human need for the transmission of virtue is manifested clearly in her declaration of the artistic state of Western Civilization in the wake of the French Revolution. The Enlightenment business of smashing idols creates a felt need for the production of new ones: "The instant we banish an illusion, we must substitute a reality; as soon as we eradicate an ancient prejudice, we stand in need of a new virtue" (*The Influence* 121).
4. Bello's link to Staël's writings on the social effects of literature are particularly clear. Gómez García has noted that parts of Staël's text annotated and translated by José García del Río appeared in the inaugural tome of *Biblioteca americana* (1823), a publication edited in London by Bello and García del Río and which also included Bello's well-known poem "Alocución a la poesía" (Gómez García 12–13).
5. Trish Lougran cites an example from a speech by US abolitionist Edward D. Barber given in 1836 in which Barber uses electricity as a metaphor for the extreme communicability of moral truth via public opinion. Individual people and places are powerless to resist this force, Barber asserts, because "like electricity, it mingles itself with all the elements of the moral world and imperceptibly becomes a part of the mental constitution" (cited in Loughran 304).
6. "El sentimiento despierta el amor de la verdad en los pueblos no habituados a pensarla porque hay una electricidad moral y el sentimiento es el mejor conductor de esa electricidad" (Hostos, *Ensayos* 37). Recent readings have tended to emphasize the progressive nature of Hostos's argument. Manuel A. Ossers Cabrera cautions that it must be read in its late nineteenth-century context and not our own (61), while Gabriela Mora finds Hostos's arguments to be more radical than those of two of his contemporaries, John Stuart Mill and Concepción Arenal (143).

7. "El sentimiento es facultad inestable, transitoria e inconstante en nuestro sexo; es facultad permanente, constante, en la mujer" (Hostos, *Ensayos* 37).
8. "Nadie mejor que ella podría dar á luz libros hermosísimos, *americanos netos*, que no fuesen tristes pinturas de las tristísimas pasiones desenfrenadas" (Acosta, *La mujer* 410).
9. "Catacismo de inmoralidad, de impiedad, de corrupción que la amenaza" (Acosta, *La mujer* xi).
10. "La grande obra de la regeneración" (Acosta, *La mujer* xi).
11. "Como escritoras que deben difundir buenas ideas en la sociedad" (Acosta, *La mujer* 386); "podría escribir nobilísimas obras literarias que llenasen de entusiasmo a sus lectores por el bien y el deseo de imitar los ejemplos que escribiese" (Acosta 406).
12. Eugenia Roldán Vera's study of the distribution and reception of Ackermann's catechisms in nineteenth-century Spanish America emphasizes the advantages of the style: "As Joseph Blanco White, another editor of Ackermann's magazines, wrote, the main advantage of the catechetical style was that it 'fixed' the attention of the reader" (*The British* 156).
13. "Puede ser leida la verdad por pura curiosidad?"; "La verdad debe ser leida para grabarla en el ánimo: para buscar en ella no el placer de la novedad, sino el fruto" (Villanueva 96).
14. "El vulgo quiere aprender la moral en novelas"; "Darsela pura, y no corrompida: no de un modo ridículo, sino con el decoro que exige la ciencia más importante de la sociedad" (Villanueva 60).
15. Villanueva's text participates in a long tradition of confluence between the Anglophone and Hispanophone world on the topic of moral literature. David T. Haberly has noted the appearance of José Luis Muñárriz's translations of Hugh Blair's *Lectures on Rhetoric and Belles Lettres* (1784). Muñárriz's translations, which appeared under several titles in the early nineteenth century, were also adaptations, since the translator "inserted literary examples to replace Blair's British references" (Haberly, "Scotland" 797).
16. The fervor surrounding monitorial schools on Joseph Lancaster's model sheds some light on the salience of book scarcity as a condition of nineteenth-century Spanish American society. Roldán Vera has noted the shift the montorial system underwent upon crossing the Atlantic—"It became a tool for the expansion of universal education and stopped being a mechanism only for the instruction of the children of the lower classes" ("Export" 259). Webster E. Browning's early twentieth-century analysis of the eventual failure of the monitorial system to take root quotes monitorial (and Christian) evangelist James Thomson on the need for "a work on the evidences of Christianity," blaming what he sees as the lack of Christian fervor in Spanish America at least in part on the absence of such a book ("Joseph" 92). Roldán Vera has noted that the lack of Spanish American

textbook production made printed educational materials a necessary import (*The British* 37).

17. "Hizo el desconsolador i alarmante descubrimiento de que en aquella república de casi un millón de habitantes entonces, no habia mas que TRESCIENTAS SESENTA BIBLIOTECAS"; "Nada más que trescientos sesenta bibliotecas! Qué miseria! Es como suelen decir los banqueros de los negocios que se les proponen. 'Ni un pobre millón me dejaría eso!'" (Sarmiento, *Las escuelas* 251–52).

18. "Trescientas sesenta bibliotecas públicas harian la gloria de Sud América, con veinte millones de habitantes i un mundo por morada" (Sarmiento, *Las escuelas* 251–52).

19. "La obra en doce volúmenes conteniendo la lista de libros prohibidos es el alfa i la homega del saber español de entonces. Saber lo que no era permitido saber!" (Sarmiento, *Las escuelas* 250). Roldán Vera points out that Sarmiento's sarcastic invocation of the index of prohibited books as the great Spanish "work" of his time is taken from the commentary of a British travel account of a bookshop in Montevideo where the traveler was able to find the index and little else of interest (*The British* 20n28). Sarmiento is, in effect, making an effort to see Spanish America through the eyes of a foreign traveler, a technique that brings to mind Montesquieu's *Persian Letters* (1721) and José Cadalso's *Cartas marruecas* (1789).

20. Sarmiento's introduction to *Ambas Américas*, an ambitious periodical he launched in 1867, makes the literal comparison between publishing and transportation infrastructure, drawing a link between political affiliation, newspaper publishing, and a nationwide sense of connection: "The parties tighten the national bond, and the great newspapers, like the *Times, Herald Tribune*, serve as connectors, like railways and canals, between cities and municipalities" (Los partidos estrechan el vínculo nacional, i los grandes periódicos, como el *Times, Herald Tribune*, ligan entre sí, como ferrocarriles i canales, todas las ciudades y aldeas) (*Ambas* 7).

21. "Los yankees, los ingleses, los franceses, los alemanes, no solo ven, oyen, huelen, gustan i palpan como nosostros, sino que saben ademas casi todos leer, escribir i calcular, lo que les habilita a ser mas industriosos, mas morales, mas religiosos" (Amunátegui 4).

22. "¡Los he hallado! Podía exclamar como Arquímedes, porque yo los había previsto, inventado, buscado aquellos catecismos" (Sarmiento, *Recuerdos* 147).

23. "Soñando congresos, guerra, gloria, libertad, la República en fin"; "Pero deben haber libros, me decía yo, que traten especialmente de estas cosas, que las enseñe a los niños" (Sarmiento, *Recuerdos* 147).

24. See Cabrera Valverde for more on del Valle in the context of human rights: "Valle is one of the first Spanish American writers to seek support in human

rights for the defense of American Independence" (Valle es uno de los primeros escritores hispanoamericanos que se apoya en los derechos humanos para defender la Independencia de América) (Cabrera Valverde n. pag.).

25. "Debe haber un sistema de *hominis cultura* para desarrollar todas las facultades del hombre" (del Valle, *Memoria* 36).
26. "Un diccionario que consagrado a las ciencias, ofreciese en la suma de sus artículos un sistema de métodos dirigidos a facilitar su adquisición" (del Valle, *Memoria* 38).
27. "La inferioridad de mis conocimientos" (del Valle, *Memoria* 39).
28. "Sería costoso su edición en un país donde es cara la imprenta y no son muchos los compadres de libros" (del Valle, *Memoria* 39).
29. It could be argued that this idea of the book in subjunctive is the impulse behind the continuing prominence of the theme of the book project in the twentieth-century novels of the Latin American "boom." In Gabriel García Márquez's *One Hundred Years of Solitude*, for example, a character seeks to solve the problem of collective memory by creating a "memory machine" the narrator describes as "a spinning dictionary that a person placed on the axis could operate by means of a lever, so that in a very few hours there would pass before his eyes the notions most necessary for life" (García Márquez 48).
30. Andrew Reynolds has argued that it would be counterproductive and counterfactual to consider the book in Spanish America in isolation from other forms of print media: "The idea of doing 'book history' intersects with, and should be viewed alongside, a larger and more diverse history of textual production" (*The Spanish* 137).
31. "La apertura de un desconocido horizonte creativo" (Gómez García 22–23).
32. Along with the geographical conundrum of seeking to write to and of America from England, Pratt also sees a certain irony in the fact that Bello's *El Repertorio Americano* would mention a cycle of epic poems on America that would in fact never be completed (*Imperial* 170). If we view that epic in subjunctive alongside Villanueva, Rodo, and Sarmiento's dreams of educational books, we might consider it as the poetic history text that was never written, yet another distinct, necessary, and hypothetical book.
33. "Ha manifestado con mucha exactitud cuan poderosa es la influencia de la literatura sobre la virtud, la felizidad, la gloria i la libertad de las naciones, i el inmenso poder que ejerce sobre estos grandes sentimientos, primeros móviles del hombre" (García del Río 20).
34. "El egoismo del estado de naturaleza combinado con la activa multiplicidad de los intereses sociales"; "la currupción sin cultura"; "Forzoso es, pues, americanos, que nos empeñemos en mejorarnos, i en adelantar nuestras facultades intelectuales" (García del Río 35).

35. Over a hundred years later the Cuban critic Roberto Fernández Retamar would argue that book scarcity continued to warp the development of intellectual culture in Latin America and to reify European and US assumptions about Latin American intellectual inferiority. Fernández Retamar confesses his suspicion "that we only read with real respect those anticolonial authors distributed from the metropolis" (que sólo leemos con verdadero respeto a los autores anticolonialistas difundidos desde las metrópolis) (Fernández Retamar 51).
36. When then-congressman Henry Clay of Kentucky addressed the US House of Representative in 1820 in support of recognition for the nascent Spanish American republics, he cited, among other factors, the vibrant state of newspaper publishing in Buenos Aires, an issue he ties implicitly with public education: "They had fostered schools with great care; there were more newspapers in the single town of Buenos Ayres (at the time he was speaking) than in the whole kingdom of Spain" (*Papers* 2:858). Andrew Reynolds has also noted the particular growth in newspaper publishing in nineteenth-century Spanish America: "By the end of the nineteenth century, journalistic production per capita in Spanish American urban centers was among the largest in the world" (*The Spanish* 4).
37. V. Barrantes wrote of Olavide in 1891, responding to a new edition of D. J. A. de Lavalle's biography. Speaking of Olavide's career as a colonial official before his move to Europe, he argues that "such an example of the protection of exceptional sons of the colonies is an achievement that Spain's detractors can only deny in vain" (Semejante ejemplo de protección á los hijos sobresalientes de las colonias es un timbre que en vano regatearán á España sus detractores) (Barrantes 42).
38. "El blanco donde dispararon los Inquisidores (que en paz descansen para siempre) sus pèrfidos tiros" ("Una proeza" 123–24).
39. "Los relámpagos precursores de la Revolución acabaron de iluminar también el alma de Olavide" (Barrantes 61); "amistoso techo en Chaverny, cerca de Blois" (62).
40. "Casi al pie del cadalso del infortunado Luis XVI" (Vélez 159).
41. One critic has called the book "a defense of Christianity as a social and religious system necessary for the wellbeing of society and its individuals" (una defensa del Cristianismo como sistema social y religioso necesario al bienestar de la sociedad y sus individuos) (E. M. Valle 147).
42. Nuñez's find has been referred to by a recent critic as "a discovery that changed the history of the Peruvian novel" (un descubrimiento que cambió la historia de la novela peruana) (Bendezu Aibar 1). See Núñez, *El nuevo* 80–81 for more on the recovery of these works.
43. Two examples of the "genre" of the *desengaño* are Agustín Pomposo Fernández's *Desengaños que a los insurgentes de N. España seducidos por los francmazones agentes de Napoleon, dirige la verdad de la religion católica*

*y la experiencia* and Rafael de Velez's *Preservativo contra la irreligión*. See Briggs for more on the diffusion of the *desengaño* in the Independence-era Americas.

44. "La sal de la chiste y la pimienta de la calumnia" (Olavide, *El evangelio* 4:302).
45. "El veneno es dulce y la triaca les parece amarga" (Olavide, *El evangelio* 4:307). Olavide's pithy formulation of the corruption of public taste echoes Campomanes's comment, in his 1775 *Discurso sobre la educación populares de los artesanos y su fomento*, that "Livy complained that the Roman public of his time, could no longer tolerate the maladies, nor suffer the remedies" (Livio se quejaba, de la pública Romana en su tiempo, ya no podía soportar los males, ni sufrir los remedios) (138). In both cases the reformer is concerned about the public's ability to recognize and embrace correction. Any notion of virtue as "natural" or inherently attractive breaks down, they want to argue, when we consider the mutability of public perception.
46. "En nuestros días el arte de la Imprenta ha llegado entre nosotros á un grado de perfeccion que nunca tuvo" (Olavide, *El evangelio* 3:377).
47. "Un libro conciso, con un método claro, y en estilo simple y proporcionado á su inteligencia" (Olavide, *El evangelio* 1:vi).
48. "Una historia que no pretende mas que contar, sostenida con los hechos, y animada por los diálogos, puede tal vez despertar la curiosidad, interesar á los lectores, y aficionarlos á la doctrina" (Olavide, *El evangelio* 1:ix–x).
49. Olavide's condemnation of certain kinds of popular novels serves to underline the genre's success in the late eighteenth and early nineteenth centuries. As Virginia Heffernan has put it: "An art form or cultural practice thrives to the degree in is considered poisonous: by contrast, it's ailing when there are MFA programs in it" (87–88).
50. Roldán Vera notes that the catechisms influenced directly at least two generations of Spanish American leaders. The older generation encountered the catechisms as adults with some control over educational policy in their respective republics—"Prominent Spanish American politicians like Simón Bolívar, Francisco de Paula Santender, Bernadino Rivadavia, and José Cecilio del Valle read Ackermann's books before they advocated their use in education"—while another generation of reader-autobiographers "who were teenagers at the time Ackermann's books were first published, wrote in their autobiographies about the influence that those (and other foreign) publications had on them, and how their reading was linked to the refashioning of their own careers in the new political order" (Roldán Vera, *The British* 173). Among this group, she names Sarmiento, José Victorino Lastarria, and José Antonio Páez.
51. Solomon Lipp has identified Olavide as a novelist who "was not interested merely in reflecting reality, but rather, in teaching an ethical lesson to improve human behavior" ("Conflict" 81).

52. "Un género mixto entre novela y didáctica" (Núñez 102); "el primer novelista americano en el tiempo aunque no en los temas" (109).
53. "Un iluso de filantropía, pero con cierta cándida y buena fé que a ratos le hace simpatico" (Menéndez y Pelayo, *Historia* 3:207).
54. "Publicada en Valencia en 1798 sin nombre de autor, se reimprimió cuatro veces en un año, y llegó hasta el último rincón de España, provocando una reacción favorable a Olavide" (Menéndez y Pelayo, *Historia* 3:215).
55. "Fue un libro muy comprado, un *best seller* como se diría actualmente"; "muy pocos fueron los que tuvieron la paciencia de leerlo hasta el final" (Dufour, "*El Evangelio*" 164). Barrantes's review of Lavalle's Olavide points out that Lavalle could trace his interest in the subject to a copy of *El evangelio* he remembered encountering as a child (40). Lavalle's reference to "a copy of *Evangelio en triunfo*, adorned with beautiful engravings" (Un ejemplar del Evangelio en triunfo, adornado de preciosas láminas) makes Barrantes think of the edition he remembers from his own childhood, and, in particular, of an illustration of Olavide "with the famous black tunic and extinguished candle of the prisoners of the faith" (con la famosa túnica negra y la vela apagada de los reos de la fe), receiving his sentence from the Inquisition (40).
56. Olavide also drew praise from Denis Diderot. His biographical essay, "Don Pablo Olavides" was written in 1782, more than a decade before the publication of *El evangelio en triunfo*. Diderot memorably describes the Inquisition as "the source of prejudices, terror and national imbecility" (la source des préjugés, de la terreur et de l'imbecilité nationale) (470). Writing about an Olavide who was still the Inquisition's prisoner, Diderot cites him as a lesson that "it is dangerous to do good against the will of the Inquisition, and to be found anywhere that tribunal exists" (il est dangereux de faire le bien contre le gré de l'inquisition, et à s'observer partout où ce tribunal subsiste) (472).
57. "Un libro edificante"; "una lógica vigorosa y una vasta y profunda erudición así teológica como filosófica" (Lavalle 116).
58. "Como el fiero sicambrio, quemó lo que antes había adornado y adoró lo que antes había quemado" (Lavalle 117).
59. "Nada hay que recuerde que aquí nació, se educó y vivió hasta la edad de 24 años, al hombre á quién se calificó de *honra de su patria*" (Lavalle 135).
60. "Severa y elocuente lección moral" (Lavalle xvi). Fifty years later, Angelica Palma would make a similar observation in *El Sol* (1931) noting the confluence between "the painful Peruvian moment" (la dolorosa actualidad peruana), the commemorative event honoring Olavide's memory in Lima, and the construction project that had replaced Olavide's old house in Lima with a high-rise apartment building: "It's OK . . . or it's bad, depending on how you look at it; but in any case, it should be made known to future generations that in this house that is now anything but *limeña*, was once that of Lima's excellent son" (Está bien . . . o está mal, según como se mira; pero de todos modos, debía hacerse saber a las nuevas generaciones que esa casa,

hoy tan poco limeña, fué la de un hijo excelso de Lima) (1). Spanish evaluations of Olavide's legacy from the period would also stress the oblivion into which he had fallen. In 1880 *El Globo* (Madrid) emphasized the "decadence" (decadencia) of Olavide's Sierra Morena colony after the reformer's imprisonment by the Inquisition death ("Nuestro" 1). Luis Arauja-Costa's 1928 book review of Ricardo León's *Jauja* invoked the forgotten Olavide as a precursor to the scientifically planned village in which León's novel takes place.

61. "El vertiginoso torbellino de intereses materiales en el que se vé envuelta nuestra jóven sociedad" (Orbegoso 3).
62. "Hasta aquí se la ha empleado a pequeño vapor"; "que trabajemos porque se le dé todo el vapor de la ciencia i del arte, para que le ayude al hombre a arrastrar con mas rapidez el carro del progreso humano" (Gorriti, *Veladas* 348).
63. "La revolucion que voi a proponerles no será violenta" (Alamos González 348).
64. Bendezu Aibar identifies Olavide as the source of a current of romanticism that he argues permeated the Peruvian novel in the nineteenth century, even as its authors tended to cite naturalists and realists as their influences (3). He also credits Olavide with creating a template for the "subversive" (subversiva) novel that would be so essential to Creole identity in the years after independence. Olavide's novels, he argues, are a "natural and inevitable antecedent" (antecedente natural e inevitable) of everything that would follow, despite the fact that Olavide himself was not widely read or remembered in his native Peru (29).

## CHAPTER 2

1. "Si quiere llegar a Dios, quiere llegar por la vía del raciocinio y no de la iluminación" (Castellanos 164).
2. "Hubiera hallado en esta figura un antecedente de su arquetípica Judith, posible hermana de Shakespeare, quizá dotada de genio como él pero sacrificada por la organización patriarcal de la sociedad" (Castellanos 34).
3. "Prototipo de la mística intellectual que tanto abundó en los conventos coloniales" (Parra 2:42).
4. "Sor Juana, que aprovecha sus horas de encierro en la celda de castigo para descubrir algún principio de geometría [ . . . ] la que en la cocina profundiza hasta los fundamentos de la química [ . . . ] la que en las rondas de niños percibe el ritmo que rige el universo" (Castellanos 164).
5. "Tras su reja de clausura se le hace patente lo que siglos más tarde iba a formular Válery: que del mejor rigor nace la mayor libertad" (Castellanos 33).
6. "El rechazo de esas falsas imágenes que los falsos espejos ofrecen a la mujer en las cerradas galerías donde su vida transcurre" (Castellanos 18). María Vicens employs the phrase "circuits of sociability" (circuitos de sociabilidad)

to refer to the vibrant community of writers and readers cultivated by Clorinda Matto de Turner and her female contemporaries (88).

7. "La hazaña de *convertirse en lo que es*" (Castellanos 18).
8. This phrase is a variation on the title of Raymond Carver's well-known short story collection *What We Talk About When We Talk About Love* (1981).
9. "Tantas cátedras, en fin, que solo sirven para hacer que sobreabundan los capellanes, los frailes, los medicos, los letrados, los escribanos y sacristanes mientras escasean los arrieros, los marineros, los artesanos y labradores" (Jovellanos 399).
10. "Las ciencias dejaron de ser para nosotros un medio de buscar la verdad y se convirteron en un arbitrio para buscar la vida" (Jovellanos, *Espectáculos* 394).
11. O'Hagan points out that in this work "America functions first and foremost as a framework for the displaced social and cultural criticism of Europe" (85) in a scheme that identifies "Pennsylvania as the embodiment of virtue and Europe as the embodiment of vice" (86).
12. Tufayl's book was not available in Spanish until Francisco Pons Boigues's 1900 translation. Menéndez y Pelayo wrote the introduction and argued for a reading of the great Spanish-born Arabic thinkers—Avempace, Averroes, and Tufayl—as outliers rather than representatives of Islamic thought, a clear attempt to "claim" these thinkers for Spain's intellectual tradition while rejecting the society and time period to which they belonged (xvi).
13. I am grateful to Jesús Rodríguez Velasco for pointing out the connections with the works by Pedro Montengón and Ibn Tufayl.
14. Not every nineteenth-century observer agreed with Sarmiento about the usefulness of the Ackermann publications. The Guatemalan politico and person of letters Antonio José de Irisarri refers to the catechisms in his autobiographical novel *El cristiano errante* (1847). In his view the catechisms are a symptom rather than a remedy for the scarcity of teachers and books, and he describes his protagonist's schoolbooks as "as bad as Ackermann's catechisms, in which one learns to know the world of Mr. Ackermann rather than the world in which we live" (tan malos, como los catecismos de Ackermann, en que se aprende a conocer el mundo del señor Ackermann, y no el mundo en que vivimos) (46).
15. "Yo me sentía Franklin; ¿y por qué no? Era yo pobrísimo como él, estudioso como él, dándome maña y siguiendo sus huellas, podíaun día llegar a formarme como él, ser doctor *ad honorem* como él, y hacerme un lugar en las letras y en la política americanas" (Sarmiento, *Recuerdos* 162).
16. Carlos Altamirano and Beatriz Sarlo have noted the tension created by Sarmiento's status as an autodidact who very much craves official recognition, and their illuminating critical treatment of Sarmiento's autobiographical self refers to "the constant tension between the autodidact and the academic" (158).
17. "La vida de Franklin fue para mí lo que las vidas de Plutarco para él, para

Rousseau, Enrique IV, Mma. Roland y tantos otros" (Sarmiento, *Recuerdos* 151). Sylvia Molloy's analysis of this passage stresses the influence of translation in Sarmiento's relationship to Franklin: "For Sarmiento, translating himself into Franklin is more than being Franklin the exemplary figure. It is also being Franklin the reader" (*At Face* 34).

18. "La vida de Franklin debiera formar parte de los libros de las escuelas primarias"; "que no habría muchacho, un poco bien inclinado que no se tentase a ser un Franklincito, por aquella bella tendencia del espíritu humano a imitar los modelos de la perfección que concibe" (Sarmiento, *Recuerdos* 151).

19. "Pero por más bien intencionado que el niño sea, renuncia desde temprano a la pretension de hacer milagros, por la razón sencilla que los que lo aconsejan se abstienen ellos mismos de hacerlos" (Sarmiento, *Recuerdos* 152).

20. "Debe estar en los altares de la humanidad, ser mejor que santa Bárbara abogada contra rayos, y llamarse el santo del pueblo" (Sarmiento, *Recuerdos* 152).

21. "Si Franklin a été un homme de genie, il a été aussi un homme de bon sens" (Mignet 10).

22. "Le genie de'un homme devient le bon ses du genre humain, et une neuveauté hardie se change en usage universel" (Mignet 12).

23. "Servicio á la educación pública y popular"; "jefes de familia" (Franklin, *El libro* 4).

24. "Consejos importantes é ingeniosos reglas de conducta para todos los estados de la vida" (Franklin, *El libro* 4).

25. "¡Ojalá la publicación de este LIBRO contribuya á la moralizacion de la juventud y á la morijeración de las masas, sin cuyos requisitos no hay órden social!" (Franklin, *El libro* 4). Bergnes's volume appeared during the regency of María Cristina and in the interim between the first and second Carlist Wars, a tumultuous time by any standard.

26. "La perserverancia y la energía de sus conatos para cultivar su razón y perfeccionarse. Él mismo fué su maestro" (Franklin, *El libro* 21).

27. That 1793 London edition follows the 1791 Paris publication in identifying a combination of pedagogy and entertainment as the prime motivator for both Franklin the writer and the individual publishers. The French editor celebrates Franklin's purpose as that of teaching and filling up leisure hours—"a été d'intruire sa posterité, en amusant ses loisirs" (Franklin, *Mémoires* v–vi)—while the London editor suggests that "The public will be amused with following a great philosopher in his relaxations, and observing in what respects philosophy tends to elucidate and improve the most common subjects" (Franklin, *Works* vii).

28. Myers cites Sor Juana's abstaining from eating cheese as an example of the "self-mortification" that was already commonplace in the published lives of saints (463).

29. "Tuve en San Juan mi casa por cárcel, y el estudio del francés por recreo" (Sarmiento, *Recuerdos* 152).
30. "Tenía mis libros sobre la mesa del comedor, apartábalos para que sirvieran el almuerzo, después para la comida, a la noche para la cena: la vela se extinguía a las dos de la mañana, y cuando la lectura me apasionaba, me pasaba tres días sentado, registrando el diccionario" (Sarmiento, *Recuerdos* 152). See Altamirano and Sarlo for a reading of this section of *Recuerdos de Provincia* that pays special attention to the implausibility of Sarmiento's claims and the problems with terms such as "reading" and "translation" in his narrative.
31. "Estuvo siempre en actividad el órgano de instrucción y de información que tengo más expedito que el el oído" (Sarmiento, *Recuerdos* 156).
32. "El día siguiente supe que don Andrés Bello y Egaña lo habían leído juntos, y hallándolo bueno. ¡Dios sea loado!, me decía a mí mismo, estoy ya a salvo!" (Sarmiento, *Recuerdos* 177).
33. "Tuve yo que asientir al fin en que el artículo era irreprochable de estilo, castizo en el lenguaje, brillante de imágines, nutrida de ideas sanas revistadas con el barniz suave del sentimiento" (Sarmiento, *Recuerdos* 178). Sylvia Molloy has traced the repeated references to "scenes of reading" in Spanish American autobiography with particular attention to Sarmiento and Franklin (*At Face* 16–18, 34).
34. "Aquellos escritores franceses, que desde la desmantelada guardilla del quinto piso, arrojan un libro a la calle y recogen en cambio un nombre en el mundo literario y una fortuna" (Sarmiento, *Recuerdos* 178).
35. Franklin's virtue chart would prompt D. H. Lawrence's well-known twentieth-century rejoinder—"I'm really not just an automatic piano with a moral Benjamin getting tunes out of me" (22)—a critique of Franklin's project as crass utilitarianism and nothing more. Ormond Seavey has argued that the textual Franklin of the autobiography is better read as a virtuous self, created "at the expense of the other selves that had to be discarded" (73), while Jay Fleigelman and Christopher Looby paint Franklin as a textual virtuoso intent on drawing attention to his own artistry. For Mitchell Robert Breitweiser, the chart represents an attempt to imagine a more independent, less subservient vision of the student. He notes that the list of virtues points to an emphasis on clarity of perception and judgment: "the avoidance of vividly presented involvements or interests that would compromise the clearheadedness that calculates whether any given expense of time is a wise investment" (Breitweiser 283).
36. "Por economía, pasatiempo y travesura"; "Conservan muchos en Copiapó el recuerdo del minero, a quien se encontraba siempre leyendo" (Sarmiento, *Recuerdos* 153).
37. "Levantose en Santiago un sentimiento de desdén por mi inferioridad, de que hasta los muchachos de los colegios participaron"; "Yo preguntara hoy si fuera necesario, a todos esos jóvenes del Semanario ¿habían hecho realmente

estudios más serios que yo? ¿También a mí querrían embaucarme con sus seis años del Instituto Nacional?" (Sarmiento, *Recuerdos* 156).

38. "Mi contacto diario con César, Cicerón y mis personajes favoritos" (Sarmiento, *Recuerdos* 157).

39. "Así, el lector empezó a apercibirse en muchos de sus trabajos que ocurrían frases, períodos, que ya habían sonado gratos a sus oídos, y páginas que los ojos se acordaban de haber visto" (Sarmiento, *Recuerdos* 100). See Molloy for more on Sarmiento's approach to plagiarism (*At Face* 27–29).

40. "Que para nosotros se convierte más bien que en reproche en muestra clara de mérito" (Sarmiento, *Recuerdos* 100).

41. "Aquello, pues, que llamamos hoy plagio, era entonces erudición y riqueza; y yo prefiriera oír segunda vez a un autor digno de ser leído cien veces" (Sarmiento, *Recuerdos* 100).

42. Almost a century after Sarmiento's encounter with Franklin's autobiography, the Spanish intellectual and traveler Ramiro de Maetzu would characterize (in 1926) the US educational system as thoroughly steeped in biography as a pedagogical genre and the discussion of biography as pedagogy as a basic educational activity. He notes that "en las escuelas de primera enseñanza y en los colegios de segunda suele ser obligatorio el estudio de la vida de Franklin, así como el de la de Washington" (in the primary and secondary schools the study of Franklin's life, as well as Washington's, tends to be obligatory). And the students, he adds, are not satisfied with the mere imitation and discussion of these exemplary lives, as "el objeto preferente de las sociedades estudiantiles de debates suele ser el parangón entre Franklin y Washington y el discernimiento de cuál de los dos heroes alcanzó la mayor estatura moral" (the preferred question for the student debating societies tends to be the comparison between Franklin and Washington and the discernment of which of the two heroes achieved a greater moral status) (283). The student societies are debating, in short, which figure's life makes better didactic reading.

43. "Más bien que ejecutado, hemos dirigido el trabajo de adaptar a la lengua que se habla en América del Sud, una Vida del Presidente Lincoln, entresacada de las varias que corren impresas" (Sarmiento, *Vida* xi).

44. "En verdad que nadie puede con propiedad llamarse autor de la biografía de hombres que han llegado por entre las ajitaciones de la vida pública a puestos tan encumbrados como Lincoln" (Sarmiento, *Vida* xi).

45. "Vése venir a Lincoln con el hacha al hombro, el emblema del trabajo que conquista la tierra, desde el seno de las selvas de Kentucky, *pioneer* del desierto, dotado de aquella ciencia moral de los Establecimientos, que hace la belleza del tipo que Cooper pasea por todas sus novelas" (Sarmiento, *Vida* xxvii).

46. "Se ha hecho abogado, orador y legislador; absorviendo en su naturaleza de esponja esas esencias de civilizacion, de gobierno, de libertad, que estan

flotantes y diluidas en la atmósfera de los Estados Unidos, y se reconcentran diariamente en cuatro mil diarios, y en millones de libros y folletos, que popularizan el saber de uno, la experiencia del otro, el resultado de la ciencia o de sus aplicaciones en toda la tierra" (Sarmiento, *Vida* xxviii).

47. "La escuela política de la América del Sur está en Estados Unidos" (Sarmiento, *Vida* xlvii).
48. Lincoln himself noted the importance of print culture in the United States in a lecture given less than two years before the Civil War. Referring to important inventions, he described printing as "but the *other* half—and in real utility, the *better* half—of writing" (142).
49. Cupertino del Campo's exuberant twentieth-century biographical compilation, which paired US and Argentinian figures (Sarmiento/Horace Mann; Bartolomé Mitre/Abraham Lincoln; etc.), would negotiate the autodidact's delicate combination of nurture and nature in Lincoln's case by remarking, of his firelight readings, that "Tal estudio, más que enseñarle algo, le reveló el caudal maravilloso de pensamiento y sensibilidad latentes que llevaba dentro de sí mismo" (These studies, more than teaching him anything, revealed the marvelous stock of latent thoughts and sensibility that he already carried around inside) (n. pag.).
50. "Debia ejercer en su espíritu una influencia parecida a la que se atribuye a la de las Vidas de Plutarco sobre la conducta pública de otros personajes" (Sarmiento, *Vida* 5–6).
51. For more on the US reception of *Facundo* and Sarmiento, see Haberly's "*Facundo*" and "The Statesman." In Sarmiento's later years, Haberly argues, he tended to attribute US prosperity less to its formal system of education and more to "inventiveness, a characteristic assisted by education but not dependent on it" ("The Statesman" 245).
52. Some seventeen years later, the *Nation* would react to another Sarmiento production, *Conflicto y Harmonías de las Razas en América*, a book dedicated to Mary Mann, with a favorable review that found Sarmiento a necessary corrective to what it saw as a particular form of decadence: "The new generation in the author's native republic, having been reared in peace, seems to be losing its way; there is dangerous retrogression; while the theory is excellent, the practice is wretched" ("Sarmiento's Spanish" 59). What the US reviewer praises, in a line of reasoning that says more about US sensibility toward its own indigenous population than it does about Sarmiento's book, is a lack of sentimentality toward the narrative of the Conquest: "He detests the Christians who hunted the free Indians or worked the enslaved to death, but has no admiration for the savages who succumbed" (59).
53. Sylvia Molloy points out the importance of what she calls "generic adjudication" and defines "autobiography is biography is history" in Sarmiento's *Recuerdos de provincia* ("The Unquiet" 194). Stressing that the text itself sought "not the pleasure of evocation but the preservation of knowledge and,

one should add, the construction of a model," Molloy highlights Sarmiento's insistence on a frame that makes his autobiography a biographical project: "He will set the stage for his life story in such a way that it will allow him to deal with it *as if* it were a biography" ("The Unquiet" 196).

54. In the same conversation in which Miller expresses her vision of an American Lincoln, Carolyn Boyd underlines Lincoln's importance for Spanish liberals and progressives. She notes that the 1873 biographical anthology *Los mártires de la república*, which was published in Barcelona, included Lincoln (along with Mazzini, Garibaldi, Kossuth, and others). What this demonstrated, she argues, was the tendency of Spanish liberals to include him in "a pantheon of republican saints that was not identified with any particular nationality" ("Interchange" 479).

## CHAPTER 3

1. "Porque el hombre más humilde se reconoce" (Labra 118).
2. Smiles goes so far as to parody what we might call today the "self-help" ad copy of his own time. Perhaps his contempt for "short cuts to science" and promises to "learn French and Latin 'in twelve lessons,' or 'without a master'" (286), stems at least in part from a desire to cordon off his own use of biographical example as a more substantive and realistic form of self-help.
3. "No por mucho madrugar amanece mas temprano, dice uno de nuestros mas sabios adagios. No por querer progresar rápidamente se consigue hacer progresos útiles" (Irisarri, *Historia del perínclito* 38).
4. "¿Son acaso los que no saben leer ni escribir los que nos han puesto en este estado? No por cierto; son los que saben leer y escribir mui bien" (Irisarri, "Próspecto" 3).
5. Virginia Heffernan has pointed out that the question of rules for reading extends from the beginnings of print culture to our own Internet age: "Separating real from false reading, and real from false readers, has been a power proposition with sinister consequences since the first century AD" (67).
6. "Una doctrina que está en contradicción con el character español; digo, al menos con el de los españoles" (*El Solfeo* 4).
7. "A actividad del incansable propagandista contra la esclavitud, nuestro ilustrado amigo D. Rafael de Labra" (*Revista de Andalucía* 192). Another Madrid newspaper, *La Unión*, placed notice of Smiles's *Los hombres de energía* alongside that of A. Jouault's *Abraham Lincoln: su juventud y su vida*, published in Barcelona in 1876, which had appeared in the original French in an 1875 Paris edition. While the pairing of biographical texts makes logical sense, it also demonstrates the degree to which the work of the British author Smiles, who published before Lincoln's ascension to the presidency, retained its relevance precisely because a new biographical figure and martyr seemed to personify the principle of his compilation.

8. Smiles's *Autobiography* proudly recounts the reception of his books in Spanish America. It mentions, for example, the 1887 publication of four of his books under the single title *El Evangelio Social* (translated by General Edelmiro Mayer). Along with favorable reviews in the Buenos Aires newspapers *L'Amico del Populo, Standard of Buenos Aires,* and *Deutsche La Plata Zeitung,* Smiles offers an account of the words, we might call them the "blurbs," of prominent citizens of Buenos Aires, including this suggestive endorsement, perhaps from Sarmiento himself: "The Ex-President of the Argentine Republic informed General Mayer that he had *Character* at his bedside and that it should be at the bedside of every man" (Smiles, *The Autobiography* 398–99).
9. "Seguir la idea de Smiles en el precioso libro llamado *Self-Help*" (Acosta, *La mujer* viii).
10. "Un conjunto razonado de biografías" (Acosta, *La mujer* vii); "porque el bien es también contagioso como el mal" (68).
11. "Nuestras Repúblicas, en donde el estado normal es el de la revolución y el excepcional el de paz y concordia" (Acosta, *La mujer* 20); "la moralización de las clases bajas" (137–38).
12. "Aquella que con sus virtudes y sus sanas obras da un ejemplo digno de ser seguido por los demás" (Acosta, *La mujer* 171); "una de las armas mas ponderosas que Dios nos ha dado" (189).
13. "Mujeres que han vivido para el trabajo propio" (Acosta, *La mujer* ix). Carmen McEvoy has noted a similarity between the "bourgeois ethic" (ethos burgués) that emerged in mid-nineteenth-century Peru and "the English paradigm of the *self-made man*" (el paradigma inglés del *self made man*) (72).
14. "La vida desnuda de toda trama novelesca, sin quitarle ni ponerle cosa alguna, sin tener que añadir ninguna aventura a la narración, de cada uno de aquellos personajes, bastaba para interesar al lector y surtía todos los efectos de un cuadro histórico-novelesco" (Acosta, *Biografías* 2).
15. "Una obra de agradable lectura y utilidad moral" (Quintana 4).
16. "Á las personas vivas se les deben en ausencia y presencia aquella contemplación y atenciones que el mundo y las relaciones sociales prescriben"; "á los muertos no se les debe otra cosa que verdad y justicia" (Quintana 6).
17. "Porque viven en sus hijos y en sus nietos, en las leyes que hicieron y en los partidos que fundaron" (Acosta, *Biografías* 3).
18. "Más bien como una curiosidad etnográfica, que no como un conocimiento útil"; "la gran mezcla de la raza indígena con la blanca que existe en Colombia"; "tiende á desaparecer" (Acosta, *Biografías* 2).
19. "La civilización de que gozamos nos viene de Europa, y los españoles son los progenitores espirituales de toda la población. Así pues, á éstos debemos atender con preferencia, si deseamos conocer el caracter de nuestra civilización" (Acosta, *Biografías* 2).

20. "Recuerdos sagrados y respetos merecidos"; "la juventud americana" (Matto, *Bocetos* 15).
21. "Á tomar los puntos culminantes de la vida de un individuo desde la cuna, explotando sus buenas acciones para ejemplo, con más satisfacción que sus vicios para anathema" (Matto, *Bocetos* 13–14).
22. "Los hijos de los hombres que pasaron por la tierra dejando virtudes y glorias como huella de su tránsito, quedan aún como buen elemento para la regeneración social á que aspiramos" (Matto, *Bocetos* 14–15).
23. "Pertenezco al número de los creyentes. Tengo fe en los futuros buenos destinos del Perú" (Matto, *Bocetos* 15).
24. See Vanesa Miseres for more on Matto's print idealism in connection with her work as a newspaper editor. Miseres argues that Matto's work on the Arequipa-based newspaper *La Bolsa* demonstrated her commitment to print culture's possible connections to workers and artisans (177).
25. "El escalpelo del anatómico"; "el escrúpulo del alquimista" (Matto, *Bocetos* 13).
26. "Estaba cosechando el campo para su obra durante dos décadas" (Gallego 158).
27. "Mediadora entre la aspereza natural i la capazidad sentimental del hombre" (García del Río 368).
28. "Mientras que la parte masculina de la sociedad se ocupa de la política [ . . . ] ¿no sería muy bella que la parte femenina se ocupase en crear una nueva literatura?" (Acosta, *La mujer* 388).
29. "El escritor puede detenerse en el camino para coger las flores envenenadas"; "lectores de todas clases, muchos cuyas inteligencias estragadas por el exceso de la civilización necesitan un alimento condimentado con descripciones cada día más violentamente exageradas"; "alimentos intelectuales sanos é higiénicos" (Acosta, *La mujer* 389).
30. "Nosotros no vemos ningún antagonoismo entre los dos sexos"; "consideramos al hombre dirigiendo la marcha de las grandes evoluciones y á la mujer influyendo en su espíritu" (Cáceres 6–7).
31. "Si en la mujer existiese la fuerza de la iniciativa y de mando, algún pueblo la habría mostrado como element dirigente y al hombre secundándola" (Cáceres 9).
32. González de Fanning argued, in "Sobre la educación de la mujer," her induction speech into the Lima Ateneo, that public force of family life would by definition provide a platform for educated women to influence politics and government. She sketches her vision of the moralizing female presence as "the priestess of good, the shaper of the future" (la sacerdotisa del bien, la obrera del porvenir) (*Lucecitas* 260–61). In an earlier newspaper article ("Las literatas"), González de Fanning promotes the cultivation of female writers as much as a form of self-education as a contribution to larger national literary culture: "And when writing becomes the costume among many women and

not just a few, pedantry and presumption will become rarer, too; these marks that so disfigure and that are so opposed to true merit" (Y cuando el escribir sea la costumbre de muchas, y no de unas pocas, serán tambien mas raras la pedanteria y presuncion; esos lunares que tanto afean y tan opuestos son al verdadero mérito) ("Las literatas" 319).

33. Diego Ignacio Parada puts the notion of female emancipation within social limits in stark terms in his impressively comprehensive 1881 collective biography of female Spanish intellectuals. Noting that he is offering the book in the hopes of shaping a contemporary debate on the education of women, he contextualizes his support of female education from the perspective of men seeking wives—"It's necessary that we put her on our level, because in the contrary case we will be forced to descend to hers" (necesario es que la pongamos a nuestro nivel, porque de lo contrario nosotros tendremos que descender hasta el suyo) (vii–viii)—and with the caveat that intellectual inequality need not overturn social norms (viii).

34. "Una heroína del hambre en el proletariado y una heroína de abnegación entre las clases directoras" (Cáceres 8).

35. "Los tiempos primitivos"; "la historia sólo guarda en sus páginas lo que puede servir de enseñanza a la posteridad, hacienda conocer la grandeza de la humanidad en sus tragedias, en sus alegrías, en sus odios, en sus virtudes y en sus ambiciones" (Cáceres 9).

36. "La manera de pensar" (Cáceres 139).

37. "Una feminist no es extranjera"; "en cualquier gran capital adonde llegue" (Cáceres 341).

38. One sign of the pervasiveness of the female collective autobiography is its mention even in texts that are not collective biographies. When Amalia Puga addressed the readership of the Spanish publication *El Album Ibero Americano* in November 1892 to gloss the accomplishment of a handful of Spanish American literary women, she notes that those who are seeking an exhaustive catalog of influential women should look elsewhere, to wit, that they should direct their attention to the apparently ubiquitous editions of collective biography: "To get to know the notable women of all eras over there is history, and, more concretely, over there are the Female Biographical Dictionaries, the Galleries of celebrated Women" (Para conocer á las mujeres notables de todas las épocas allí está la Historia, allí está, más concretamente, los Diccionarios Biográficos Femeninos, las Galerías de Mujeres célebres) (Puga 201).

39. Leona S. Martin's study identifies a number of these "pan-Hispanic women's networks" in the late nineteenth century and defines their common themes as "an overarching concern with gender issues, a clear awareness of their important roles as nation builders, and a political stance that privileged internationalism and pan-Hispanic ideals" ("Nation" 440).

40. "Atenas del Nuevo Mundo"; "el estudio perfecto fisiológico"; "el pensamiento social"; "torrentes de inspiracion" (Serrano, "Inmortales" 99).
41. "Afanosa é infatigables educacionista"; "Con su eficaz iniciativa estimuló á la pléyade femenina juvenil, para que de lleno y sin temor á las añejas preocupaciones, invadiera el campo de las lecturas y conquistara frescos y hermosos laureles" (Serrano, "Inmortales" 99).
42. "Un trato más suave, más feminino y más amable" (Serrano, "Inmortales" 99).
43. The Baronesa de Wilson, who appeared in Parada's *Escritoras y eruditas epañolas* (1881), published a two-volume collective biography of her own, *El mundo literario americano* (1903), which included male and female writers from all of the former colonies of Spanish America plus Brazil, Haiti, and the United States. Her book offered a brief biography of Acosta, as well as salutes to Matto, Cabello, and Juana Manuela Gorriti, all of whom she recounted as friends from the *veladas literarias* in 1870s Lima.
44. "Al uso laudable que han sabido hacer del sagrado depósito que su madre patria les confiara en todos los géneros de cultura" ("Notas" 153).
45. "Llamada por la naturaleza á otras funciones, no menos dignas y trascendentales" ("Notas" 153).
46. "Un ejemplar, no ya de fantasía y sensibilidad exquisita, sino de austera penetración, de severo juicio, de grave y reposado análisis" ("Notas" 153).
47. "Cuando se hayan desvanecido los últimos restos de las nubes que se interpusieron entre los hijos de una misma patria y formemos todos los hijos de España un mismo pueblo" ("Notas" 156).
48. "Aurora Cáceres, como buena americana, ama á la vieja madre española" ("La mujer" 3).
49. "Esos alegatos indigestos de feminismo" ("La mujer" 3).
50. "Entre las mejores hablistas castellanas" ("La mujer" 3).
51. "Una historia feminina"; "ese gesto antestético de la sufragista ó de las académicas" (*Por Esos* 894).
52. "Consultando más a su corazón que á los estólidos libros de hombres" (Mazol 6).
53. "Una literatura nueva, una ciencia nueva, un idioma nuevo, la forma, tono y estilo que mejor se ajuste al sexo" (Mazol 6).
54. "Ni un miserable portero de la Academia Española! ¡¡Ni un *encerador* de la Embajada!!" (Mazol 5).
55. "La dulce voz de la Sra. Cáceres, sonaba algo así como el rezo de una hija sobre latumba de una madre. Nunca pareció más muerta que entonces España; ya no oye . . . ya no entiende, ni siquiera á los que hablan su lengua . . . ¡*Muerta!*" (Mazol 6).
56. "En los colegios fraceses"; "hasta presentarse en labios de una mujer" (Mazol 6).
57. "Paréceme que va siendo hora de que se levanten por vergüenza algundo de

los académicos barbudo, para ceder ese asiento a éstas mujeres que, contra viento y marea, han conquistador palmas que no todos los académicos han ganado" (Mazol 6).
58. This need and fascination with the transatlantic counterpart would be shared though not necessarily reciprocal. Arbaiza has argued that, in Acosta's case (and in that of the Colombian *Regeneración* with which she associates her project), the Creole perspective on Spain was something other than subaltern. Speaking of "Spanish American Hispanism," Arbaiza identifies it as "a bold postcolonial turn in which the American authors instrumentalized their bonds with the former colonizer and even reversed the subaltern position" (125). For these postcolonial Creoles, Spain represented less a place of cultural authority than "a museum of their own traditions" (132).
59. "De lo contrario, muy pronto, ante la pléyade de escritores castellanos brotados de las repúblicas americanas, la de nuestros académicos quedará esfumada" (Mazol 6).
60. This prominence of Spanish American intellectuals in Europe represents a rough equivalent to what Andrew Reynolds has referred to as *modernismo*'s "inverted conquest" of the metropolis (*The Spanish* 139).
61. Martin characterizes Staël as a "model of the woman of letters" (modelo de mujer de letras) for Serrano ("La baronesa" 16).
62. "Una de las pocas mujeres de verdadero genio vital" (Acosta, *La mujer* 244); "las mujeres pueden tener talento, inteligencia, más perspicacia generalmente que los hombres, pero el *genio creador* es extraño a su naturaleza" (245).
63. "La mujer que se dedica á las letras, no constituye un género aparte" (Cáceres, *Mujeres* 323); (El siglo XIX se inició para la mujer, con la más grande, con la mujer coloso, como la llama un crítico, la señora Staël) (325–26).
64. "La mujer en todo tiempo y lugar tiene una gran misión delante de sí, y ojalá que no la olvidara nunca" (Acosta, *La mujer* 247–48); "La sociedad se ve amenazada con volver á la barbarie, y en manos de la mujer está el impedirlo" (248).
65. "La época de turbulencias y conjuraciones políticas que durante más de ochenta años obscurecieron el horizonte social"; "acerca del papel que hará la mujer en el nuevo orden de cosas que se prepara" (Acosta, *La mujer* 383–84).
66. "La condición actual de nuestras sociedades exige de la mujer un esfuerzo mayor de energía, su condición pasiva de compañera infantil, inconsciente, ha cesado" (Cáceres 345).
67. "La compañera, no sólo del amor, sino también de las tristezas, del trabajo y de los ideales que alegran la vida" (Cáceres 345).
68. "Debería constituirse en confederación para ayudarse, defenderse y darse mutuamente gloria" (Acosta, *La mujer* 395).
69. "Á pintar con gráficos colores la hermosa naturaleza de *las Américas* nuestra América, las costumbres históricas acaecidos en estos paises en los siglos pasados y en el presente" (Acosta, *La mujer* 405).

70. "La descripción pormenorizada de las costumbres desordenadas de una clase de la sociedad limeña, remedo de la corrupción europea, malamente transplantada al Nuevo Mundo" (Acosta, *La mujer* 405).
71. "Cosa excepcional en Hispanoamérica" (Acosta, *La mujer* 405).
72. "Libros hermosísimos, *americanos netos*"; "aptitudes como escritora, como pensadora, como moralista" (Acosta, *La mujer* 405).
73. "La misión de la mujer hispanoamericana"; "cristianizar, moralizar y suavizar las costumbres" (Acosta, *La mujer* 410).
74. "La idea de la transformación" (Gallego 161).
75. "El más antiguo y mejor representado hogar literario femenino" (Cáceres 189).
76. "Ninguna escritora ha adaptado mejor su vida ni sus obras han recibido mayor influencia de su patria" (Acosta, *La Mujer* 190).
77. Sara Beatriz Guardia points out that more than politics and religion were behind the public's turning against Matto: "there was also a strong dose of jealousy and envy" (hubo también una fuerte dosis de celos y envidia) (213).
78. "Lo que más nos sorprende en ella es su carácter, formado de energías, ajenas á la peruana, y su laboriosidad poco común" (Cáceres 190).
79. "La suerte la ha convertido en una luchadora, en una heroína del destino" (Cáceres 190).
80. "Este ave acostumbrada al alto vuelo de los Andes, fácilmente abandonó el Perú, para trasladarse á la República amiga, la Argentina" (Cáceres 190).
81. "Un diario importante de Arequipa"; "intrépido diario político" (Cáceres 191).
82. "La persecución fanática, á la venganza política y aún a la regional" (Cáceres 190).
83. It's difficult to gauge just how much of Staël's influence is present beyond both Cáceres's and Acosta's acknowledgement of her as an early prototype of the woman of letters. Charlotte Julia von Leyden's biography of Staël had appeared in German, English, and French in the fervor of the 1889 centenary of the French Revolution, and a glance at the Spanish-language database Hemeroteca Digital reveals that Staël remained a frequently cited figure throughout the nineteenth century.

## CHAPTER 4

"Para nosotros, defender y difundir la cultura es una misma cosa: aumentar en el mundo el humano tesoro de conciencia vigilante."

1. "Este paréntesis que la pluma nos impone en medio del trabajo" (Gorriti, *La tierra* 149).
2. "'Oasis' efímero de cofraternidad americana" (Batticuore, *El taller* 20).
3. The contextual links between educational reform and the ongoing project of independence points to the broader notion of education as a project for shaping the society of the future. As Linda K. Gerber puts it, "No dream

dies harder than the one that promises that we will save the world if we can only square things for the next generation" (218–19).

4. This belief in a narrative of progress as particular intellectual cultivation of the New World would figure in US conceptions of Latin America from the early days of the independence movement onward. Henry Clay's speech before the House of Representatives in favor of Spanish American independence would justify his position with a concept of shared American-ness. Clay argued that "these governments will be animated by an American feeling, and guided by an American policy" (83). Clay's position was by no means the obvious one in a nation that still remembered Spain as a crucial ally in its own War of Independence against Great Britain.

5. Julio N. Galofre's 1894 evaluation of Mercedes Cabello, which appeared in the Venezuelan journal *El Cojo Ilustrado*, used similarly mystical terms to refer to the writer's art, citing the manipulative force of "the magic hand of a sharp and harmonious narration" (la mano mágica de una narración nítida y armoniosa) (311–12).

6. "El sentimiento es el mejor conductor de esa electricidad" (Hostos, "La educación" 37).

7. "El sentimiento es facultad inestable, transitoria e inconstante en nuestro sexo; es facultad estable, permanente, constante, en la mujer" (Hostos, "La educación" 37).

8. "Daos madres que lo enseñen científicamente a sus hijos, y ellas os darán una patria que obedezca virilmente a la razón, que realice concienzudamente la libertad, que resuelva despacio el problema capital del Nuevo Mundo" (Hostos, "La educación" 38).

9. "No en la fuerza corruptora, no en el moral indiferente, no en el predominio exclusivo del bienestar individual"; "en la ciencia, en la moralidad y en el trabajo" (Hostos, "La educación" 38).

10. Peruvian poet Juan Francisco de Larriva gave the development of steam power a political turn in his poem "Al vapor," which José Domingo Cortés included in his 1871 collection *Parnaso peruano*, which was in fact published in Valparaíso, Chile. Francisco de Larriva likens steam power to other inventions such as the printing press, the compass, and the telegraph, and he blends the march of technological progress into a political march "against vacillating absolutism" (contra el absolutismo vacilante) (362) and the New World as a fitting location for industrial progress. While "the light comes to us from the Old World / And hatred and horror and oppression with it" (La luz nos viene del antiguo mundo / Y odio y horror y opresion con ella), New World steam power will, in the poet's vision, transform that dangerous light into something more socially healthful: "On the wings of steam, with swift flight, / It will turn out more pure than what first came" (En alas del vapor, con raudo vuelo, / Mas pura tornará de lo que vino) (363).

11. "Haced que todos sepan leer, i el sacerdote podrá estar presente en todas

partes" (Amunátegui 354); "El día en que todas las mujeres sepan leer, no quedarán ignorantes en el mundo" (374).

12. "La mujer es el mejor de los maestros" (Amunátegui 374).
13. "La regeneración religiosa sólo puede venir por ellas" (Arenal 102); "Podrán inocular con su fe en un mundo corroído por la duda, gangrenado por la indiferencia" (103).
14. This notion of America as asylum from the world might be called the converse emotion to the "desire for the world" that Mariano Siskind discusses with regard to *Minha Formaçáo* (Rio de Janeiro, 1900), the intellectual autobiography of Brazilian intellectual and diplomat Joaquim Nabuco. Siskind finds Nabuco, along with Jorge Luis Borges, as examples of a cosmopolitan sensibility that projects "a horizontal, universal, discursive field" that the New World can share with the Old (Siskind 6). What's particularly American is the necessity for "desire": the notion is that the real world of literary and cultural production is somewhere else and the cosmopolitan literary field is a bridge to that world. The American writer-educators that I will be examining feel connected to the Old World, too, but they fear rather than desire most of its products.
15. "No está llamada al púlpito, ni á la turbulencia de la tribuna sino á la enseñanza de la familia, la paz del hogar y el embellecimiento de la sociedad, por sus virtudes unidas á una educación esmerada" (Matto, *Elementos* 3).
16. "Elementos de retórica y poética, historia universal, lenguas vivas, caligrafía, dibujo, música y labores propias del sexo" (*Reglamento* 26).
17. "El seno del hogar doméstico, à la vez que la sociedad en general, reclaman el estudio de la retórica para la mujer, que es la señalada para embellecer uno y otra. Coma maestra, como amiga tambien, está llamada á instruir, aconsejar, y derramar los consuelos entre los que sufren y lloran. Madre, exhorta, manda, disuade; esposa, suplica, persuade y comparte; y en todos estos casos la elocuencia le prestará su apoyo dejándole el triunfo reservado á la mujer virtuosa é ilustrada" (Matto, *Elementos* 7).
18. In his 1924 essay "Las reivindicaciones feministas," the Peruvian essayist and political activist José Carlos Mariátegui would include feminism in his own cartography of Marxist revolution, arguing that "Feminism, as a pure idea, is essentially revolutionary" (El feminismo, como idea pura, es esencialmente revolucionario) (Mariátegui 232), while condemning the sentimental attachment to the traditional domestic sphere as "a defense of women's servitude" (una defensa de la servidumbre de la mujer) (234).
19. "Está dotada de mas sensibilidad, mas perspicacia y mayor belleza moral que el varón" (Matto, *Elementos* 68).
20. "¿Qué sirven mujeres / que en vez de cuidarnos / la ropa y la mesa, / nos hablen de Byron, / del Dante y Petrarca, / cual si esos señores, / lecciones les dieran / del modo que deben / zurcir calcetines / ó hacer un guisado?" (Matto, *Elementos* 60–61).

21. "Acercad a la mujer al santuario de la ciencia para que ella a su vez pueda acercar al hombre al altar de Dios" (Cabello, "Influencia" 40).
22. Vásquez's study focuses, among other topics, on the legacy of Bronson Alcott and Harriet Beecher Stowe, and he argues that an association between the feminine and the role of mediator gave women writers and readers leverage in Protestant New England, where narratives of religious conversion held a particular fascination. Vásquez sees "the convergence of religious and educational reform ideology" in the idea of the female writer (89), and he notes a similar synthesis in the narratives of Harriet Beecher Stowe, narratives in which "moral and intellectual enlightenment were inevitably linked" (241).
23. Fuentes Castro, a contemporary of the Lima group whose writings appeared in many of the same publications, described the press's social role in clearly educational terms as that of "correcting vices and reforming society" (corregir los vicios y reforma la sociedad) (*Notas* 80).
24. Pinto Vargas's biography of Cabello recounts Serrano's return to Lima in 1892 to promote a new hypothetical book of her own. According to the Lima press, she was planning to publish a twenty-volume, 10,000-page, "Historia de América" that would cover the entire region, country by country (633).
25. "Sacerdotes del deber"; "por América, y para América"; "*Enseñar al que no sabe*, son palabras del Evangelio, divinas y elocuentes frases que encierran en sí el pensamiento más grande y la felicidad de la humanidad" (Serrano, *La ley* 7).
26. Alcott's introduction to this volume, which purported to reproduce on the page classroom discussions on religious and philosophical topics, linked the origins of Christianity to the science of pedagogy. Calling the Gospels examples "of the true method of imparting instruction," Alcott identified Jesus Christ as an exemplary pedagogue: "His manner and style are models" (*Conversations* xxxiv–xxxv).
27. "Más tarde la humanidad buscará los nombres de los propagandistas, de los innovadores, de aquellos que han contribuido á la grande obra de la civilización y les consagrará eterno reconocimiento" (Serrano, *La ley* 14).
28. "Verdadero y sublime apóstol del progreso" (Serrano, *La ley* 11). Elsewhere Serrano praises Brooks as the inspiration of the development of the public school system in the United States while giving Mann credit for its development and summing up the Bostonian's character in a phrase that could have been pulled from Samuel Smiles: "the most dignified and concrete example of what the love of work and the desire for usefulness can do" (el ejemplo mas digno y mas palpable, de lo que puede el amor al trabajo y el deseo de ser útil) (100–101).
29. "El arma omnipotente contra el oscurantismo" (Serrano, *La ley* 28).
30. "Corrección de estilo para acostumbrar su oido á la pureza del idioma; buena forma, naturalidad en las imágenes, nada de exajerados cuadros que exalten

la infantil imaginación y sobre todo, en las anecdotas, cuentos e historietas, argumentos y desenlaces de fácil comprensión" (Serrano, *La ley* 33).

31. "Emplear sucesivamente el encanto del relato con el ejemplo de los vicios y defectos, el premio ó castigo de ellos, interesando la imaginacion del niño y apelando y haciendo vibrar las fibras de sus sentimientos, la sensibilidad y buen corazón" (Serrano, *La ley* 33).

32. "Que siembran la perturbación"; "sentimientos nobles" (Serrano, *La ley* 35).

33. Ross raises this question as part of the librarian's dilemma when addressing the influence of books and writers on readers: "Is the reader engaged in a cognitive activity of skill building? Or is the reader duped, dumbed down, tranquilized or deceived?" (638). Debates over the educational utility of reading tend to swing back and forth, as Serrano's arguments do, between reader- and writer-centered perspectives, according to the most pressing argumentative need.

34. "De un texto literario implica asfixiar la multivariedad que el mismo ofrece, y conduce al receptor/multiplicador a manipular una única línea de sentido" (Díaz Rönner 22).

35. "Belleza en el orden moral"; "el sacrificio de la propia tranquilidad ó de la propia existencia, en beneficio de los demás o de la patria" (González de Fanning, *Lecciones* 49).

36. "Debe enseñarse á los niños á apreciarla por medio de lecturas apropiadas, y, más aùn [sic], por medio de ejemplos prácticos" (González de Fanning, *Lecciones* 49).

37. "Tan claras y bien explicadas las materias, que el menos inteligent ó más niño podía discutirlas y analizarlas" (Serrano, *La ley* 31–32).

38. "El profesor conversaba extensamente en su obra, hacia reflexiones y apreciaciones y ponia ejemplow, que cautivaron el párvulo y le dieron placer por el aprendizaje" (Serrano, *La ley* 31–32).

39. "Es de aquellos que pudiera decirse humanos, pues comprende los sentimientos del corazón humano así lata en las nevadas estepas de la Siberia ó en las ardientes regiones de los trópicos" (González de Fanning, *Educación* 78).

40. "Muy mal dotado estará el niño ó muy viciada será la educación doméstica que haya recibido, si al leer *Corazón* no se siente inclinado á imitar los bellos ejemplos que este cinematógrafo moral va presentando a la vista, especialmente si tiene una madre discreta y cuidadosa que, evitando la lectura atropellada e inconsciente, fije su atención en cada rasgo saliento y se lo recuerde cuando la oportunidad lo requiere" (González de Fanning, *Educación* 80).

41. "Cada capítulo tiene su acción y su enseñanza propias; son como perlas engarzadas que se juntan sin tocarse y sin confundirse, realizando cada una la nítida belleza de sus vecinas" (González de Fanning, *Educación* 79).

42. "Medio de grabar en los corazones de los niños el sentimiento de cofraternidad nacional" (González de Fanning, *Educación* 79).

43. "La era de la integración nacional"; "no es un chabacano nacionalismo, sino un patriotismo neto, limpio, cordial" (Bermúdez xxvii).
44. "Un lectorcito mexicano—en forma inconsciente tal vez—pueda leer Durango donde dice Turin, Distrito Federal donde se escribe Roma" (Bermúdez xvii).
45. "En cada país, por que el que más y el que menos todos tienen sus héroes y sus luchas, su norte laborioso su alegre sur, sus hermosas playas, sus ajetreados puertos y su señorial capital" (Bermúdez xxvii).
46. "Es una reducción de la sociedad algo así como una preparación microscópica, donde el observador puede analizar á su sabor los resortes del alma" (Munilla, *El Imparcial* 3).
47. "El suave y tierno escritor de los niños, de los obreros, de las almas cándidas, el que tenía por tintero un corazón y por pluma una rama de olivo" (*El Imparcial* 8).
48. As recently as 2010, the Galician-born Spanish writer José María Merino would take the publication of a new Spanish edition of *Corazón* to praise De Amicis for sublimating, a bare ten years after Italian unification, "all the aspects, that I dare to call utopian, of the historical optimism corresponding to the political moment that the country was living and to the author's own ideology" (todas las facetas, que me atrevo a llamar utópicas, del optimismo histórico correspondiente al momento político que el país estaba viviendo y a la propia ideología del autor) (40). What Merino stresses, writing from a Spanish moment in which the question of Catalan independence had come to be seen by some as an existential threat to the Spanish state, is De Amicis's ability to fashion a patriotism that manages to transcend national chauvinism: "a nation that has as its goal that its human components should be citizens fraternal and equal in rights" (una nación que tiene como finalidad que sus componentes humanos sean ciudadanos fraternos e iguales en derechos) (40).
49. "No logran su objeto los padres que compran libros y los entregan a los niños que principiando la lectura con la vehemencia propia de su edad la abanondan luego con la inconstancia natural de la misma. Es preciso enseñarles á comprender, á jugar, á comparar acertadamente; solo así se consigue que asimilen y seleccionen lo útil, lo bueno y lo bello; lo demás es arrojar la semilla á merced del viento que la arrastra, a arremolina y la esteriliza" (González de Fanning, *Lecciones* 80).
50. "Fomenta el amor al trabajo y á la vida arreglada; respeto al deber; honradez y exactitud"; "la ociosidad que es la causa más frecuente de los vicios" (González de Fanning, *Lecciones* 7).
51. González de Fanning's desire to adapt foreign materials for American students was not at all unusual in her historical context. The Chilean poet Marín del Solar—best known for her elegy of Diego de Portales—sketched out her thoughts on education in a document believed to have been written

ca. 1840, but not published until Miguel Luis Mariátegui included it in his 1892 study *La alborada poética en Chile*. Like González de Fanning, Marín de Solar gives advice on useful texts. She recommends Claude Fleury's *Catecismo histórico*, first published in French but widely available in Spanish by the end of the eighteenth century along with anecdotes from the Old and New Testament. The key component to her approach is the memorization and communication of a story—that the young woman should learn to narrate in her own words (Marín de Solar 509–10). In his catechism Fleury offers his own justification for the use of anecdote, arguing that "everyone is capable of understanding and of retaining a story" (Todo el mundo es capaz de entender, y de retener en sí una historia) (Fleury 34–35), and citing the frequent use of parables in the Gospels as proof of narrative's divine imprimatur as a pedagogical tool) (42–43).

52. Textbook emphasis on American geography also made value judgments that tended to favor rural life over city life, given the predominantly rural nature of US society (Elson 25). Elson's survey of US textbooks also detects a widespread tendency to evaluate New World nature as superior: "European scenery is compared with American in every book, much to the advantage of American" (36). On the other hand, some Spanish American commentators such as Sarmiento and Juana Manso stressed the difficulties posed by American nature. In her novel *La familia del Comendador*, first published in 1854, Manso describes the isolating effects of undeveloped natural spaces as a condition common to both Spanish America and Brazil, and thus a key element of regional identity (*La familia* 127).

53. "Todo lo que quieran saber les vamos a decir, y de modo que lo entiendan bien, con palabras claras y con láminas finas" (Martí, *La Edad* 4).

54. "Con los caballeros de mañana, y con las madres de mañana" (Martí, *La Edad* 4); "niño de América" (Martí 5).

55. Armando García emphasizes the importance of "freedom and resistance" among those civil virtues promoted by *La Edad de Oro* and also notes its curious longevity as a pedagogical text, a periodical frozen in time as a book: "Over a hundred years later it remains a teaching tool in elementary schools throughout Spanish-speaking Latin America" (19).

56. Patricia Clancy counts fifty-three "editions or reprints" of Leprince's *Almacén* during the nineteenth century and notes that these reprints often contained "various modifications to the historical, geographical and religious content" (282). Its literary reach was so large in part because it quickly became a global project that "was very soon translated into all of the European languages, including Russian, Swedish, and Greek" (Clancy 282).

57. Leprince de Beaumont's experience echoes a number of other educational responses to book scarcity complicated by language and travel (or exile). The Venezuelan reformer Simón Rodríguez translated Chateaubriand's *Atala* into Spanish in 1805 in order to give the French students at his Spanish-language

academy a readable narrative in the target language. The famed educational experiments of the exiled French revolutionary schoolteacher Joseph Jacototo (1770–1840) also took book scarcity as a point of departure. Faced with a classroom full of Flemish-speaking students and few resources, he developed a reading comprehension approach in which students were challenged to "read" *Télémaque* in French by responding to basic, but increasingly complicated questions, whose answers could be found in the text.

58. "Una gran luchadora por los derechos de la mujer" (Marrero 177).
59. "¿Para qué sirve este libro en la mano?" (Serrano, *Almacén* 19).
60. "Debe de reprimir sus caprichos, y conformarse con la voluntad de sus padres ó maestros" (Serrano, *Almacén* 134); "La mejor prenda de una jóven es la moderación y la sencillez" (289).
61. "La Independencia se hizo en este país por los blancos y para los blancos" (Acosta, *Conversaciones* 112–13)
62. "Las gentes del pueblo eran mucho más felices en tiempos de los españoles"; "simulacros de escuelas"; "Como en los campos jamás vuelvan á ver un libro ni un papel ¿qué bien es que se les hace obligándolos a que aprendan lo que jamáss han de practicar" (Acosta, *Conversaciones* 112–13).
63. "Todo el mundo, hasta los seres más estúpidos, tienen un german dentro de sí" (Acosta, *Conversaciones* 168).
64. "Las malas costumbres, los malos hábitos, los vicios y errores del pueblo" (Acosta, *Conversaciones* 272–73).
65. "Un alimento mental propio para sus cortas y poco maduras facultades" (Acosta, *Conversaciones* 275); "una educación que le proporcione resignación y consuelo" (276).
66. "La parte enteramente blanca de la población, que ha heredado la civilización de sus antepasados"; "la democracia completa es muy difícil en Colombia" (Acosta, *Conversaciones* 275).
67. Ballesteros Rosas compares Acosta's belief in the need to recover a shared Hispanic heritage to that of Uruguayan intellectual José Enrique Rodó, who posited a Latin American identity, symbolized by Ariel, as a counterpoint to the materialistic North American colossus he marked as Caliban (300). She also points out the cosmopolitanism of Acosta's global feminism, particularly in her activities as a professional magazine editor. Along with her own essays on female emancipation, she published translations of texts by Dinah Maria Mulock Craik and Paul Leroy-Beaulieu (297).
68. "Cada una de las cajas que contiene un juego de matrices de un mismo tipo con que trabaja una linotipia" (Serrano, *Almacén*).
69. Sandlin, O'Malley, and Burdick have pointed out the degree to which teaching functions as a social norm and is shaped by shared assumptions: "Our very frameworks for understanding what pedagogy *is* and *looks like / feels like* extend from our own cultural constructs of what counts as teaching and learning in an institutional setting" ("Mapping" 364).

70. Vásquez's formulation puts the gendered locus of reform in the domestic sphere—"education is a way to revise domesticity" (247)—while positing this domestic revision as a foothold for broad social change.
71. "Sobre la base de una nacionalidad en gran medida común a todos ellos" (Goldgel, *Cuando* 28).

## CHAPTER 5

1. Hipólito Escolar has pointed out that this interdependence between newspapers and book publishers was an essential condition of the Spanish literary scene, too. He argues that this structural phenomenon affected content as writers whose books appeared in newspaper installments viewed themselves less as timeless literary artists and sought "communication with the public, entertaining it and imbuing it with liberal and social ideals, which they considered modern, at the same time that they obtained good economic benefits" (comunicación con el público, entreniéndole e imbuyéndole ideas liberales y sociales, que consideraban modernas, al tiempo que obtenían buenos beneficios económicos) (224–25). The newspaper, by this reckoning, provides the book author with a forum in which economic gain and political altruism need not conflict.
2. Rocío del Águila stresses the subversive nature that gender lends to the project of social networking and professionalization. Speaking of Gorriti, Matto, and their contemporaries, she argues that "they cannot be accused of not taking an active interest in the sociological situation of the woman, because, as we have seen, the changes that they propose through their participation and works break the traditional conception of power" (no se les debe acusar de no interesarse activamente en la situación sociológica de la mujer, porque como se ha visto, los cambios que proponen a través de su participación y obras quiebran la concepción tradicional del poder) (55).
3. Here I am to some degree echoing Francesca Denegri's comment about *El Correo del Perú*, a contemporaneous publication she describes as dedicating more or less fifty percent to advertising and fifty percent to "the production of a national literature, in which women stood out" (la producción de una literatura nacional, en la cual las mujeres destacaban) (153–54).
4. "Una versión feminizada del naturalismo canónico" (Peluffo, *Lagrimas* 206).
5. "Tomada, mojor que del espontáneo Cervantes, de los místicos, escritores catizos por excelencia" (Pardo Bazán, *La cuestión* 170).
6. "Un des plus monstruex jargond de la langue française" (Zola, *Les romanciers* 374); "moins d'art et plus de solidité" (376).
7. "La imitación de una afectación" (Valera, "Folletín" 1226).
8. "El verdadero naturalismo"; "la sencilléz, el candor, la total carencia de artificio de quien habla ó escribe de buena fe, porque tiene algo que decir" (Valera, "Folletín" 1226).
9. "Los Padres escribían, por lo común, á fin de que los entendiesen los peque-

ñuelos, las mujeres ignorantes y la gente vulgar, y á fin de enseñar algo que juzgaban de mayor provecho para la salud de las almas. Así es que miraban más al fondo que á la forma de que decían, y eran, y no podían menos de ser, muy naturales" (Valera, "Folletín" 1226).

10. See Peluffo, "Emilia," for an in-depth reading of Pardo Bazán's prologue to *Lucecitas*. Peluffo focuses on the context from which Pardo Bazán was writing as a way of explaining what she refers to as the Spanish author's exercise in "the art of writing ambiguous prologues" (el arte de escribir prólogos ambiguos) ("Emilia" 66). Peluffo argues that while contemporary readers might take the modesty of González de Fanning's vision of female authorship with a dose of irony, such a reading was not possible for Pardo Bazán "who was looking for allies in the other continent against an elitist and masculine vision of the republic of letters" (que busca en el otro continente aliadas contra una visión elitista y masculinizante de la república de las letras) (69).

11. "Guardamos el comunismo y la tacañería para las novelas" (Pardo Bazán, *La cuestión* 174). Sarmiento had addressed Spanish America's market potential decades earlier in his 1843 address to the Facultad de Humanidades. After emphasizing the paucity of important texts originating in Spain by citing Larra—"*let us translate and cry*" (*lloremos y traduzcamos*) (*Ortografía* 12)—he points out that an entire expatriate publishing industry had sprung up in Paris, London, Burgundy, and other European cities to fulfill this excess demand (*Ortografía* 45).

12. William DeForest's well-known editorial "The Great American Novel" had made a similar argument on the pages of *The Nation* in 1868. Like Pardo Bazán, DeForest identifies a culture of piracy as an essential condition of the New World literary landscape. While Pardo Bazán worries about European authors who do not receive compensation for their labor, DeForest views the problem from the perspective of the New World, where "the American author is undersold in his own market by the stolen brain-labor of other countries" ("The Great" 28–29). Part of the problem is cultural, too, as "The American reader must have his book cheap" and thus "To charge the English price for a good novel might provoke an indignation meeting, if not a riot" (29).

13. "La novela no se considera allí pasatiempo ni mero deleite estética, sino una institución, el quinto poder del Estado"; "las novelas son los sermones de la época actual" (Pardo Bazán, *La cuestión* 158).

14. "Propósito moral y docente, empeño de corregir y convertir, afán de salvar al lector" (Pardo Bazán, *La cuestión* 159).

15. "Detiene su escalpelo"; "los últimos pliegues del alma" (Pardo Bazán, *La cuestión* 159).

16. "La vie passionnelle et intellectuelle" (Zola, *Le roman* 2).

17. "L'observation montre, l'experience instruit" (Zola, *Le roman* 11); "En un

mot, nous devons óperer sur les caractères, sur les passions, sur les faits humains et sociaux, comme le chimiste et le physicien opèrant sur les corps bruts, comme le phsiologiste opère sur les corpts vivants" (16).
18. "Nous sommes, en un mot, des moralistes expérimentateurs, montrant par l'experience de quelle façon se comporte une passion dans un milieu social" (Zola, *Le roman* 24).
19. "Tiene que ser la fotografía que estereotipe los vicios y las virtudes de un pueblo, con la consiguiente moraleja correctiva para aquellos y el homenaje de admiración para estas" (Matto, *Aves* 1). Marcel Velázquez Castro identifies the prologue to *Aves sin nido* as "a crucial text because it marks a new period in the development of the Peruvian novel: the consciousness of the novelistic genre in our literary tradition" (es un texto crucial porque marca un nuevo periodo en el devenir de la novela peruana: la conciencia del género novelístico en nuestra tradición literaria) (55).
20. "En sus hojas contine muchas veces el secreto de la reforma de algunos tipos, cuando no su extinción" (Matto, *Aves* 1). Thomas Ward has referred to Matto's synthesis of morality and naturalism as "pedagogical naturalism" (naturalismo pedagógico), which he judges to be "an oximoron" (un oxímoron) (99).
21. "El novelista observador que, llevando el correctivo en los puntos de su pluma, penetra los misterios de la vida, y discurre ante la multitud ese denso velo que cubre los ojos de los moradores ciegos y fanatizados a un mismo tiempo" (Matto, *Índole* 250).
22. "Dulces suspiros de brisa y blancos rayos de luna"; "si hallan el correctivo condimentado con morfina, con ajinjo y con todos aquellos amargos repugnantes para las naturalezas perfectas, no sólo nos leen, nos devoran" (Matto, *Herencia* 24).
23. "Una distribucion mas general i justa de recompensas y castigos" (Gómez Hermosilla 316).
24. "Se encaminan mas directamente al Corazon, para hacerle amar lo que es perfecto y detestar lo defectuoso" (Gómez Hermosilla 321).
25. "En los países, como el nuestro, la LITERATURA se halla en su cuna" (Matto, *Aves* 1).
26. "De mejorar la condición de los pueblos chicos del Perú"; "y aun cuando no fuese otra cosa que la simple conmiseración, la autora de estas páginas habrá conseguido su propósito" (Matto, *Aves* 2).
27. "Señalando puntos de no escasa importancia para los progresos nacionales; y *haciendo*, a la vez, literatura peruana" (Matto, *Aves* 2).
28. "Tendrían su cantor, su novelista o su historiador que los inmortalizase con la lira o la pluma, pero que, en lo apartado de mi patria, apenas alcanzan el descolorido lápiz de una hermana" (Matto, *Aves* 2).
29. "¿Por qué el novelista no ha de imitar al médico que busca y estudia los medios que pueden evitar ciertas enfermedades?" (Cabello, *Sacrificio* 81).

30. "Su parte más grosera, más baja y ruin para mostrarla, como lo único real y verdadero" (Cabello, *Sacrificio* 81).
31. "¿Y por qué olvidar que en el alma humana hay un lado noble, elevado, bello, que es el que el novelista debe estudiar, debe estimular, y mostrar como el único medio de reformar las costumbres?" (Cabello, *Sacrificio* 81).
32. "Francamente, sepa usted, señorita, que la costumbre es ley, y que nadie nos sacará de nuestras costumbres" (Matto, *Aves* 16).
33. "Será necesario pues en adelante dividir á los novelistas en dos categorías, colocando á un lado á los que, como decía Cervantes, escriben papeles para entretener doncellas, y á los que pueden hacer de la novela un medio de investigación y de estudio, en que el arte preste un poderoso concurso á las ciencias que miran al hombre, desligándolo de añejas tradiciones y absurdas preocupaciones" (Cabello, *Blanca* vii).
34. Hipólito Escolar notes that in nineteenth-century Spain the growing economic importance of the female reader and subscriber was accompanied by cultural resistance from male figures of authority. He cites an article by "Cayetano del Rosell, who would become director of the National Library" (Cayetando del Rosell, que llegaría a ser director de la Biblioteca Nacional) which focused on "an impertinent female reader" (una lectora impertinente) (Escolar, *Historia* 223). He also argues that worries about the motives of male writers and their relationships with readers left an opening to female novelists, who were seen as less of a threat (223).
35. "En tanto el romanticismo ha dañado los corazones por exceso de ficción e idealismo, la escuela naturalista los ha dañado por carencia de ideales, por atrofía del sentimiento y supresión completa del ser moral" (Cabello, *La novela* 21).
36. "Un reflejo de la francesa"; "si ni aun en la patria de Monroe, Miss Stowe y Longfellow, han alcanzado este beneficio" (Cabello, *La novela* 31).
37. "Será la que innove el naturalismo, convirtiéndolo en el realismo psicológico y filosófico" (Cabello, *La novela* 31).
38. "Carecen de ese algo indefinible, inexplicable, que hace palpitar las páginas del libro, como si los animara el alma" (Cabello, *La novela* 32).
39. Decades before Sarmiento had argued that Spain and Spanish America alike were satellites in literary orbit of France, enthralled by popular novels published in newspapers and reprinted in Spanish (*Ortografía* 40), and that Spain had become a toothless colonial power in cultural as well as political terms (38).
40. "Es como buscar la idea de una facultad sin objeto, de un principio sin consecuencia, de una causa sin efecto" (Cabello, *La novela* 35).
41. "sería como decir la ciencia por la ciencia, negando su influencia en todos los conocimientos que tienden a estudiar y curar las dolencias de la humanidad" (Cabello, *La novela* 35).

42. "El placer no es un fin; y dado que lo fuese, de allí nacerá una acción benéfica o maléfica para nuestro espíritu" (Cabello, *La novela* 35).
43. David S. Reynolds cites *Uncle Tom's Cabin* as a contributor to the freeing of the serfs in Russia in 1861 (174) and as a spur to antislavery movements in Cuba and Brazil in the decades following (176).
44. Surwillo notes that even in a climate in which translated novels were generally popular, *Uncle Tom's Cabin* managed to set a record in 1853, as it "appeared in more editions in a single year than any other imported novel before in that century" (769).
45. See Mackay for more on the circulation and influence of *Uncle Tom's Cabin* in Russia.
46. The prologue to an 1853 edition published in Mexico City by Vicente Segura Argüelles is particularly telling. Criticizing the book for presenting an unrealistically violent picture of slavery, its author explains that it has been necessary to provide "some notes in those places where it seems to us that the author has strayed from the truth" (algunos notas en aquellos lugares que nos parezca se ha desviado la autora de la verdad) (Stowe, *La cabaña* vii). While this may seem an extreme example, the repeated charge of exaggeration would prompt Stowe to publish *A Key to Uncle Tom's Cabin* to demonstrate the veracity of her sources and point out that in many cases verisimilitude had required her to make her novel *less* violent than the source materials (*The Key* 1).
47. "Fué arma más poderosa para la causa de la libertad de los negros que todos los discursos doctrinales pronunciados en este sentido en el Congreso de Washington y en los *meetings* abolicionistas" (Cueto 630).
48. "Cierta gallarda confianza en el futuro de la humanidad" (Valera, "Novela-Programa" 38).
49. "Hay ahí cierta emulación, cierta petulancia juvenil, que son útiles, porque persuaden á muchos de que América logrará lo que Europa no ha logrado; resolverá problemas que aquí tenemos por irresolubles, y realizará ideales que nosotros, ya cansados, agotados y viejos, abandonamos por irrealizables y quiméricas" (Valera, "Novela-Programa" 38).
50. "La poesía lírica de ahí inculca en sus mejores obras que querer es poder" (Valera, "Novela-Programa" 39).
51. "La primera novela, verdaderamente nacional, con el sabor de la tierruca" (Ariel 1255). Stowe's role as a touchstone for reviewers was by any measure hemispheric. Exiled Cuban intellectual José Martí cited Stowe in his 1895 review of US novelist Helen Hunt Jackson's *Ramona*. Martí, who had published a Spanish-language translation of Jackson's novel in New York in 1887, notes that public opinion in the United States considers it "without the weaknesses of Beecher [Stowe]'s book, another *Cabin*" (sin las flaquezas del libre de la Beecher, otra *Cabaña*) (1). Written from New York City,

Martí's review appeared in a December 1895 issue of *La Opinión*, published in Asunción, Paraguay.
52. "Ese fin, altamente humanitario y filosófico que persiguió la autora de la *Cabaña del Tío Tom* allá en la patria de Francklin" (Ariel 1255).
53. Just as Ariel seems to be praising Matto for going beyond the confines of Lima's Creole society in her pursuit of Peruvian reality, DeForest had praised *Uncle Tom's Cabin* as the closest approximation to "the Great American Novel" because it extended its literary gaze beyond the confines of the author's native New England. It therefore contained "national breadth" as well as "truthful outlining of character, natural speaking, and plenty of strong feeling" ("The Great" 28).
54. "Es esta indubnlemente la época de la mujer emancipada de hecho, en los dominios del pensamiento, y el Perú no podía evadirse de la imposición del siglo" (Ariel 1255).
55. "300.000 ejemplares, que se agotaron en pocos días" (Acosta, *La mujer* 172–73).
56. Muñoz makes the morally unassailable nature of Stowe's achievement a cornerstone of her argument. If conventional wisdom holds that learning opposes religion or at least a scholar's personal religious sentiment, what about Stowe, whose social effect was "extremely meritorious and Christian?" (meritísima y cristiana) (Muñoz, "De la mujer" 41).
57. "Cristianizar no sólo al 'Otro,' sino a los propios cristianos, con el fin de causar misericordia en ellos mismos" (Schmidt-Welle 135).
58. "La contradicción entre la reivindicación de los 'Otros' y la supuesta necesidad de la modernización a expensas de la cultura de ellos" (Schmidt-Welle 144).
59. Geraldine Scanlon has noted that Pardo Bazán's status as an important female writer provoked a similar logical shift in the debate over naturalism. Her relative comfort with the new movement and adoption of naturalist techniques in her own fiction "gave a dimension of sexual politics to the literary controversy" (dio una dimensión de política sexual a la polémica literaria) (131).
60. "Porque la misión de la mujer es fecundar y sentir, entre tanto que el destino del hombre es pensar y examinar" (Neira de Mosquera 188).
61. "La inteligencia no escoge sexos. La república literaria no se fija en el autor, sino en la obra" (Neira de Mosquera 188).
62. "Como hay el hombre aptitudes para las investigaciones científicas, hay extraordinaria idoneidad en la mujer para entregarse á las estéticas lucubraciones del arte" (Puga 201).
63. "Encontrar el poema de la existencia en la vida afectiva enlazada á la vida intelectual" (Gimeno de Flaquer 242).
64. "Las mujeres que, sin énfasis ni pedantería, cultivan su entendimiento y

ayudan, en las letras ó en las artes, á la civilización general y al lustre de la patria" (Cueto 637).
65. "Cuando el escribir sea la costumbre de muchas y no el privilegio de unas pocas, serán también más raras la pedantería y presunción"; "'Sólo sé que no sé nada,' ha dicho el sabio, y en verdad que la vanidad y petulancia parecen ser atributos exclusivos de la ignorancia" (Gónzalez de Fanning, *Lucecitas* 246).
66. "Cierta sumisión y dulzura que delatan la adaptación del espíritu femenino al molde en que lo han vaciado tantos siglos de sujeción moral y material" (Pardo Bazán,"Prólogo" vii).
67. "Una mujer útil en el más amplio sentido de la palabra"; "Las letras constituyen su descanso, su ameno solaz—sola nobilísimo, de nunca ponderada eficacia y virtud para curar los dolores del alma" (Pardo Bazán, "Prólogo" vii).
68. "Servían para confirmar el carácter 'moral' de la obra de Fanning" (Peluffo, "Emilia" 69).
69. "Establecer una polarización entre la proyección estética y el sustrato ideológico de la obra" (Peluffo, "Emilia" 67). Elsewhere Peluffo has shown how the prologue can be read more charitably as an attempt to contextualize González de Fanning's relatively timid vision of female emancipation within a larger spectrum, "that there are different ideological positions within the process of cultural democratization" (que ha diferentes posiciones ideológicas dentro del proceso de la democratización cultural) (*Lágrimas* 276).
70. "No escapó jamás al panfleto"; "Pero los personajes la vencieron. Como en obra de Priandello: la vencieron" (Tamayo Vargas 70).
71. "Lleno de enseñanzas" (Tamayo Vargas 148); "el tono mitad romántico, mitad pedagógico"; "hondas raíces hasta nuestro tiempo" (95).
72. The critique of realism and realist readers by the narrator of Herman Melville's *The Confidence-Man* (1857) argues that it is absurd that a reader who ostensibly seeks artistic escape from reality "should yet demand of him who is to divert his attention from it, that he should be true to that dullness" (207).
73. Denegri has noted, "It is not until the War of the Pacific, with González Prada and Clorinda Matto, that we find reference to Indians as 'Peruvians'" (no es sino hasta la Guerra del Pacífico, con González Prada y Clorinda Matto, que encontramos referencias a los indios como "peruanos") (Denegri 76).
74. "Los rusos exigen de la novela más que nosotros"; "Solicitan que el novelista sea el profeta, vale, de un porvenir mejor" (Pardo Bazán, *La revolución* 265–66).
75. "La novela seria y honda muere aquí sin eco" (Pardo Bazán, *La revolución* 276–77).

76. "El público hace al escritor, y no el escritor al público" (Fuentes Castro, "Literatura" xxxii).
77. "Zola al lado de Tolstoy es un novelista que adolece de miopía intelectual" (Cabello, *El conde* 16). Cabello goes to some metaphoric lengths to express her opinion of Zola as superficial in comparison to his Russian contemporary. She describes Tolstoy as a moral scientist, a kind of Pasteur—"Tolstoy, like the *bacteriologist*, discovers families and worlds unknown to the masses" (Tolstoy á semejanza del *bacteriologista*, descubre familias y mundos desconocidos por el vulgo) (Cabello, *El conde* 17)—and finds Zola, in contrast, to suffer from "the confusion of an artist who, being able to photograph souls, is content to photograph bodies" (la equivocación del artista que pudiendo fotografiar almas se contenta con fotografiar cuerpos) (19).
78. "Tolstoy filósofo es menos filósofo que Tolstoy novelista" (Cabello, *El conde* 8). In Cabello's formulation religious and literary goals cannot completely coexist. Speaking again of a Tolstoy who is divided between offices, she maintains that "the apostle diminishes the novelist and the mystic [diminishes] the thinker" (el apóstal empequeñece al novelista y el místico al pensador) (4).
79. "Como se condensan en la atmósfera los fluidos eléctricos, para luego desatarse en horrible tempestad" (Cabello, *El conde* 25–26).
80. "La causa de su esclavitud no reside en ella misma sino en las pasiones concupiscentes del hombre" (Cabello, *El conde* 11–12).
81. "El hombre de hoy es la obra del hombre de ayer, y el hombre de mañana será la obra del hombre de hoy" (Cabello, *El conde* 47–48).
82. "Este mundo en que se alimenta nuestro espíritu, podemos formarla y edificarla a nuesto albedrío" (Cabello, *El conde* 60).
83. "Elevando con admirable tino el sentimiento del bien hasta la altura en que se puede ser comprendido por cualquiera y ejercer fácilmente su saludable influencia en todas las clases sociales" (Rev. 10).
84. Henry James responded to Besant's idealistic vision of the novelist's office with a demand for specifics—finding "morality" too vague a term—and positing a simpler set of rules, that "No good novel will ever proceed from a superficial mind" (83). On the subject of the works themselves, James proves equally elegant (and cutting), arguing the necessity "that it be interesting" is the genre's first and last aesthetic principle (Besant and James 84). On the other hand, even Edgerton's critique of the sentiments expressed in *What Is Art?* acknowledges the difficulty of parsing out boundaries between art and ethics and calls the tradition of didactic narration "as old as literature itself" ("The Critical" 160).
85. Gustavo Adolfo Otero names Mexico and Bolivia as nations that suffered similarly from "the excess of optimism in the markets and a failed calculation of production and consumption" (el exceso de optimismo en los mercados y el cálculo fallido de la producción y el consumo) (141).

86. "Entre el 'deseo civilizador' y la realidad de su ejecución podermos entender la paradoja de nuestra modernidad" (Marín Colorado 273).
87. "La sincera convicción de haber cumplido esctríctamente con nuestro deber" (Acosta, *Una holandesa* 270).
88. Carolina Alzate points out Acosta's tendency to mingle questions of gender identity and national identity—"*la patria*" and "*la mujer*" (111). In this sense her work could be said to transcend the divide between the tropes of gender emancipation and Creole identity outlined by Pratt.
89. "Los acontecimientos políticos nos han fatigado, y nos fatigarán aún mas las profundas y sombrías meditaciones impropias de un país que se halla en la actividad y con todos los movimientos de la niñez" (Seguín 389).
90. "En el Perú todos somos cubanos del corazón" (Cabello, *Sacrificio* 94). Tamayo Vargas declares that Cabello should be viewed as "Americanist," and he praises her ability to discern "this need to form a 'new world,' apart from the disordered appetites of a Europe in eternal struggle, a poor Europe, that looked with astonished eyes at the productive magnificence of the other continents" (Esta necesidad de formar un "mundo nuevo," ajeno a los apetitos desordenados de una Europa en eterna pugna, de una Europa pobre, que mira con ojos asombrados la magnificencia productora de los otros continentes) (Tamayo Vargas 56).
91. "Sin método, sin discernimiento"; "un caos de principios mal fundados" (Cabello, *El conspirador* 94).
92. "En pugna con vicios que gozan del privilegio de arraigados" (Matto, *Aves* 97).
93. "La condición esencial del arte es la moralidad" (Mendiola 61); "la misión del arte es educar" (60–61).

## CONCLUSION

1. It is possible to label the 1895 coup, which Matto opposed, as an at least somewhat progressive event, given the electoral and social reforms that the Piérola regime managed to enact and that were enacted by subsequent elected governments (see Dobyns and Doughty 206–07, 222–23).
2. "La educación moral debe recibirse toda la vida" (García y García, *Tendencias* 69–70).

# BIBLIOGRAPHY

Acosta de Samper, Soledad. *Biografías de hombres ilustres ó notables, Relativas á la época del Descubrimiento, Conquista y Colonización de la parte de América denominada actualmente EE. UU. de Colombia.* Bogota: Imprenta de "La Luz," 1883.

———. *Conversaciones y lecturas familiares sobre historia, biografía, crítica, literatura, ciencias y conocimientos útiles.* Paris: Garnier Hermanos, 1896.

———. *La mujer en la sociedad moderna.* Paris: Garnier Hermanos, 1895.

———. *Una holandesa en América.* 1888. Ed. Catharina Vallejo. La Habana/Bogotá: Fondo Editorial Casa de las Américas/Universidad de los Andes, 2006.

Acree, William Garrett, Jr. *Everyday Reading: Print Culture and Collective Identity in the Río de la Plata, 1780–1910.* Nashville: Vanderbilt UP, 2011.

Adams, Henry. *The Education of Henry Adams.* Boston: Massachusetts Historical Society, 2007.

Águila, Rocío del. "(A)filiaciones femeninas: Gorriti y la genealogía de la escritura en Lima." *Decimonónica* 10.1 (2013): 45–63.

Aguirrea, Beatriz E. "La escritura y la búsqueda de la subjetividad femenina. Tres protagonistas de Soledad Acosta de Samper." *Estudios de Literatura Colombiana* 21 (Jul.–Dec. 2007): 15–34. Web. Dialnet. 29 Dec. 2014.

Alamos González, Bernicio. "Enseñanza superior de la mujer." *Veladas literarias de Lima 1876–1877.* Vol. 1. Gorriti. 347–85.

Alcott, Bronson. *Conversations with Children on the Gospels.* Conducted and edited by A. Bronson Alcott. Vol. 1. Boston: James Munroe, 1836.

———. *Notes of Conversations, 1848–1875.* Ed. Karen English. Madison, NJ: Fairleigh Dickinson UP, 2007.

Allen, James Sloane. "Tolstoy's Prophecy: 'What Is Art?' Today." *New Criterion* 17.4 (Dec. 1998). Web. EBSCOhost. 9 Mar. 2012.

Alonso, Carlos. *The Burden of Modernity: The Rhetoric of Cultural Discourse in Spanish America.* New York: Oxford UP, 1998.

Altamirano, Carlos, and Beatriz Sarlo. "The Autodidact and the Learning

Machine." Ed. Tulio Halperín Donghit et al. Berkeley: U of California P, 1994. 156–68.

Alzate, Carolina. "El *Diario íntimo* de Soledad Acosta de Samper: Configuración de una voz autorial femenina en el siglo XIX." *Revista de Critica Literaria Latinoamericana* 31.62 (2005): 109–23. Web. JSTOR. 29 Dec. 2014.

Amunátegui, Miguel Luis, and Gregorio Víctor Amunátegui. *De la instrucción primaria en Chile; lo que es, lo que debería ser.* Santiago: Imprenta del Ferrocarril, 1856.

"Aphorisms on Teaching History." *American Journal of Education* 8.20 (Mar. 1860): 101–110. Web. Google Books. 26 Jul. 2016.

Arauja-Costa, Luis. "'Jauja' por Ricardo León." *La Época del Domingo* (7 Jul. 1928): 1. Web. Hemeroteca Digital. 15 Apr. 2014.

Arbaiza, Diana. "Spain as Archive: Constructing a Colombian Modernity in the Writings of Soledad Acosta de Samper." *Journal of Latin American Cultural Studies: Travesia* 21.1 (2012): 123–44. Web. doi:10.1080/13569325.2012.6624 79. 21 Jan. 2014.

Ard, Patricia. "Seeds of Reform: The Letters of Mary Peabody Mann and Domingo F. Sarmiento, 1865–1868." PhD Diss. State U of New Jersey, 1996. Web. Proquest. 8 May 2013.

Arenal, Concepción. *La mujer del porvenir.* Ed. Vicente de Santiago Mulas. Madrid: Castalia, 1993.

Ariel. Rev. of *Aves sin nido*, by Clorinda Matto de Turner. *El Perú Ilustrado* (11 Jan. 1890): 1255.

Avellaneda, Gertrudis Gómez de. *Albúm cubano de lo bueno y lo bello.* Havana: Impr. del Gobierno y Capitanía General, 1860.

Baldwin, James. "Everybody's Protest Novel." *Notes of a Native Son.* 1955. Rpt. Boston: Beacon Press, 2012.

Ballesteros Rosas, Luisa. "Soledad Acosta de Samper y el papel de la mujer intelectual colombiana en la historia y sociopolítica del siglo XIX." *Retomando la palabra: Las pioneras del siglo XIX en diálogo con la crítica contemporánea.* Ed. Claire Emilie Martin and María Nelly Goswitz. Madrid/Frankfurt am Main: Iberoamericana/Vervuert, 2012. 289–302.

Baroud, Mahmud. *The Shipwrecked Sailor in Arabic and Western Literature: Ibn Tufayl and His Influence on European Writers.* London: I.B. Tauris, 2012.

Barrantes, V. "Nuevas noticias del filósofo Olavide." *La España Moderna (Revista Ibero-Americana)* 3.29 (May 1891): 39–63. Web. Hemeroteca Digital. 15 Apr. 2014.

Batticuore, Graciela. *El taller de la escritura: veladas literarias de Juana Manuela Gorriti: Lima-Buenos Aires (1876/7–1892).* Buenos Aires: Beatriz Viterbo, 1999.

Bello, Andrés. *Selected Writings of Andrés Bello.* Trans. Frances M. López-Morillas. Ed. Iván Jaksić. New York: Oxford UP, 1997.

Bendezu Aibar, Edmundo. *La novela peruana: De Olavide a Bryce*. Lima: Lumen, 1992.

Bermúdez, María Elvira. Prologue. *Corazón*. By Edmondo de Amicis. 3rd ed. Mexico City: Porrúa, 1973. IX–XXXIII.

Besant, Walter, and Henry James. *The Art of Fiction*. Boston: DeWolfe and Fiske, 1884.

Blanchot, Maurice. *The Book to Come*. Trans. Charlotte Mandell. Stanford: Stanford UP, 2003.

Booth, Alison. *How to Make It as a Woman: Collective Biographical History from Victoria to the Present*. Chicago: U of Chicago P, 2004.

Breitwieser, Mitchell Robert. *Cotton Mather and Benjamin Franklin: The Price of a Representative Personality*. New York: Cambridge UP, 1985.

Briggs, Ronald. "A Napoleonic Bolívar: Historical Analogy, *Desengaño*, and the Spanish/Creole Consciousness." *Journal of Spanish Cultural Studies* 11.3–4 (Dec. 2010): 337–52.

Brooks, Charles. "Moral Education: The Best Methods of Teaching Morals in the Common Schools." *American Journal of Education (1855–1882)* 1.3 (Mar. 1856): 336–44. Web. Google Books. 26 Jul. 2016.

———. *Remarks on Europe Relating to Education, Peace, and Labor, and Their Reference to the United States*. New York: C.S. Francis, 1846. Web. The Making of the Modern World. 10 Oct. 2012.

Browning, Webster E. "Joseph Lancaster, James Thomson, and the Lancasterian System of Instruction, with Special Reference to Hispanica America." *Hispanic American Historical Review* 4.1 (Feb. 1921): 49–98. Web. JSTOR. 17 Dec. 2012.

Burga, Manuel, and Alberto Flores Galindo. *Apogeo y crisis de la república aristocrática*. 2nd ed. Lima: Rikchay Peru, 1981.

Cabello de Carbonera, Mercedes. *Blanca Sol (novela social)*. 2nd ed. Lima: Imprenta y Librería del Universo, 1889.

———. *El conde León Tolstoy*. Lima: El Diario Judicial, 1896. Web. Hathi Trust. 16 Jun. 2011.

———. *El conspirador (autobiografía de un hombre público)*. Lima: E. Seguí, 1892.

———. "Influencia de la mujer en la civilización." *Mercedes Cabello de Carbonera: Una mujer en el otro margen*. Ed. Carlos Cornejo Quesada. Lima: Museo Contisuyo, 2009. 25–55.

———. *La novela moderna: Estudio filosófico*. Lima: Hora del Hombre, 1948.

———. *Sacrificio y recompensa*. Buenos Aires: Stockcero, 2005.

Cabrera Valverde, José Mario. "Los derechos humanos y la Ilustración en el ensayo 'América' y en otros escritos de José Cecilio del Valle." *Istmo: Revista Virtual de Estudios Literarios y Culturales Centroamericanos* 13 (Jul.–Dec. 2006): n. pag. Web. istmo.denison.edu. 19 Jan. 2012.

Cáceres, Aurora. *Mujeres de ayer y de hoy*. Paris: Garnier, 1910.

Caldas, Francisco José de. *Obras de Caldas, recopiladas y publicadas por Eduardo Posada*. Bogota: Imprenta Nacional, 1972. Web. Hathi Trust.

Campo, Cupertino del. *Prohombres de América*. 2nd ed. Buenos Aires: Asociación de Difusión Interamericana, 1944.

Campomanes, Pedro Rodríguez de. *Discurso sobre el fomento de la industria popular (1774); Discurso sobre la educación popular de los artesanos y su fomento (1775)*. Ed. John Reeder. Madrid: La Fábrica Nacional de Moneda y Timbre, 1975.

Caruso, Marcelo. "New Schooling and the Invention of a Political Culture: Community, Rituals and Meritocracy in Colombian Monitorial Schools, 1821–1842." *Imported Modernity and Post-Colonial State Formation: The Appropriation of Political, Educational, and Cultural Models in Nineteenth-Century Latin America*. Ed. Eugenia Roldán Vera and Marcelo Caruso. Frankfurt am Main: Peter Lang, 2007. 277–306.

Castellanos, Rosario. *Mujer que sabe latín . . .* Mexico City: Fondo de Cultura Económica, 2012.

Castells, Manuel. "Materials for an Exploratory Theory of the Network Society." *British Journal of Sociology* 51.1 (Jan.–Mar. 2000): 5–24.

Caulfield, Sueann. "The History of Gender in the Historiography of Latin America." *Hispanic American Historical Review* 81.3–4 (2001): 449–90. Web. hahr.dukejounals.org. 19 Jan. 2014.

Chamberlin, Vernon A., and Ivan A. Schulman, eds. *La Revista Ilustrada de Nueva York: History, Anthology, and Index of Literary Selections*. Columbia: U of Missouri P, 1976.

Clancy, Patricia A. "Mme. Leprince de Beaumont: Founder of Children's Literature in France." *Australian Journal of French Studies* 16 (Jan. 1979): 281–87. Web. Proquest. 21 Jan. 2015.

Clay, Henry. "The Emancipation of South America." *The World's Famous Orations. America: II. (1818–1865)*. Ed. William Jennings Bryan. New York: Funk and Wagnalls, 1906. 76–86.

———. *Papers of Henry Clay*. Ed. James F. Hopkins. Lexington: U of Kentucky P, 1959.

Conway, Christopher. *Nineteenth-Century Spanish America: A Cultural History*. Nashville: Vanderbilt UP, 2015.

Craik, George L. *The Pursuit of Knowledge Under Difficulties*. 3rd ed. 2 vols. London: C. Knight, 1831–1834. Web. Hathi Trust. 14 Jun. 2013.

Cueto, Leopoldo Augusto de. "Noticias literarias: Observaciones sobre algunas leyendas y novelas de la sra. doña Gertrudis Gómez de Avellaneda—(Obras literarias, t. V.)." *Revista de España* 7.21 (1871): 627–38. Web. Hathi Trust. 20 Sept. 2013.

DeForest, William. "The Great American Novel." *The Nation* (9 Jan. 1868): 27–29. Web. EBSCOhost. 12 May 2015.

Denegri, Francesca. *El abanico y la Cigarrera: La primera generación de mujeres ilustradas en el Perú*. Lima: "Flora Tristán" Centro de la mujer peruana / Instituto de Estudios Peruanos, 1996.

Díaz Rönner, María Adelia. *Cara y cruz de la literatura infantil*. Buenos Aires: Lugar Editorial, 2001.

Diderot, Denis. "Don Pablo Olavides." *Oeuvres complètes de Diderot*. Vol. 6. Paris: Garnier Frères, 1875. 467–72. Web. Hathi Trust. 2 May 2014.

"Un discurso del Dr. Toloso Latour." *El Dia* [Madrid] (11 Dec. 1893): 1. Web. Hemeroteca Digital.

Djikic, Maja, Keith Oatley, and Mihnea C. Moldoveanu. "Opening the Closed Mind: The Effect of Exposure to Literature on the Need for Closure." *Creativity Research Journal* 25.2 (2013): 149–54. Web. Taylor and Francis. 14 Aug. 2013.

Djikic, Maja, Keith Oatley, Sara Zoeterman, and Jordan B. Peterson. "On Being Moved By Art: How Reading Fiction Transforms the Self." *Creativity Research Journal* 21.1 (2009): 24–29. Web. EBSCOhost. 14 Aug. 2013.

Dobyns, Henry F., and Paul L. Doughty. *Peru: A Cultural History*. New York: Oxford UP, 1976.

Dónoan. "Soledad Acosta de Samper, la narrativa y el pensamiento original de una mujer que lucha contra el olvido y apuesta por una memoria viva como argumento de una educación y cultura nacional." *Revista Antropos* 213 (2007): 197–202.

Dufour, Gerard. "*El Evangelio en triunfo* en el dispósitivo político del Príncipe de la Paz." In *Ideas en sus paisajes: Homenaje al profesor Russell P. Sebold*. Ed. Guillermo Carnero and Ignacio Javier López y Enrique Rubio. Alicante: U de Alicante, 1999. 159–66.

Eagleman, David. "The Moral of the Story." *New York Times Book Review* (5 Aug. 2012): 17.

Edgerton, William B. "The Critical Reception Abroad of Tolstoy's *What Is Art?*" *American Contributions to the Eighth International Congress of Slavists, Zagreb and Ljubljana, September 3–9, 1978*. Vol. 2. Ed. Victor Terras. Columbus, OH: Slavica, 1978. 146–65.

———. "Tolstoy and Magalhães Lima." *Comparative Literature* 28.1 (Winter 1976): 51–64. Web. JSTOR. 12 Mar. 2012.

"Educational Biography: Señor D.F. Sarmiento. Alonzo Potter, D.D., L." *American Journal of Education (1855–1882)* 45.16 (Dec. 1866): 592–98. Web. Google Books. 26 Jul. 2016.

"Educational Lessons from South America. Drawn from the Experience of the United States." *American Journal of Education* 44 (Sept. 1866): 533–38. Web. American Periodicals. 26 Jul. 2016.

"An Efficient Ministry and Working Church Essential to Religious Prosperity, Second Paper." *The Bible Christian Magazine* (May 1871): 208. Web. Google Books. 7 Feb. 2016.

Elson, Ruth Miller. *Guardians of Tradition: American Schoolbooks of the Nineteenth Century*. Lincoln: U of Nebraska P, 1964.
"En casa de la Pardo Bazán." *El Perú Ilustrado* 148 (8 Mar. 1890): 1523.
Escolar, Hipólito. *Historia del libro español*. Madrid: Gredos, 1998.
Fernández Retamar, Roberto. *Todo Calibán*. San Juan: Ediciones Callejón, 2003.
Ferrús Antón, Beatriz. "Cuando las 'obreras del pensamiento' escriben del amor: Juana Manso, Carlota Garrido de la Peña y Mercedes Práxedes Muñoz." *Anales de Literatura Hispanoamericana* 43 (2014): 255–69.
Fleury, Claudio, abad de Loc-Dieu. *Catecismo histórico que contiene en compendio la historia sagrada y la doctrina cristiana*. Vol. 1. Trans. Juan Interian de Ayala. Madrid: D. Antonio de Sancha, 1773. Web. Hathi Trust. 14 Jan. 2015.
Fliegelman, Jay. *Prodigals and Pilgrims: The American Revolutions Against Patriarchal Authority 1750–1800*. New York: Cambridge UP, 1982.
Franklin, Benjamin. "The Autobiography." *The Norton Anthology of American Literature*. Vol. 1. Ed. Nina Baym, et al. New York: Norton, 1994. 487–600.
———. "Information to Those Who Would Remove to America." *The Norton Anthology of American Literature*. Vol. 1. Ed. Nina Baym et al. New York: Norton, 1994. 459–64.
———. *El libro del hombre de bien, Opúsculos morales, económicos y políticos estractados de Benjamin Franklin*. Barcelona: Imprenta de Don Antonio Bergnes, 1843.
———. *Mémoires de la vie privée de Benjamin Franklin, ecrits par lui-méme, et adressés a son fils*. Paris: Chez Buisson, 1791. Web. Sabin Americana. Gale, Cengage Learning. Columbia U., 28 Oct. 2013.
———. *Works of the Late Doctor Benjamin Franklin: Consisting of His Life*. Vol. 1. London: Printed for G.G.J. and J. Robinson, 1793. Web. Sabin Americana. Gale, Cengage Learning. Columbia U., 28 Oct. 2013.
Fuentes Castro, Paulino. "Literatura fosforescente." *El Correo del Perú* (31 Dec. 1874): xxxii.
———. *Notas literarias y Hojas para el pueblo*. Lima: Impr. Liberal, 1882.
Gallego, Solangii. "Soledad Acosta de Samper: Imaginar, escribir e historiar la nación." PhD Diss. Indiana U., 2012. Web. Proquest. 5 Feb. 2014.
Galofre, Julio N. "Mercedes Cabello de Carbonera." *El Cojo Ilustrado-Reimpresión*. Caracas: Ediciones "Emar" C.A., 1894. 311–12.
Gannett, Ezra Styles. *An Address Delivered before the Boston Sunday School Society: On the Celebration of the Fiftieth Anniversary of the Sunday School Institution, at the Federal Street Church, September 14, 1831*. Boston: Printed for the Society, 1831. Web. Google Books. 7 Feb. 2016.
García, Armando. "José Martí and the Global Dimension of Late Nineteenth-Century Nation Building." PhD Diss. Washington State U. 2006. Web. Proquest.
García del Río, Juan. "Consideraciones sobre la influencia de la literatura en la sociedad." *La Biblioteca Americana, o miscelánea de literatura, artes i ciencias*.

By García del Río and Andrés Bello. London: G. Marchant, 1823. Web. Hathi Trust. 18 Sept. 2014.

García Márquez, Gabriel. *One Hundred Years of Solitude*. Trans. Gregory Rabassa. New York: Harper, 2006.

García y García, Elvira. *Tendencias de la educación femenina: Correspondientte a la misión social que debe llenar la mujer en América*. Lima: Imp. Nacional de Federico Barrionuevo, 1908.

Gargurevich, Juan. *Historia de la prensa peruana, 1594–1990*. Lima: La Voz, 1991.

Gates, Henry Louis, Jr., and Hollis Robbins. Introduction. *The Annotated Uncle Tom's Cabin*. Ed. Gates and Robbins. New York: Norton, 2007. xi–xxx.

Gerber, Linda K. *Toward an Intellectual History of Women*. Chapel Hill: U of North Carolina P, 1997.

Giles, Paul. *Transatlantic Insurrections: British Culture and the Formation of American Literature, 1730–1860*. Philadelphia: U of Pennsylvania P, 2001.

Gimeno de Flaquer, Concepción. "Conferencia de la Sra. D.a. Concepción Gimeno de Flaquer." *El Album Ibero Americano* 23.21 (7 Jun. 1905): 242. Web. Hemeroteca Digital. 25 Feb. 2014.

Goldgel, Víctor. *Cuando lo nuevo conquistó América: Prensa, moda y literatura en el siglo XIX*. Buenos Aires: Siglo Veintiuno, 2013.

Gómez García, Juan Guillermo. "Marginala. La independencia literaria en América Latina." *Ideas y Valores* 144 (Dec. 2010): 5–27. Web. Proquest. 16 Sept. 2014.

Gómez Hermosilla, José M. *Arte de hablar en prosa y verso*. Ed. Vicente Salvá. Paris: Librería de Garnier Hermanos, 1866.

Gómez Ocampo, Gilberto. "El proyecto feminista de Soledad Acosta de Samper: Análisis de *El corazón de la mujer*." *Revista de Estudios Colombianos* 5 (1988): 13–22.

González de Fanning, Teresa. *Ambición y abnegación*. Lima: Imp. de Torres Aguirre, 1886.

———. *Educación femenina: Colección de artículos pedagógicos, morales y sociológicos*. Lima: "El Lucero," 1905. Web. Nineteenth Century Collections Online. 2 Oct. 2014.

———. *Indómita*. Lima: Tip. de "El Lucero," 1904.

———. *Lecciones de economía doméstica*. Lima: Sanmartí, 1917.

———. "Las literatas." *El Correo del Perú* 40 (1 Oct. 1876): 319.

———. *Lucecitas*. Madrid: Imprenta de Ricardo Fe, 1893.

———. *Roque Moreno: Novela histórica*. Lima: Tip. de "El Lucero," 1904.

González Echevarría, Roberto. "A Brief History of the History of Spanish American Literature." *Discovery to Modernism*. Vol. 1 of *The Cambridge History of Latin American Literature*. Ed. González Echevarría and Enrique Pupo-Walker. Cambridge: Cambridge UP, 1996. 7–32. Web. Cambridge Histories Online. 1 May 2015.

Gooding, David. "'In Nature's School': Faraday as Experimentalist." *Faraday*

*Rediscovered: Essays on the Life and Work of Michael Faraday, 1791–1867*. Ed. Gooding and Frank A. J. L. James. New York: Stockton, 1985. 105–35.

Gorriti, Juana Manuela. *La Tierra Natal. Lo íntimo*. Buenos Aires: Fondo Nacional de las Artes, 1999.

———. *Veladas literarias de Lima 1876–1877*. Vol. 1. Buenos Aires: Imprenta Europa, 1892. Web. Hathi Trust. 29 Apr. 2014.

Goswitz, María Nelly. "Del salón finisecular y las Veladas Literarias de Juana Manuela Gorriti al salón virtual. Escritoras Latinoamericanas del Diecinueve (ELADD)." *No hay nación para este sexo. La Re(d)pública transatlántica de las letras: Escritoras españolas y latinoamericanas (1824–1936)*. Ed. Pura Fernández. Madrid/Frankfurt am Main: Iberoamericana/Vervuert, 2015. 133–46.

Guardia, Sara Beatriz. *Mujeres peruanas: El otro lado de la historia*. 5th ed. Lima: s.n., 2013.

Guerlac, Suzanne. "Writing the Nation (Mme de Staël)." *French Forum* 30.3 (Fall 2005): 43–56. Web. Proquest. 26 Feb. 2014.

Haberly, David T. "*Facundo* in the United States: An Unknown Reading." *Ciberletras* 14 (Dec. 2005): n. pag. *www.lehman.cuny.edu/ciberletra/v14/haberly/htm*. 3 Feb. 2016.

———. "Francis Bond Head and Domingo Sarmiento: A Note on the Sources of Facundo." *Modern Language Notes* 120.2 (Mar. 2005): 287–93. Web. Proquest. 3 Feb. 2016.

———. "Reopening *Facundo*." *Bulletin of Hispanic Studies* 85.1 (2008): 47–61. Web. Proquest. 3 Feb. 2016.

———. "Scotland on the Pampas: A Conjectural History of Facundo." *Bulletin of Spanish Studies* 83.6 (2006): 789–813. Web. Proquest. 3 Feb. 2016.

———. "The Statesman and the Castaway: Domingo Sarmiento and Guillermo Bonaparte." *Hispania* 89.2 (May 2006): 239–47. Web. JSTOR. 3 Feb. 2016.

Heffernan, Virginia. *Magic and Loss: The Internet as Art*. New York: Simon & Schuster, 2016.

Hostos, Eugenio María de. "La educación científica de la mujer." *Ensayos*. Barcelona: Linkgua, 2007. 37–44.

———. *Ensayos*. Barcelona: Linkgua, 2007.

Hugo, Victor. *Les rayons et les ombres*. Paris: Hetzel, 1840. Web. Hathi Trust. 12 Sept. 2014.

"Interchange: The Global Lincoln." *Journal of American History* 96 (Sept. 2009): 462–99. Web. Proquest. 30 Apr. 2013.

Irisarri, Antonio José de. *El cristiano errante: Novela que tiene mucho de historia*. Santiago, Chile, 1929. Rpt. Guatemala: Editorial del Ministerio de Educación Pública, 1960.

———. *Historia crítica del asesinato cometido en la persona del Gran Mariscal de Ayacucho*. Madrid: Editorial-América, 1917.

———. *Historia del perínclito Epaminondas del Cauca por el Bachiller Hilario de Altagumea, antiguo jefe de ingenieros, artillería y bombadas de S.M.C.* New York: Hallet, 1863.

———. "Próspecto." *La Verdad Desnuda* 1.1 (1 Jun. 1839): 1–6.

Jaksić, Iván. *Andrés Bello: Scholarships and Nation-Building in Nineteenth-Century Latin America.* Cambridge: Cambridge UP, 2006. Web. Google Books. 8 Jul. 2015.

Jenckes, Kate, and Patrick Dove. "Aesthetics." *Dictionary of Latin American Cultural Studies.* Ed. Robert McKee Irwin and Mónica Szurmuk. Gainesville: UP of Florida, 2012. 136–42. Web. Ebrary. 3 Jul. 2014.

"Journal of the Union, New York, Jun. 1, 1842." *Journal of the American Temperance Union* 6 (Jun. 1842): 88.

Jovellanos, Gaspar Melchor de. *Espectáculos y diversions públicas. Informe sobre la Ley Agraria.* Ed. Guillermo Carnero. 2nd ed. Madrid: Cátedra, 1998.

Juana Inés de la Cruz, Sor. *Poems, Protest, and a Dream.* Trans. Margaret Sayers Peden. New York: Penguin, 1997.

Kete, Mary Louise. *Sentimental Collaborations: Mourning and Middle-Class Identity in Nineteenth-Century America.* Durham: Duke UP, 2000.

"La mujer de ayer y de hoy." *Heraldo de Madrid* (4 Jan. 1910): 3. Web. Hemeroteca Digital. 17 Jan. 2014.

Labra, Rafael M. *Estudios biográfico-políticos.* Madrid: "La Guirnalda," 1887. Web. Hathi Trust. 9 Dec. 2013.

LaGreca, Nancy. *Rewriting Womanhood: Feminism, Subjectivity and the Angel of the House in the Latin American Novel, 1887–1903.* University Park: Pennsylvania State UP, 2009.

Lanier, Jaron. *You Are Not a Gadget: A Manifesto.* New York: Knopf, 2010.

Larriva, Juan Francisco de. "Al vapor." *Parnaso peruano.* Ed. José Domingo Cortés. Valparaiso: Imprenta Albion de Cox y Taylor, 1871. 361–65. Web. Hathi Trust. 6 Jun. 2015.

*La Unión* (14 Jan. 1879): 4. Web. Hemeroteca Digital. 20 Dec. 2013.

*La Unión* [Madrid 1878] (18 Jan. 1879): 4. Web. Hemeroteca Digital. 20 Dec. 2013.

Lavalle, J. A. de. *Don Pable de Olavide. (Apuntes sobre su vida y sus obras).* Lima: Imprenta del Teatro, 1885. Web. Hathi Trust. 23 Apr. 2014.

Lawrence, D. H. *Studies in Classic American Literature.* New York: Penguin, 1977.

Leprince de Beaumont, Jeanne Marie. *The Young Misses Magazine, containing dialogues between a governess and several young ladies of quality her scholars.* London: F. Wingrave, 1793. Web. Eighteenth Century Collections Online. 25 Feb. 2015.

Levander, Caroline Field, and Robert S. Levine. Introduction. "Essays beyond the Nation." *Hemispheric American Studies.* Ed. Levander and Levine. New Brunswick: Rutgers UP, 2007. Web. Proquest Ebrary. 27 Feb. 2016.

Lincoln, Abraham. *The Portable Abraham Lincoln*. Ed. Andrew Delbanco. New York: Viking Penguin, 1992.

Lipp, Solomon. "Conflict and Conciliation in Pablo de Olavide." *Dieciocho* 20.1 (1997): 77–84.

Looby, Christopher. *Voicing America: Languages, Literary Forms, and the Origins of the United States*. Chicago: U of Chicago P, 1996.

Lougran, Trish. *The Republic in Print: Print Culture in the Age of U.S. Nation Building, 1770–1870*. New York: Columbia UP, 2007.

Ludmer, Josefina. "Tretas del débil." *La sartén por el mango: encuentro de escritoras latinoamericanas*. Río Piedras: Ediciones Hurucán, 1985. 47–54.

"Luis Blanc, miembro del gobierno provisional de Francia, en el seno de la comisión de gobierno para los trabajadores." *El Espectador, periódico progresista* (11 Apr. 1848): 1–2. Web. Hemeroteca Digital. 8 Feb. 2016.

Machado, Antonio. *Juan de Mairena II*. Ed. Antonio Fernández Ferrer. Madrid: Cátedra, 1995.

Mackay, Thomas. Preface. *The Autobiography of Samuel Smiles*. By Samuel Smiles. Ed. Mackay. 1905. Rpt. London: Routledge/Thoemmes, 1987. vii–xiii.

Maetzu, Ramiro de. *Norte América desde dentro*. Madrid: Editora Nacional, 1957.

Mahler, Anne Garland. "The Global South in the Belly of the Beast: Viewing African American Civil Rights through a Tricontinental Lens." *Latin American Research Review* 50.1 (2015): 95–116.

Mann, Horace. "Third Annual Report of the Secretary of the Board of Education." *Common School Journal* 3.24 (15 Dec. 1841): n. pag. Web. American Periodicals. 8 Sept. 2011.

Mann, Mary Peabody. *Vida de Abran Lincoln, precedida de una Introduccion*. Rev. ed. *Christian Examiner* 80.1 (Jan. 1866): 133–38. Web. EBSCOhost. 17 May 2013 and 18 Nov. 2013.

Manso, Juana. *La familia del Comendador y otros textos*. Buenos Aires: Colihue/Biblioteca Nacional, 2006.

Mariátegui, José Carlos. *Invitación a la vida heróica: Antología*. Ed. Alberto Flores Galindo and Ricardo Portocarrero Grados. Lima: Instituto de Apoyo Agrario, 1989.

Marín Colorado, Paula Andrea. "Soledad Acosta de Samper y Luis Segundo de Silvestre: Retórica de la 'limpieza de sangre' y procesos de subjetivación en el campo de la novela colombiana de la segunda mitad del siglo XIX." *Lingüística y Literatura* 61 (2012): 255–76. Web. Dialnet. 25 Sept. 2014.

Marín del Solar, Mercedes. "Plan de estudios de una niña." *La alborada poética en Chile después del 18 de septiembre de 1810*. By Miguel Luis Amunátegui. Santiago: Imprenta Nacional, 1892. 508–15.

Marrero Marrero, María del Carmen. "Un modelo educativo en el siglo XVIII: Leprince de Beaumont." *El Guiniguada* 6–7 (1995–1998): 175–87. Web. Dialnet. 21 Jan. 2015.

Martí, José. *La Edad de Oro*. Middlesex: Echo Library, 2008.

———. *Ensayos y crónicas*. Ed. José Olivio Jiménez. Madrid: Cátedra, 2004.

———. "'Ramona,' de Helen Hunt Jackson." *La Opinión* [Asunción, Paraguay] (7 Dec. 1895): 1. Web. World Newspaper Archive. 25 Jan. 2014.

Martin, Leona S. "La Baronesa de Wilson canta a Colombia y a Soledad Acosta de Samper." *Revista de Estudios Colombianos* 30 (1986): 15–23. Web. *www.colombianistas.org*. 7 May 2014.

———. "Nation Building, International Travel, and the Construction of the Nineteenth-Century Pan-Hispanic Women's Network." *Hispania* 87.3 (Sept. 2004): 439–46. Web. JSTOR. 7 May 2014.

Martineau, Harriet. *Miscellanies*. Vol. 1. Boston: Hilliard, Gray, 1836. Web. Social Theory. 7 Mar. 2014.

Masiello, Francine. "Literacy, Gender, and Transnational Meddling." *Literacy: Interdisciplinary Conversations*. Ed. Deborah Keller-Cohen. Cresskill, NJ: Hampton Press, 1994. 229–48.

Mather, Cotton. *Bonifacius: An Essay Upon the Good, That Is to Be Devised and Designed by Those Who Desire to Answer the Great End of Life and to Do Good While They Live*. Boston: Printed by B. Green, for Samuel Gerrish, 1710. Web. Sabin Americana. Gale, Cengage Learning. Columbia U. 7 Aug. 2013.

Matto de Turner, Clorinda. *Aves sin nido*. Havana: Casa de las Américas, 1974.

———. *Bocetos al lápiz de Americanos célebres*. Vol. 1. Lima: Bacigalupi, 1890. Web. Hathi Trust. 22 Mar. 2012.

———. *Elementos de literatura. Segun el Reglamento de Instruccion Pública para uso del bello sexo*. Arequipa: Imprenta de "La Bolsa," 1884.

———. *Herencia*. Lima: Instituto Nacional de Cultura, 1974.

———. *Índole*. Lima: Instituto Nacional de Cultura, 1974.

Mazol, Ricardo. "El debut de Aurora Cáceres." *El Motín* (27 Jan. 1910): 5–6. Web. Hemeroteca Digital. 17 Jan. 2014.

McCallister, Rick. "The Dawn of Modernity in Central America: José Cecilio del Valle." *Journal of Hispanic Philology* 18.1–3 (Fall 1993–Spring 1994): 127–40.

McEvoy, Carmen. *Homo Politicus: Manuel Pardo, la política peruana y sus dilemas 1871–1878*. Lima: ONPE/PUCP/IRA/IEP, 2007.

McFadden, Margaret H. *Golden Cables of Sympathy: The Transatlantic Sources of Nineteenth Century Feminism*. Lexington: UP of Kentucky, 1999.

McGuffey, William Holmes. *McGuffey's Newly Revised Eclectic Fourth Reader: Containing Elegant Extracts in Prose and Poetry with Rules for Reading, and Exercises in Articulation, Defining, Etc*. Cincinnati: Winthrop B. Smith, 1848.

Mcleod, Glenda. *Virtue and Venmo: Catalogs of Women from Antiquity to the Renaissance*. Ann Arbor: U of Michigan P, 1991.

Melville, Herman. *The Confidence-Man*. Ed. John Bryant. New York: Modern Library, 2003.

Mendiola, Rómulo. "El realismo en la novela." *El Correo del Perú* (14 Feb. 1875): 52 and (21 Feb. 1875): 60–61.

Menéndez y Pelayo, Marcelino. *Historia de los heterodoxos españoles.* 3 vols. Madrid: Librería católica de San José, gerente V. Sancho-Tello, 1880–1881. Web. Hathi Trust. 22 Apr. 2014.

———. Prólogo. *El filósofo autodidacto de Abentofail; novela psicológica.* By Ibn Tufayl. Zaragoza: Tip. de Comas Hermanos, 1900.

Mignet, François-Auguste. *Vie de Franklin: Á l'usage de tout le monde.* Paris: Pagnerre, 1848. Web. The Making of the Modern World. Gale Group. 24 Oct. 2013.

Mignolo, Walter. *Local Histories/Global Designs: Coloniality, Subaltern Knowledges, and Border Thinking.* Princeton: Princeton UP, 2012. Web. Proquest Ebrary. 27 Feb. 2016.

Miseres, Vanessa. "De artesana de la palabra a obrera del pensamiento: Clorinda Matto de Turner y sus reflexiones en torno a la prensa en *La Bolsa* de Arequipa (1884)." *Boletín del Instituto Riva Agüero* 35 (2009–2010): 171–88.

Molloy, Sylvia. *At Face Value: Autobiographical Writing in Spanish America.* Cambridge: Cambridge UP, 1991.

———. "The Unquiet Self: Mnemonic Strategies in Sarmiento's Autobiographies." *Sarmiento: Author of a Nation.* Ed. Tulio Halperín Donghit, et al. Berkeley: U of California P, 1994. 193–212.

Mora, Gabriela. "Hostos feminista: Ensayos sobre la educación de la mujer." *Revista de Estudios Hispánicos* 24.2 (May 1990): 143–60. Web. Proquest. 9 May 2014.

Morrison, Toni. "Rootedness: The Ancestor as Foundation." *What Moves at the Margin: Selected Nonfiction.* By Morrison. Ed. Carolyn C. Denard. Jackson: UP of Mississippi, 2008. 56–64.

Munilla, José Ortega. Rev. of *Corazón* by Edmondo de Amicis. *El Imparcial* (2 Jan. 1893): 3. Web. Hemeroteca Digital. 7 Oct. 2014.

Muñoz, Juana N. "De la mujer." *La Escuela Moderna* (Jan.–Dec. 1908): 38–46. Web. Hemeroteca Digital. 27 Sept. 2013.

Murphy, Gretchen. "The Hemispheric Novel in the Post-Revolutionary Era." *The Cambridge History of the American Novel.* Ed. Leonard Cassuto, Clare Virginia Eby, and Benjamin Reiss. New York: Cambridge UP, 2011. 553–70.

Myers, Kathleen A. "Sor Juana's *respuesta*: Rewriting the *vitae*." *Revista Canadiense de Estudios Hispánicos* 14.3 (Spring 1990): 459–79. Web. JSTOR. 10 Feb. 2014.

Neira de Mosquera, Antonio. "La doctora Guzmán y la cerda." *Semanario Pintoresco Español* (12 Jun. 1853): 188–90. Web. Hathi Trust. 26 Sept. 2013.

"Notas Bibliográficas." *Revista de España* (Jan. 1887): 152–57. Web. Hemeroteca Digital. 24 Dec. 2013.

"Nuestro grabado." *El Globo* [Madrid] (6 Mar. 1880): 1. Web. Hemeroteca Digital. 15 Apr. 2014.

Núñez, Estuardo. *El nuevo Olavide: Una semblanza a través de los textos ignorados.* Lima: n. pub., 1970.

O'Hagan, Clara. "Pedro Montengón's *Eusebio*: Atoning for Spain's Colonial Abuses in the Eighteenth Century." *Dieciocho: Hispanic Enlightenment* 33.1 (2010): 81–100.

Obaldía, Claire de. *The Essayistic Spirit: Literature, Modern Criticism, and the Essay.* New York: Oxford UP, 1995.

Olavide, Pablo de. *El evangelio en triunfo, ó historia de un filósofo desengañado.* 4 vols. 8th ed. Madrid: Imprenta de Don Joseph Doblado, 1803.

Orbegoso, Rosa Mercedes R. de. "Charla literaria." *Perú Ilustrado* (18 Jun. 1887): 4.

Ossers Cabrera, Manuel A. "Una relectura de 'La educación científica de la mujer,' de Eugenio María de Hostos." *Confluencia* 6.2 (Spring 1991): 61–65. Web. Proquest. 9 May 2014.

Otero, Gustavo Adolfo. *La cultura y el periodismo en América.* Quito: Casa Editorial Lobermann, 1953.

Palma, Angelica. "Impresiones." *El Sol* [Madrid] (6 Mar. 1931): 1. Web. Hemeroteca Digital. 15 Apr. 2014.

Parada, Diego Ignacio. *Escritoras y eruditas españolas.* Madrid: M. Minuisa, 1881.

Pardo Bazán, Emilia. *La cuestión palpitante. Con un prólogo de Clarín.* Madrid: V. Saiz, 1883. Web. Hathi Trust. 8 Sept. 2014.

———. *La revolución y la novela en Rusia (Lectura en el Ateneo de Madrid).* Madrid: Publicaciones Españolas, 1961.

———. Prólogo. *Lucecitas por María de La Luz.* Teresa González de Fanning. Madrid: Imprenta de Ricardo Fé, 1893.

Parfait, Claire. *The Publishing History of Uncle Tom's Cabin 1852–2002.* Aldershot: Ashgate, 2007.

Parker, Franklin D. "José Cecilio Del Valle: Scholar and Patriot." *Hispanic American Historical Review* 32.4 (Nov. 1952): 516–39. Web. JSTOR. 19 Jan. 2012.

Parra, Teresa de la. *Obra escogida.* Mexico City/Caracas: Fondo de Cultura Económica/Monte Ávila Latinoamericana, 1992.

Peluffo, Ana. "Emilia Pardo Bazán lee *Lucecitas* de Teresa González de Fanning." *Siglo Diecinueve* 13 (2007): 65–71. Web. Informe Académico. 30 Sept. 2014.

———. *Lágrimas andinas: Sentimentalismo, género y virtud republicana en Clorinda Matto de Turner.* Pittsburgh: Instituto Internacional de Literatura Iberoamericana, 2005.

———. "Rizomas, redes y lazos transatlánticos: América Latina y España (1890–1920)." *No hay nación para este sexo. La Re(d)pública transatlántica de las letras: Escritoras españolas y latinoamericanas (1824–1936).* Ed. Pura Fernández. Madrid/Frankfurt am Main: Iberoamericana/Vervuert, 2015. 207–24.

———. "The Scandal of Naturalism in Nineteenth-Century Peru." *Au Naturel: (Re)Reading Hispanic Naturalism*. Ed. J. P. Spicer-Escalante and Lara Anderson. Newcastle-upon-Tyne: Cambridge Scholars, 2010. 117–34.

Peraita, Carmen. "Elocuencia y fama: El catálogo de mujeres sabias en la Respuesta de Sor Juna Inés." *Bulletin of Hispanic Studies* 77.2 (2000): 73–92. Web. Taylor and Francis. 7 Feb. 2014.

Pinto Vargas, Ismael. *Sin perdón y sin olvido: Mercedes Cabello de Carbonera y su mundo*. Lima: Universidad de San Martín de Porres, 2003.

Pomposo Fernández, Agustín. *Desengaños que a los insurgentes de N. España seducidos por los francmazones agentes de Napoleon, dirige la verdad de la religión católica y la experiencia*. Mexico City: M. de Zúñiga y Ontiveros, 1812.

Popkewitz, Thomas S. *A Political Sociology of Education Reform: Power/Knowledge in Teaching, Teacher Education and Research*. New York: Teachers College Press, 1991.

*Por Esos Mundos* 11.190 (Nov. 1910): 894. Web. Hemeroteca Digital. 17 Jan. 2014.

Portal, Magda. *El Aprismo y la mujer*. Lima: Editorial cooperativa aprista "Atahualpa," 1933. Web. Latin American Women Writers. 4 Sept. 2015.

Pratt, Mary Louise. "'Don't Interrupt Me': The Gender Essay as Conversation and Countercanon." *Reinterpreting the Spanish American Essay: Women Writers in the 19th and 20th Centuries*. Ed. Doris Meyer. Austin: U of Texas P, 1995. 10–26.

———. *Imperial Eyes: Travel Writing and Transculturation*. 2nd ed. New York: Routledge, 2008.

Puga, Amalia. "La literatura en la mujer." *El Album Ibero Americano* 5.17 (7 Nov. 1895): 201–04. Web. Hemeroteca Digital. 25 Feb. 2014.

"Pursuit of Knowledge." *Common School Journal* 5.3 (Feb. 1843): 43–44.

Quintana, Manuel José. *Obras del excmo. señor D. M. José Quintana*. Paris: Garnier, 1882. Web. Google Books. 26 Feb. 2016.

*Reglamento general de instrucción publica, del Perú*. Lima: Imprenta del Estado, 1876. Web. Google Books. 9 Jun. 2015.

Rev. of *Sacrificio y recompensa*. *El Perú Ilustrado* 9 (9 Jul. 1887): 10.

*Revista de Andalucía* (1 Jan. 1877): 192. Web. Hemeroteca Digital. 20 Dec. 2013.

Reynolds, Andrew. *The Spanish American Crónica Modernista, Temporality and Material Culture: Modernismo's Unstoppable Presses*. Lewisburg: Bucknell UP, 2012.

Reynolds, David S. *Mightier than the Sword: Uncle Tom's Cabin and the Battle for America*. New York: Norton, 2011.

Richards, Zalmon. "VI. The Teacher as Artist." *American Journal of Education (1855–1882)* 14.34 (Mar. 1864): 69–80 Web. American Periodicals. 26 Jul. 2016.

Roca, Pedro. "Vida y obras de D. Francisco Pons y Boigues." *Revista de archivos, bibliotecas y museos* 4.12 (Dec. 1900): 714–23.

Rodríguez, José Ignacio. "Las novelistas de los Estados Unidos de América." *La*

*Revista Ilustrada de Nueva York: History, Anthology, and Index of Literary Selections*. Ed. Vernon A. Chamberlin and Ivan A. Schulman. Columbia: U of Missouri P, 1976. 136–59.

Roldán Vera, Eugenia. *The British Book Trade and Spanish American Independence*. New York: Routledge, 2003.

———. "Export as Import: James Thomson's Civilising Mission in South America, 1818–1825." *Imported Modernity and State Formation: The Appropriation of Political, Educational, and Cultural Models in Nineteenth-Century Latin America*. Ed. Roldán Vera and Marcelo Caruso. Frankfurt am Main: Peter Lang, 2007. 231–76.

Rorty, Richard. "Dewey and Posner on Pragmatism and Moral Progress." *The University of Chicago Law Review* 74.3 (Summer 2007): 915–27. Web. JSTOR. 22 Feb. 2016.

Rosanvallon, Pierre. *The Demands of Liberty: Civil Society in France Since the Revolution*. Trans. Arthur Goldhammer. Cambridge: Harvard UP, 2007.

Ross, Catherine Sheldrick. "Reader on Top: Public Libraries, Pleasure Reading, and Models of Reading." *Library Trends* 57.4 (Spring 2009): 632–56. Web. Wilson. 25 Jan. 2012.

Sandlin, Jennifer A., Michael P. O'Malley, and Jake Burdick. "Mapping the Complexity of Public Pedagogy Scholarship: 1894–2010." *Review of Educational Research* 81.3 (Sept. 2011): 338–75. Web. Sage Journals. 10 Dec. 2012.

Sarmiento, Domingo Faustino. *Ambas Américas, revista de educación, biografía i agricultura*. New York: Hallet and Breen, 1867. Web. Making of American Books. 6 Nov. 2012.

———. "III. The Dignity of the Schoolmaster's Work." *American Journal of Education (1855–1882)* 16.42 (Mar. 1866): 65–74. Web. American Periodicals. 26 Jul. 2016.

———. *Las escuelas: Base de la prosperidad i de la república en los Estados Unidos*. New York: 1866. Rpt. New York: D. Appleton, 1890.

———. *Ortografía, instrucción pública 1841–1854*. Vol. 4 of *Obras completas de Sarmiento*. Buenos Aires: Editorial Luz del Día, 1949.

———. *Recuerdos de provincia*. Barcelona: Linkgua, 2006.

———. *Vida de Abrán Lincoln, décimo sesto president de los Estados Unidos. Precedida de una introducción por D. F. Sarmiento*. 2nd ed. New York: D. Appleton, 1866.

"Sarmiento's Spanish America." *The Nation* 942 (19 Jul. 1883): 59–60. Web. EBSCOhost. 18 Nov. 2013.

Scanlon, Geraldine. "Emilia Pardo Bazán (1851–1921)." *Mujeres para la historia: Figuras destacadas del primer feminismo*. Ed. Rosa María Capel. Madrid: Abada, 2004. 119–48.

Schlau, Stacey. *Spanish American Women's Use of the Word: Colonial through Contemporary Narratives*. Tuscon: U of Arizona P, 2001.

Schmidt-Welle, Friedhelm. "Harriet Beecher Stowe y Clorinda Matto de Turner:

Escritura pedagógica, modernización y nación." *Iberoamericana* 1.4 (2001): 133–46. Web. JSTOR. 10 Jul. 2014.

Scott, Nina M. "'La gran turba de las que mercieron nombres': Sor Juana's Foremothers in 'La Respuesta a Sor Filotea.'" *Coded Encounters: Writing, Gender, and Ethnicity in Colonial Latin America*. Ed. Francisco Javier Cevallos-Candau et al. Amherst: U of Massachusetts P, 1994. 206–23.

Seavey, Ormond. *Becoming Benjamin Franklin: The Autobiography and the Life*. University Park: Pennsylvania State UP, 1988.

Seguín, Manuel M. "El americanismo en literatura." *El Correo del Perú* (29 Nov. 1874): 378–80 and (6 Dec. 1874): 388–89.

Serrano, Emilia, Baronesa de Wilson. *Almacén de las señoritas*. Paris: Ch. Bouret, 1886.

———. *América y sus mujeres*. Barcelona: Fidel Giró, 1890.

———. "Inmortales americanas: Mercedes Cabello de Carbonera." *Albúm Salón* (Jan. 1902): 38. Web. Hemeroteca Digital. 26 Jul. 2016.

———. *La ley del progreso (páginas de instrucción pública para los pueblos sudamericanos)*. Quito: Imprenta Nacional, 1880.

———. *El mundo literario americano*. 2 vols. Barcelona: Casa Editorial Maucci, 1903.

Silva, Carmen P. de. "Justicia á la mujer." *El Album Ibero-Americano* (30 Jun. 1901): 280. Web. Hemeroteca Digital. 27 Sept. 2013.

Simpson, James. *Necessity of Popular Education as a National Object; With Hints on the Treatment of Criminals, and Observations on Homicidal Insanity*. Boston: March, Capen, and Lyon, 1834.

Siskind, Mariano. *Cosmopolitan Desires: Global Modernity and World Literature in Latin America*. Evanston: Northwestern UP, 2014.

Smiles, Samuel. *The Autobiography of Samuel Smiles*. Ed. Thomas Mackay. 1905. Rpt. London: Routledge/Thoemmes, 1987.

———. *Self-Help; With Illustrations of Character and Conduct*. New York: Harper and Brothers, 1860.

———. *Vida y trabajo o caracteres peculiares de los hombres según su laboriosidad, cultura y su genio*. Trans. G. Núñez de Prado. Barcelona: Ramón Sopena, 1887.

*El Solfeo* (30 Dec. 1876): 4. Web. Hemeroteca Digital. 20 Dec. 2013.

Sommer, Doris. "Schiller and Company, or How Habermas Incites Us to Play." *New Literary History* 40 (2009): 85–103. Web. Proquest. 13 Sept. 2012.

Staël Holstein, Madame de. *De la littérature considérée dans ses rapports avec les institutions sociales*. Paris: Charpentier, 1860.

———. *The Influence of Literature Upon Society*. Vol. 2. Boston: W. Wells and T. B. Wait, 1813.

Stowe, Harriet Beecher. *La cabaña del Tío Tomás*. Mexico City: Impr. de Vicente Segura Argüelles, 1853.

———. *A Key to Uncle Tom's Cabin; Presenting the Original Facts and Documents*

*Upon Which the Story Is Founded, Together with Corroborative Statements Verifying the Truth of the Work*. Boston, 1854. Rpt. Salem, NH: Ayers, 1987.

Sullivan, Dolores P. *William Holmes McGuffey: Schoolmaster to the Nation*. Rutherford, NJ: Fairleigh Dickinson UP, 1994.

Surwillo, Lisa. "Representing the Slave Trader: Haley and the Slave Ship; Or, Spain's 'Uncle Tom's Cabin.'" *PMLA* 120.3 (May 2005): 768–82. Web. JSTOR. 28 Feb. 2014.

Tamayo Vargas, Augusto. *Perú en trance de la novela: Ensayo crítico-biográfico sobre Mercedes Cabello de Carbonera*. Lima: Ed. Baluarte, 1940.

Tauber, Zvi. "Aesthetic Education for Morality: Schiller and Kant." *Journal of Aesthetic Education* 40.3 (Autumn 2006): 22–47. Web. JSTOR.

Tolstoy, Leo. "The Kreutzer Sonata." Trans. Louise and Aylmer Maude. *The Great Short Works of Leo Tolstoy*. New York: Harper and Row, 1967. 353–449.

———. *War and Peace*. Ed. George Gibian. New York: Norton, 1966.

———. *What Is Art?* Trans. Richard Pevear and Larissa Volokhonsky. New York: Penguin, 1995.

Trivedi, Saam. "Artist-Audience Communication: Tolstoy Reclaimed." *Journal of Aesthetic Education* 38.2 (Summer 2004): 38–52. Web. Project Muse. 7 Mar. 2011.

"Una proeza de la Inquisición." *El duende de los cafées* (30 Aug. 1813): 123–24. Web. Hemeroteca Digital. 15 Apr. 2014.

Urraca, Beatriz. "Juana Manuela Gorriti and the Persistence of Memory." *Latin American Research Review* 34.1 (1999): 151–73. Web. JSTOR. 28 Oct. 2009.

Valera, Juan. "Folletín: Apuntes sobre el nuevo arte de escribir novelas por D. Juan Valera." *El Perú Ilustrado* 139 (4 Jan. 1890): 1226.

———. "Novela-Programa." *La España Moderna (Revista Ibero-Americana)* 2.18 (1 Jun. 1890): 31–54. Web. Hemeroteca Digital. 20 Sept. 2013.

Valle, Enid M. "La estructura narrativa de *El Evangelio en triunfo* de Pablo de Olavide y Jáuregui." *Pen and Peruke: Spanish Literature of the Eighteenth Century*. Ed. Monroe Z. Hafter. Spec. issue of *Michigan Romance Studies* 12 (1992): 135–51.

Valle, José Cecilio del. *Escritos inéditos*. Ed. Ramón Oquelí. Tegucigalpa: Secretaría de Cultura y las Artes, 1996.

———. *Memoria sobre la educación*. Comayagüela, DC, Honduras: Ministro de Educación Pública, 1968.

Vásquez, Mark G. *Authority and Reform: Religious and Educational Discourses in Nineteenth-Century New England*. Knoxville: U of Tennessee P, 2003.

Velázquez Castro, Marcel. *El revés del marfil: Nacionalidad, etnicidad, modernidad y género en la literatura peruana*. Lima: Universidad Nacional Federico Villarreal, Editorial Universitaria, 2002.

Vélez, P. P. M. [no title] *America y España* (1 Apr. 1912–30 Jun. 1912): 161. Web. Hemeroteca Digital. 15 Apr. 2014.

Velez, Rafael de. *Preservativo contra la irreligión*. 1813. Mexico City: M. Fernández de Jáuregui, 1814.

Velleman, Barry L. "Introducción: Sarmiento y los Mann: 1847, 1865." *Mi estimado Señor: Cartas de Mary Mann a Sarmiento (1865–1881)*. Ed. Velleman. Buenos Aires: Instituto Cultural Argentino Norteamericano, 2005. 23–56.

———, ed. *"Mi estimado Señor": Cartas de Mary Mann a Sarmiento (1865–1881)*. Buenos Aires: Instituto Cultural Argentino Norteamericano, 2005.

Vicens, María. "Entre las vacaciones y el trabajo: Sociabilidad y profesionalización en *Viaje de recreo* de Clorinda Matto de Turner." *Decimonónica* 12.2 (Summer 2015): 82–102.

*Vida Socialista* (3 Jul. 1910): 8. Web. Hemeroteca Digital. 3 Oct. 2014.

Villanueva, Joaquín Lorenzo de. *Catecismo de los literatos*. London: Ackermann, 1828.

Vogüé, Eugène-Melchior de. *The Russian Novelists*. Trans. Jane Loring Edmands. Boston, 1887. Rpt. New York: Haskell House, 1974.

Ward, Thomas. "Rumbos hacia una teoría peruana de la literatura: Sociedad y letras en Matto, Cabello y González Prada." *Bulletin of Hispanic Studies* 78.1 (Jan. 2001): 89–101. Web. Proquest. 22 Nov. 2013.

Webster, Noah. *A Collection of Essays and Fugitiv Writins: On Moral, Historical, Political and Literary Subjects*. Boston: I. Thomas and E. T. Andrews, 1790. Web. Sabin Americana. Gale, Cengage Learning. Columbia U. 15 Oct. 2002.

Woolf, Virginia. *A Room of One's Own*. New York: Harvest, 1979.

Worthen, Edward H. "Edmondo de Amicis, an Italian Hispanist of the Nineteenth Century." *Hispania* 55.1 (Mar. 1972): 137–43. Web. JSTOR. 7 Oct. 2014.

Zola, Émile. *Le roman expérimentale: Le roman expérimentale. Lettre à la jeunesse. Le naturalisme et théâtre. L'argent dans la littérature. Du roman. De la critique. La république et la littérature*. Paris: G. Charpentier, 1890. Web. Hathi Trust. 9 Sept. 2004.

———. *Les romanciers naturalistes*. Paris: G. Charpentier & E. Fasquelle, 1893. Web. Hathi Trust. 4 Sept. 2014.

Zunshine, Lisa. "Why Fiction Does It Better." *The Chronicle of Higher Education* (9 Dec. 2013): n. pag. Web. *chronicle.com/article/Theres-No-Substitute-for/143363/13*. Dec. 2013.

# INDEX

Page numbers in **boldface** refer to illustrations.

Acker, Paul, 97
Ackermann catechisms, 17, 23–24, 29, 42, 133, 194n12, 198n50, 201n14
Acosta de Samper, Soledad, 1, 18, 104–5, 149, 219n67, 228n88
    biographical collections, 14, 75, 82–85, 87, 89–94, 97–101, 107
    on "book in subjunctive" concept, 29
    on novels, 155
    portrait of, **139**
    on publication, 4, 189
    transatlantic profile of, 92–94, 96, 109
    on women writers, 22–23, 90, 97–98, 100, 114, 166
Acosta de Samper, Soledad, works
    *Conversaciones y lecturas familiares*, 133, 138, 140–43, 144
    *Una holandesa en América*, 177–78
Acree, William, Jr., 111, 192n10
Adams, Henry, 50, 176
aesthetics, 1, 5–7, 13, 15–18, 151, 154–55
    González de Fanning on, 122–23, 126, 131
    Staël on, 103, 105–6
Águila, Rocío del, 220n2
Alamos González, Benicio, 45, 117
*Albúm Salón*, 92

Alcott, Bronson, 18, 117, 119, 145, 215n26
Allen, James Sloane, 179
Alonso, Carlos, 25
Alzate, Carolina, 228n88
*Americanismo*, 72–73
*American Journal of Education*, 19, 76, 92, 110
Amicis, Edmondo De, 124–29, 131–32, 135, 145, 217n48
Amunátegui, Miguel Luis and Gregorio Víctor, 28, 113–14
Arbaiza, Diana, 96–97, 211n58
Arenal, Concepción, 114
autodidacticism, 16, 17, 47–73, 77–78, 131, 137

Bacigalupi, Peter, 152
Bacon, Francis, 158
Baldwin, James, 15, 171, 192nn15–16
Ballesteros Rosas, Luisa, 143, 219n67
Barnard, Henry, 19, 76–77, 92
Barrantes, Vicente, 43, 197n37, 199n55
Batticuore, Graciela, 108–9
Beecher, Henry Ward, 109
Bellamy, Edward, 164–66
Bello, Andrés, 21, 32–34, 36–38, 61, 82, 132, 193n4
Bendezu Aibar, Edmundo, 45, 200n64
Berg, Mary, 150
Bermúdez, Elvira, 126–28

247

Besant, Walter, 150, 175, 227n84
*Biblioteca Americana, La*, 32–34, 87, 132, 193n4
biographical collections, 16, 17, 50–51, 72, 76–101, 107, 187, 209n38. *See also individual titles*
Blair, Hugh, 158, 194n15
Blanchot, Maurice, 36
Blanco White, José María, 82
Boccaccio, Giovanni, 87
Bolet Peraza, Nicanor, 157
Bolívar, Simón, 27, 32, 163
"book in subjunctive" concept, 17, 23, 29–31, 36–37, 45–46, 62–63, 196n29, 196n32
    autobiographical tendencies in, 41, 74–75
    feminism and, 88, 98, 99–106
books and publishing, 17, 19–46, 57–58, 149
    copyright infringement, 156, 221n12
    encyclopedias and, 30–31
    European influence on, 12–13, 25–27, 36
    growth of, 77–78, 118, 120, 143, 187
    male bias of, 48
    morality and, 19–20, 23–26, 30, 35, 36, 40–42, 84, 90
    motives for, 8–12
    periodicals and, 31, 36, 60–61, 92, 149, 195n20, 197n36, 220n1
    scarcity of, 17, 27–30, 33–34, 64, 146, 187, 194n16, 197n35, 218n57
    technology of, 41, 192n9
    textbooks, 111, 114, 118, 120–24, 187–88, 218n52
    *See also* literature; novels; reading, act of
Booth, Alison, 87–88
Boyd, Carolyn P., 72–73, 74, 206n54
Brooks, Charles, 5–6, 7, 19–21, 24, 29–30, 82, 112

    on biographies, 75
    on Europe, 9, 19, 25–27, 109
    Serrano and, 119, 120, 215n28
Burga, Manuel, 176
Burke, Edmund, 26

Cabello de Carbonera, Mercedes, 1, 2, 18, 149–50, 175–76, 180, 189
    Acosta on, 22–23, 100–101
    death of, 185
    on lower classes, 82–83
    on novels, 152, 155, 159–63, 173–75, 227n77
    on publication, 4
    Tamayo Vargas on, 169–70, 228n90
    on Tolstoy, 227nn77–78
    on women's education, 45, 108, 176
Cabello de Carbonera, Mercedes, works
    *Blanca Sol*, 22, 100, 117, 129, 150, 160–61, 177–78, 184
    *El conde Leon Tolstoy*, 173–74, 176
    *El conspirador*, 117, 170, 177, 178
    "Influencia de la mujer en la civilización," 116–17
    "Mujer escritoria," 116
    *La novela moderna*, 161–62
    *Sacrificio y recompensa*, 159–60, 175, 178
Cáceres, Aurora, 4, 22, 102–5
    on Matto, 102–3
    *Mujeres de ayer y de hoy*, 14, 75, 85, 87, 90–92, 94–100, 107
    on Staël, 97–98
    transatlantic profile, 92, 94–95
Caldas, Francisco José de, 52
Campo, Cupertina del, 205n49
Campomanes, Pedro Rodríguez de, 35, 40, 51, 198n45
Carlyle, Thomas, 26
Castellanos, Rosario, 47–49, 187
Castells, Manuel, 191n4
catechism form, 24, 122–23, 133–34, 194n12, 198n50

Caulfield, Sueann, 145
Cervantes, Miguel de, 42, 128, 152, 154, 160
Checa Godoy, Antonio, 176
Christine de Pizan, 87, 88
Cicero, Marcus Tullius, 55, 64
Clancy, Patricia, 218n56
classroom narratives, 17–18, 117, 122–26, 131–41, 144–45, 151
Clay, Henry, 197n36, 213n4
Comte, Auguste, 104
Conway, Christopher, 189
Cooper, James Fenimore, 67
*Corazón*. *See* Amicis, Edmondo De
*Correo del Perú, El*, 116, 152, 173, 178, 180, 220n3
*costumbrista* writing, 83, 160
Craik, George S., 75, 77–79, 81, 83
Creole culture, 13–14, 84–85, 94, 97, 138, 200n64, 211n58
Cuerto, Leopoldo Augusto de, 163, 168

Defoe, Daniel, 53–54
DeForest, William, 170, 184, 221n12, 225n53
Delgado, Abel de la E., 176
Denegri, Francesca, 4, 150, 220n3
*desengaño*, 40, 197n43
Dewey, John, 181
Díaz, José Domingo, 132
Díaz Rönner, María Adelia, 122
Diderot, Denis, 30, 43, 199n56
Dove, Patrick, 7
Dufour, Gerald, 43

*Edad de Oro, La*, 132–33, 218n55
Edgerton, William, 172, 179, 227n84
education. *See* classroom narratives; female education; novels: educational; pedagogy
Egaña, Mariano, 61–62
electricity metaphor, 5, 8, 20–22, 45, 112, 121, 173, 193n5. *See also* "moral electricity"

eloquence, 20–21, 115–16
Emerson, Ralph Waldo, 21, 79–80
Escolar, Hipólito, 220n1, 223n34
essay genres, 13, 192n11
European influences, 9, 12–13, 19, 25–27, 36, 100, 111, 188, 214n14
  on Creole culture, 84–85
  decadence, 111, 149, 165
  French influence, 223n39
  on Spanish American novels, 148, 155–56, 161–62
*Eusebio*. *See* Montengón, Pedro

Feijoo, Benito Jerónimo, 40
female education, 2, 22, 45, 108, 110, 113–17, 151, 192n10
  Acosta on, 23, 141
  Cabello on, 116–17, 176, 178
  Parada on, 209n33
  Serrano on, 138
  Staël on, 104–5
  Tolstoy on, 173–74
female reader concept, 110–18, 142, 145, 223n34
feminism. *See* gender issues
Fernández Retamar, Roberto, 197n35
Ferrús Antón, Beatriz, 192n11
Flaubert, Gustave, 150
Fleury, Claude, 133, 135, 144, 217n51
Flores Galindo, Alberto, 176
*Frankenstein* (Shelley), 8
Franklin, Benjamin, 42, 50–66, 68, 75, 78, 107–8, 132, 144, 202n27
  influence on Sarmiento, 54–58, 62, 66, 68, 188
  Mather's influence on, 144
  virtue chart, 62–63, 203n35
Fuentes Castro, Paulino, 118, 173, 215n23
Funes, Gregorio, 64–66

Gallego, Solangii, 87, 101
Galofre, Julio N., 213n5
García, Armando, 218n55

García del Río, Juan, 32–33
García Márquez, Gabriel, 196n29
García y García, Elvira, 16, 189
Gates, Henry Louis, Jr., 15–16
gender issues, 12–14, 89–106, 131, 145,
    192n10, 214n18
  female emancipation, 13–14, 47,
    91–92, 103, 105, 109–10, 112–13,
    165–68, 209n33
  social novel and, 151, 167–68
  Tolstoy on, 173–74
  *See also* female education
Gerber, Linda K., 212n3
Giles, Paul, 60
Gimeno de Flaquer, Concepción, 167–68
Giner de los Ríos, Hermenegildo, 124, 128
Goldgel, Víctor, 7, 146
Gómez de Avellaneda, Diego Ignacio, 87
Gómez de Avellaneda, Gertrudis, 163, 168
Gómez García, Juan Guillermo, 32
Gómez Hermosilla, José F., 157–58
González de Fanning, Teresa, 1, 2, 7,
    149, 176, 180, 189
  on De Amicis, 124–26, 131–32
  on reading, 129–31, 145
  on women's role, 131, 208n32, 226n69
  on writing, 91, 118, 130, 136, 155, 208n32
González de Fanning, Teresa, works
  *Ambición y abnegación*, 177
  *Educación femenina*, 124–25
  *Indómita*, 177
  *Lecciones de economía doméstica*, 122–23, 129, 131
  "Las literatas," 130, 168–69, 208n32
  *Roque Moreno*, 177
  "Sobre la educación de la mujer," 208n32
González Echevarría, Roberto, 147–48, 179

González Prada, Manuel, 191n5
Gooding, David, 20
Gorriti, Juana Manuela, 1–2, **3**, 5, 8,
    44–45, 108, 116–17, 185. See also
    *veladas literarias*
Goswitz, María Nelly, 191n3
Gottschall, Jonathan, 118
Guardia, Sara Beatriz, 212n77
Guerlac, Suzanne, 20–21

hagiography, 55, 72, 154, 202n28
Heffernan, Virginia, 198n49, 206n5
hemispheric consciousness, 9–12, 73, 145, 147, 188
historiography, 34–38, 41, 91, 93–94
Hostos, Eugenia María de, 7, 23, 45, 112–13, 117–18
  electricity metaphor, 5, 22, 45, 112, 193n6
Howe, Julia Ward, 176
Hugo, Victor, 14–15, 18

Ibn Tufayl, 54, 201n12
*Index Librorum Prohibitorum*, 28, 195n19
Irisarri, Antonio José de, 80–81, 82, 201n14
"I Sing the Body Electric" (Whitman), 8

Jackson, Helen Hunt, 14, 170, 224n51
James, Henry, 150, 175, 181, 227n84
Jenckes, Kate, 7
Jovellanos, Gaspar Melchor de, 35, 40, 51–52
Juana Inés de la Cruz, 47–51, 58–60, 88, 107–8

Kete, Mary Louise, 192n8

Labra, Rafael M. de, 74, 81
LaGreca, Nancy, 4, 150, 175–76, 181, 193n18
Lanier, Jaron, 192n9
Larriva, Juan Francisco de, 213n10

# INDEX

Larriva de Llona, Lastenia, 100
Las Casas, Bartolomé de, 94
Lavalle, José Antonio de, 43–44, 199n55
Lawrence, D. H., 203n35
Leibnitz, Gottfried Wilhelm, 105
Leprince de Beaumont, Jeanne Marie, 133, 134–37, 141, 143–44, 146, 218nn56–57
Levander, Caroline Field, 9–10
Levine, Robert S., 9–10
Lima, depictions in fiction of, 100, 103, 176–77, 178, 184
Lincoln, Abraham, 9, 19, 50, 62, 66–73, 74, 205nn48–49, 206n54
Lipp, Solomon, 198n51
literature
    didacticism in, 122, 166, 169, 184
    pedagogical utility of, 2, 5, 7, 8, 11, 15–21, 166–67
    utility of, for female emancipation, 14, 83, 93
    *See also* novels
Locke, John, 80
Lougran, Trish, 193n5
Lynn, Kenneth, 171, 192n15

Maetzu, Ramiro de, 204n42
magazine, etymology of, 143–44
Mahler, Anne Garland, 11–12, 147
Mallarmé, Stéphane, 36
Mann, Horace, 9, 68
    on biographies, 74–75, 87
    *Common School Journal*, 31, 75
    European tour, 6, 25, 28, 109
    on light reading, 81–82, 130
    Serrano and, 119, 120, 215n28
    on US publishing, 27, 28–29, 109, 147
Mann, Mary Peabody, 4, 68–71, 73
Manso, Juana, 18, 218n52
Mariátegui, José Carlos, 214n18, 217n51
Marín Colorado, Paula Andrea, 177
Marín del Solar, Mercedes, 217n51
Marrero Marrero, María del Carmen, 135

Martí, José, 18, 132–33, 170, 224n51
Martin, Leona S., 2, 4, 8, 107, 209n39
Martineau, Harriet, 175
Masiello, Francine, 110
Mather, Cotton, 144
Matto de Turner, Clorinda, 1, 2, 102, 128, 149–50, 180, 189, 191n5
    death and legacy of, 185
    on Lima, 176
    magazine editorship, 8, 92, 102–3, 152, 155, 186, 208n24
    on novels, 155, 157–60
    Peluffo on, 6
    sentiment in, 6, 166–67, 171
    Stowe and *Aves sin nido*, 150, 165
    writing motivation of, 4, 7, 18
Matto de Turner, Clorinda, works
    *Aves sin nido*, 102, 157–60, 170–71, 174, 177, 178, 222nn19–20
    *Bocetos al lapis de Americanos célebres*, 85–86, 96
    *Elementos de literatura*, 114–16, 117, 122
    *Herencia*, 157, 176, 177
    *Índole*, 157
Mazol, Ricardo, 95–96
McEvoy, Carmen, 207n13
McFadden, Margaret, 4, 89
McGuffey's Readers, 18, 109, 116, 122, 132, 135, 144
Mcleod, Glenda, 88
Melville, Herman, 226n72
Mendiola, Rómulo, 180
Menéndez y Pelayo, Marcelino, 42–43, 155, 201n12
Merino, José María, 217n48
meta-literary discourse, 148–50, 157, 160
Mier, Servando Teresa de, 27
Mignet, François-Auguste, 56–57
Mignolo, Walter, 10
Miller, Nicola, 72
modernism, 12, 99, 179, 211n60
Molloy, Sylvia, 71, 201n17, 203n33, 204n39, 205n53
Montengón, Pedro, 53, 132, 141, 201n11

"moral electricity," 5, 9, 20, 21–22, 25, 29, 112, 124
morality. *See* books and publishing: morality; novels: moral
More, Thomas, 164, 165
Morrison, Toni, 183–84
Munárriz, José Luis, 158
Muñoz, Juana D., 225n56
Murphy, Gretchen, 11, 188

naturalism, 89–90, 150, 152, 154, 156, 159, 162, 225n59
Neira de Mosquera, Antonio, 163, 167
networks, 8–9, 45, 92–99, 119, 186, 191nn4–5, 220n2
    Martin on, 2, 4, 8, 107, 209n39
Newman, John Henry, 48
Nietzsche, Friedrich, 71
Novalis, 36
novels
    "American" distinction, 100–102
    educational, 50, 111, 133–34, 166–67
    historical, 83
    moral, 24–25, 42, 151, 184
    naturalist, 89–90, 128, 152, 154
    opposition to, 40–41, 79–80, 161, 198n49
    picaresque, 80, 154
    popularity of, 40, 184, 198n49, 223n39
    protest, 15, 171
    realist, 2, 24, 152, 159–60, 170, 226n72
    sentimental, 6, 14–15
    social, 14, 15, 18, 128, 149–81, 185
    theory and purpose of, 148–62, 167, 170–76, 178–81, 183–84, 227n84
    *See also* literature
Núñez, Estuardo, 40, 42

Obaldía, Claire de, 148–49
O'Hagan, Clara, 53, 201n11

Olavide, Pablo de, **39**, 51, 155, 197n41, 199n56
    *El evangelio en triunfo*, 8, 38–44, 63, 74–75, 119, 199n55
Old World threats. *See* European influences
Ortega Munilla, José, 128
Otero, Gustavo Adolfo, 227n85

Palma, Angelica, 199n60
Parada, Diego Ignacio, 87, 209n33
Pardo Bazán, Emilia, 92, 150, 155–56, 158, 161, 165–66
    on copyright infringement, 156, 221n12
    on González de Fanning, 168–69, 221n10
    on naturalism, 152, 225n59
    on Russian fiction, 172–73
    on Valera, 154
Parfait, Claire, 192n15
Parra, Teresa de la, 49, 187
"pedagogical Americanism," 9–12
pedagogy, 7, 12–14, 19, 28–30, 32–33, 41, 130, 140–42
    biographies and, 74–77, 85–87, 91, 204n42
    educational periodicals, 132–33, 143–44
    example and imitation, 56–57, 64, 68, 70–72, 75, 77, 111, 204n42
    reform efforts, 51–52, 86, 109–10, 113–14, 117–19, 124, 142, 212n3
    *See also* classroom narratives; literature: pedagogical utility of
Peluffo, Ana, 4, 7
    on "cosmopolitan modernity," 152
    on González de Fanning, 169, 221n10, 226n69
    on Matto, 6, 170
Peraita, Carmen, 88
periodicals. *See under* books and publishing; pedagogy; *and individual titles*
*Perú Ilustrado, El*, 8, 18, 102, 152, 155, 165
    illustrations from, **39, 139, 153**

# INDEX

Pestalozzi, Johann Heinrich, 112
Pirandello, Luigi, 170
plagiarism, 64–66
Plutarch, 55, 58, 68, 74, 94
Popkewitz, Thomas, 109
Portal, Magda, 185
Pratt, Mary Louise, 13, 32, 192n11
Puga, Amalia, 167, 209n38

Quintana, Manuel José, 83–84

Raumer, Karl Georg von, 76
reading, act of, 112, 121, 124, 129–31, 135–37, 146, 181, 216n33
*Repertorio Americano, El*, 32, 33–34, 132, 196n32
Reynolds, Andrew, 12, 196n30, 197n36, 211n60
Reynolds, David S., 170, 224n43
Richards, Zalmon, 76–77
Robbins, Hollis, 15–16
Rodó, José Enrique, 219
Rodríguez, José Ignacio, 14
Roldán Vera, Eugenia, 45, 194n12, 194n16, 195n19
romanticism, 36, 97, 148, 161, 200n64
Rorty, Richard, 158
Rosanvallon, Pierre, 21
Ross, Catherine Sheldrick, 111, 216n33
Rousseau, Jean-Jacques, 7, 52, 53, 55, 99, 121, 132, 141
Russian fiction, 2, 172–74

Sand, George, 89
Sanz, Miguel José, 132
Sarmiento, Domingo Faustino, 5–6, 25, 27, 50–51, 54–73, 76–77, 107–10, 119–20
    Ackermann catechisms and, 22–23, 29, 54, 123, 133, 188
    Franklin and, 54–58, 62, 66, 68, 188
    Lincoln and, 62, 66–73, 74, 77
    on periodicals, 195n20
    on plagiarism, 64–66, 69

    on publishing, 4, 92, 147, 221n11, 223n39
Sarmiento, Domingo Faustino, works
    *Conflicto y Harmonías de las Razas en América*, 205n52
    "The Dignity of the Schoolmaster's Work," 77, 110, 118
    *Education popular*, 31
    *Las escuelas*, 5–6, 27–29, 108, 110
    *Facundo*, 69
    *Recuerdos de provincia*, 17, 29, 32, 54–55, 203n30, 205n53
    *Vida de Abrán Lincoln*, 66–71, 76
Scanlon, Geraldine, 225n59
Schiller, Friedrich, 18, 54, 122, 162, 181
Schlau, Stacey, 2, 4, 191n5
Schmidt-Welle, Friedhelm, 166–67
Schopenhauer, Arthur, 174
Scott, Nina, 88–89
Scott, Walter, 175
Seguín, Manuel María, 178
sentiment
    literature and, 6, 14–16, 129, 166–67, 171, 175, 192n8, 192n15
    women and, 22, 112, 116–18, 171
Serrano, Emilia, 1–2, **3**, 5–6, 7, 44, 119–22, 189, 215n24
    Acosta and, 92–93
    classroom narrative style of, 18
    cosmpolitan sensibility of, 109
Serrano, Emilia, works
    *Almacén de las señoritas*, 133, 134, 137–38, 144
    *América y sus mujeres*, 87
    *La Ley del progreso*, 5–6, 108, 119, 123–24, 126
    *El Mundo literario americano*, 87, 210n43
Shelley, Mary, 8
Shelley, Percy Bysshe, 26
Simpson, James, 75
Siskind, Mariano, 214n14
Skinner, Lee, 150
Smiles, Samuel, 9, 76, 78–83, 87, 206n2, 206n7, 207n8

Sommer, Doris, 150, 181
Staël, Germaine de, 5, 103–5, 107, 185, 188, 193nn3–4
   on eloquence, 20–21
   influence on Lima circle, 14, 22, 32–33, 87, 97–98, 151, 186, 189, 212n83
   steam power metaphor, 45, 114, 117, 213n10
Stowe, Harriet Beecher, 98–99, 150, 161, 172, 179–80, 215n22, 224nn43–44
   critical reception of, 15, 170–71, 184, 192nn15–16, 224n46, 224n51, 225n53
   popularity in Spanish America, 9, 14, 18, 163–69, 186
   symbolic reputation of, 66, 89
Surwillo, Lisa, 163

Tamayo Vargas, Augusto, 169–70
Tauber, Zvi, 34
Tolstoy, Leo, 18, 150, 171–75, 179–80, 227nn77–78, 227n84
Toussaint L'Ouverture, 74, 81
Tristan, Flora, 185
Turgot, Anne Robert Jacques, 66

Urraca, Beatriz, 97, 119

Valera, Juan, 1, 150, 152, 154–56, 164–66, 185
Valle, José Cecilio del, 27, 30–31, 75, 159, 195n24
Vargas, Pinto, 4
Vásquez, Mark G., 118, 145, 215n22
*veladas literarias*, 1–2, 3, 5, 9, 11, 32, 44–45, 108, 176
   Cáceras on, 102
   Goswitz on, 191n3
Velázquez Castro, Marcel, 222n19
Velleman, Barry, 71
Villanueva, Joaquín Lorenzo de, 24–25, 29, 194n15
Vogüé, Eugène-Melchoir de, 172–73
Voltaire, 40, 42, 43

Ward, Thomas, 150, 222n20
War of the Pacific, 44, 176, 178
Washington, George, 32, 42, 68, 77, 103
Webster, Noah, 35–38, 132
Wilson, Baronesa de. *See* Serrano, Emilia
Woolf, Virginia, 47–49, 88
Worthen, Edward H., 128

Zola, Émile, 18, 128, 152, 156–59, 173, 227n77
Zunshine, Lisa, 181